T0298773

Leading Organizations in Hazardous Times

Does your organization have the capacity to respond to risk it has not anticipated or prepared for? Is its approach to risk explicit and understood by employees? Does it have a robust risk culture? Do employees take responsibility for managing risk? If your response to these questions is guarded or uncertain, this book will have value for you and your organization.

Organizations and leaders in a widening risk environment face four realities which challenge their ability to manage risk: (1) the two-dimensional nature of risk—risk itself and behavior in response to risk, (2) the diversity of attitudes and behavior in relationship to risk, (3) the influence on behavior of cognitive, psychological and contextual factors that are part of social dynamics and (4) the compounding effect of social dynamics that make risk difficult to manage. These realities add up to a conundrum: *The challenge for organizations and leaders lies not in risk itself but in social dynamics that shape behavior in response to risk.*

Whether triggered by an internal problem or external event, risk management failures often result from a lack of understanding of causative factors and behavior in response to risk. Effective leaders make risk a core part of their agenda. They put people at the center of strategy and face challenges head-on that impact their organizations' ability to manage risk. Among the challenges are:

- the toll on organizational resources of a growing array of risk factors
- risk "blind spots" in the organization warranting attention
- cultural weaknesses and vulnerabilities elevating exposure to risk
- employee disengagement from risk and responsibility for managing it,
- variation in attitudes and behavior that make risk difficult to detect and mitigate,
- turning risk into advantage by envisioning it as an opportunity or strength in contrast to a threat or weakness.

Leading Organizations in Hazardous Times: The Social Dynamics of Risk builds capability in risk management by enhancing leader understanding of risk behavior and factors contributing to risk culture. It encourages leaders to invest in continuous learning to navigate asymmetries of attitude and behavior, managing, and leadership style that underlie organizational success and failure.

Leading Organizations in Hazardous Times

The Social Dynamics of Risk

Richard L. Alfred

Routledge
Taylor & Francis Group

A PRODUCTIVITY PRESS BOOK

First published 2025
by Routledge
605 Third Avenue, New York, NY 10158

and by Routledge
4 Park Square, Milton Park, Abingdon, Oxon, OX14 4RN

Routledge is an imprint of the Taylor & Francis Group, an informa business

ISBN: 9781032371702 (hbk)
ISBN: 9781032371696 (pbk)
ISBN: 9781003335658 (ebk)

DOI: 10.4324/9781003335658

Typeset in Garamond
by Deanta Global Publishing Services, Chennai, India

Contents

Foreword

I was honored to be asked to write the Foreword to Dick Alfred's new book, especially because I had not met him personally. His invitation followed on the heels of my correspondence with him about his previous book, *Catastrophic Risk: Business Strategy for Managing Turbulence in a World at Risk*. I thought this previous book was poignant and important because it brought into sharp focus existential risks, like climate change, inequality and global business. These threats challenge the survival of not only business but most of humanity. I felt that they, and other threats like them, were receiving too little attention in management discourse and appreciated Dick shining light on them.

You can imagine my delight when Dick said he was writing a second book that spoke to the social dynamics of risk—the social processes that contribute to and are affected by catastrophic risks. To be able to write the Foreword allowed me to speak to topics close to my professional work and my personal values. You see, I care deeply about risk, especially risks so destructive that they will affect the prosperity of future generations, which is the heart of sustainable development. Today's generations need to steward the environment so that our children can prosper and meet their needs.

I have studied sustainability for the better part of three decades, so risk is very much at the top of my mind. I take a systems view with business as both the catalyst to and victim of catastrophic risk. There is no single person or business that can be blamed, although some have more impact and influence than others. Mitigating catastrophic risk is the domain of everyone.

Yet, the discussion of risk, both in research and practice, is often faint or muted. I believe this is because risk is invisible. The forces that catalyze risk are often difficult to see and causal inferences sometimes impossible to make. For decades, even the best weather scientists did not fully agree that climate was changing at a rate that presented a risk to humanity and that it was caused by industrial activity. Similarly, the causes of income inequality and global conflict are deeply embedded and hotly disputed. But just because risk is invisible does not make it any less important. In fact, it's the lack of awareness and action that makes discussion about risk and its consequences all the more important.

The invisible nature of risks and the fact that they are not actualized or seen by everyone means that they are open to individual biases, social construction and manipulation. Businesses, governments and societies either inadvertently or intentionally ignore risks or construct them in ways that suit their interests. Even though most natural scientists around the world agree that climate is changing because of human activity, I still encounter students in my classes who dispute its existence or its importance to business. The invisibility of climate change gives space for people to take a normative position, more so than business activities that are assumed to be "real," such as revenues and costs on balance sheets.

It is for these reasons that this book, *Leading Organizations in Hazardous Times: The Social Dynamics of Risk* is so very important. Dick offers a comprehensive view of how risk is understood, shaped and potentially mitigated. He speaks deeply about the importance of cognition and affect in sensing risk, the social and institutional forces that shape our understanding of risk, and resulting behavior. To generate ideas and recommendations for change, he draws from a broad range of disciplines, including psychology, social psychology and organizational behavior. But, fear not, abstract ideas are grounded in vivid examples from practice, Dick's professional experience and the popular press. For example, I was struck by Dick's account of the catastrophic Deepwater Horizon oil spill which blended information from federal reports, media sources and experience with organizations to describe management failures that crippled the ability of individuals to identify and act on risk.

Dick is asking us, whether we are in business or other sectors of society, to pay attention to the mechanics and dynamics of risk. Given that risks are often invisible, leaders must employ a thoughtful and balanced approach to risk, organizations must build robust risk cultures and everyone in an organization must be tasked to see and report risks. This places the responsibility on individuals to speak up when they see risks and on leaders to listen to them. To build risk intelligence, organizational members, from top to bottom, need to be familiar with potential risks and have the agency to act on them. These individual actions are the very heart of an organization's risk culture.

I am writing this Foreword at a time of intensifying polarization on issues that present catastrophic risks. I sit on the side that worries about the impacts of climate change, pandemics, unregulated artificial intelligence, income and social inequality and rogue capitalism. There are many on the other side that dismiss these issues. It is the specter of polarization that makes this book even more important, because Dick does not take a normative position. He simply states the impact on business which can speak to either end of the spectrum. And, he offers a pathway for leaders and employees into organizational structures and processes that will help to shield business, community and society from the harmful effects of catastrophic risk.

By seeing and responding to risk, organizations will ensure their own prosperity and that of shareholders, stakeholders and society. Most importantly, they will ensure the prosperity of future generations.

Pratima (Tima) Bansal,
Canada Research Chair in Business Sustainability,
Ivey Business School

Preface

I became interested in risk more than a decade ago when scientific evidence of climate change became irrefutable and events on the national and world stage challenged the boundaries of reason and belief. Things happened that were beyond my imagination. Non-stop media images of risk of our own making: extreme weather caused by climate change, anxiety surrounding AI, hyperbolic rhetoric of leaders, the growing threat of global warfare, civil disorder and gun violence, partisan antipathy, declining confidence in government and more. Doing nothing was not an option. I did something—I crafted a book describing the evolving world of catastrophic risk and actions organizations and leaders would need to take to mitigate its effects and consequences. *Catastrophic Risk: Business Strategy for Managing Turbulence in a World at Risk* was published in 2021. Its impact was negligible and, given the changing world around us, I was left to question *Why?*

The "*Why*" is our tendency to look past risk for light at the end of the tunnel. We are hard-wired to avoid threats and to rely on hope to counter the uncertainty and anxiety that are part of risk. Hope provides a sense of control and possibility—without it we are lost. *Catastrophic Risk* was not a "feel good" book; it did not offer a rosy picture of the future. Its purpose was to provide an unequivocal analysis of risks that would impact our quality of life and to call on organizations, particularly business, to put people first in times of crisis. It was unquestionably a tough read, but one that offered important lessons about risk and behavior that led to the book you are holding. These lessons were four: (1) risk has two dimensions—the risk itself and behavior in response to risk; (2) risk behavior is incredibly diverse; (3) the diversity of behavior is influenced by individual, group and setting factors that are part of social dynamics; and (4) social dynamics compound the effect and consequences of risk and render it difficult to manage.

Leading Organizations in Hazardous Times: The Social Dynamics of Risk began with these lessons. It is designed to address a conundrum facing organizations and leaders in a widening risk universe: *The challenge lies not in the risk itself but in social dynamics that shape behavior in response to risk.* This challenge and its resolution through the efforts of organizations and leaders is the raison d'etre of this book.

For Whom This Book Is Intended

The term VUCA (Volatile, Uncertain, Complex, and Ambiguous) is often used to describe the environment of growing risk in which organizations operate. Leaders who understand risk and know how to create opportunity from it will be difference makers in the future. This book is intended for difference makers, informal and otherwise, who will be the architects of organizational success in hazardous times.

A Challenge

In its most dangerous form, risk is ambiguous. It develops slowly and has unclear impact, making it easy to underestimate or ignore. The 2023 wildfire in Maui, the Fukushima nuclear accident in Japan, the Deepwater Horizon oil platform explosion in the Gulf of Mexico and the *Challenger* space shuttle disaster are examples of risk events that were unanticipated and of uncertain outcome. In each of these events, leaders struggled with risk because they failed to recognize weak signals or downplayed early warning signs.

Climate change is a perfect example of ambiguous risk with a significant impact. Weather extremes have led to rising rates of morbidity and mortality and increased susceptibility to health risks, including stress, depression and anxiety. Yet, despite the danger posed by climate change, we adapt rather than mobilize in response to root cause. As temperatures rise, we increase our fluid intake, wear lightweight clothing and avoid strenuous activity. We forgo action on root cause—for instance, taking steps to lower our carbon footprint—because greater effort is required. We know what we have to do to make a difference, but the simplicity of convenience wins out.

Let's get personal and find out what you would do when facing a choice about risk:

You are a homeowner whose growing concern about climate change has reached a point where personal action is warranted. You have figured out what it will take to reduce your carbon foot-print—get rid of your gas-powered car, use public transportation, install solar panels on the roof of your home, conserve electricity and change to a plant-based diet. Your past experience with a climate action group was positive and this is an incentive to act. Action comes with a cost however—climate action will require behavioral change on your part and it will disrupt your life routine. It will also meet with disfavor from neighbors who do not like the idea of rooftop solar panels because of concern about their property value. Beyond cost is the matter of benefit which is uncertain. You are only one person doing your part to address climate change and you wonder just how much impact your efforts will have. If you are one of many, your effort may be worthwhile. If you are acting alone, your effort may be fruitless. Taking everything into account, will your choice be to act or to forgo action?

Now, let's change the venue to organizations and ask what you would do in the position of a senior executive charged with building a robust risk culture for your company:

Facing pressure to reduce your company's vulnerability to risk in a volatile business environment, the governing board and CEO of your company have charged you with developing a culture in which risk is everyone's business. The CEO and leadership team expect steady progress toward a robust culture through policy, structural and management changes. It will be a tough slog. Standing in the way are employees with diverse attitudes toward risk, many of whom believe that risk is not part of their job—it is the responsibility of management. Making things even more difficult are informal leaders urging caution out of concern that added responsibility could affect job performance. Caught in the middle are managers who are expected to bring employees along with change while keeping relationships on positive footing. Watching with interest from outside are competitors seeking advantage, stakeholders asking tough questions about your company's approach to risk, and regulatory bodies looking into its risk management practices. Given

*these competing interests, how will you go about building a robust
risk culture?*

Each situation involves social dynamics which complicate decision-making about risk. Group dynamics are at work in the form of pressure from neighbors, company executives and informal leaders. Environmental factors are in play in the form of stakeholder expectations, competitor practices and regulatory agency protocols. And there are your personal feelings and biases about risk and their effect on decision-making. These forces are interconnected, and they will have a lot to do with how you go about building a risk culture.

What's Inside

This book is divided into three parts that describe the relationship between risk, social dynamics and behavior and implications for organizations and leaders in hazardous times.

Part I, "The Changing Face of Risk," takes the reader into the modern world of "manufactured risk." The opening chapter ("A Risk Society") describes the specter of rapidly accelerating interconnected risks arising from human activity. Six habitats of risk are presented with climate change and AI singled out as imminent threats to humanity because of their insidious nature. The focus in Chapter 2 ("Risk and Response") shifts to forms of manufactured risk and social dynamics influencing behavior in response to risk. Risks are described in terms of their origin as "known," "ambiguous" and "unforeseen" with ambiguous risks particularly vexing because of unclear warning signs and unpredictable consequences. Social dynamics mediate our relationship with risk. Cognitive, psychological and cultural factors integral to social dynamics are described, and their impact on risk behavior is examined through the lens of social science research. Chapter 3 ("Modeling Social Dynamics") presents a working model of factors which shape risk perception and behavior. Illustrations drawn from risk culture research and disaster risk analysis are used to describe social dynamics contributing to risk behavior. A multi-factor model derived from analysis is presented and used as a basis for description and analysis of social dynamics in chapters that follow.

Part II, "Social Dynamics of Risk," examines interrelated forces that shape behavior in response to risk. Chapter 4 ("Risk and Cognition") describes how the brain works to protect us from harm and its powerful effect on thought and behavior in response to risk. Everything starts with the brain. It is the driving force behind what we think and do, the social dynamics we create and how we respond to threats. Chapter 5 ("Eclipse of Societal Guardrails") turns the focus to social forces and their effect on risk perception and behavior. Forces precipitating cohesion and change are described, and social capital and exchange are profiled as behavioral modes shaping our response to risk. In Chapter 6 ("Group Dynamics and Risk Behavior") group dynamics and their effect on risk behavior are described. The impact of group membership is examined through illustrations of individual and group behavior in situations involving disaster and organizational change. Core elements of group dynamics—conformity, cohesion and groupthink—are defined and their impact on risk behavior in a three spheres framework is described. Chapter 7 ("The Shaping Power of Institutions") examines the impact of organizations and the media on risk behavior. Risk behavior develops through exposure to organizational norms and media content which channel risk into a two-dimensional framework of "event" and "attitude." Risk attitudes in organizations are varied and wide-ranging thereby complicating the efforts of leaders to manage them. In Chapter 8 ("A Perfect Storm") the impact of interconnected social dynamics forces on risk attitude is described. Attitudes are profiled on a continuum ranging from flow to asymmetry to paradox based on alignment of social dynamics forces and described in terms of the challenge they pose to organizations and leaders in managing risk.

Part III, "Leading and Managing Risk," moves to the domain of actions organizations and leaders must employ to effectively manage risk. Chapter 9 ("Building Risk Intelligent Organizations") describes the importance of building a risk intelligent risk culture in a widening risk universe. Sources of culture failure are presented and attributes of strong and weak risk cultures are examined using corporate examples. The chapter closes with a multi-dimensional Risk Culture Framework which can be used to assess organizational risk culture. Chapter 10 ("The Asymmetry of Leading") takes the reader to skills and capabilities leaders will need to develop to effectively manage risk. Chief among them are skills in bridging asymmetries of attitude, managing and leadership style that leaders will need to cultivate as part of their risk management arsenal. Asymmetric leadership is modeled using a seven-factor framework and corporate examples are provided to demonstrate real-world application of the framework.

Look Beyond What You See ... and Act

This book is written for a future that is well on its way, but yet to be fully realized. It is written with leaders in mind who possess dual capability—an ability to effectively manage risk in the present and to look beyond and envision a future rife with opportunity. These leaders, whomever they may be and wherever we will find them, will seek and find advantage in risk and act on it.

Richard L. Alfred
Ocean Park, Maine

Acknowledgments

The catalyst for this book was deep interest in the social dynamics of risk evolving from research and observation of events and conditions driving behavior in modern society. Social dynamics was a topic that received all too limited attention in my 2021 book *Catastrophic Risk: Business Strategy for Managing Turbulence in a World at Risk*. It became a nagging oversight and a "must do" in order to flesh out our understanding of risk—an understanding based on the realization that risk itself is only one part of the equation. The other part of the equation is human behavior in response to risk which conditions its effect and consequences.

I am indebted to Kate Thirolf, Associate Professor, University of Maryland Global Campus, for her contribution to the book. Kate signed on as a co-author early on in book development, contributed in important ways to the outline of the book and authored the chapter on Cognition. She is a creative thinker and skilled writer who unfortunately had to withdraw from authorship because of family matters. Cognition is a knowledge field quite apart from thinkers in disciplines outside of neuroscience and psychology. In taking the book into the realm of neuroscience, Kate opened a new door to the relationship between risk and behavior and added depth to our understanding of social dynamics.

Good fortune comes in many forms, and for me it is my partner in life and work, Patricia Carter. Pat is a vital part of the thought process that went into this book—its early development, chapter narrative and finish editing. She is a brilliant content editor who has a knack for being in the right place at the right time when an idea, a sentence or a word is needed to get a message across. The last set of eyes on the book before it was delivered to the publisher belonged to Pat. I owe a similar debt of gratitude to Kris Mednansky, Senior Editor, Business Improvement-Health Care Management at Taylor & Francis Group. Kris is the editor every author wants to work with—patient, quick to respond to an inquiry and acutely aware of author problems and concerns. She is an incredible resource and working with her on this book and its precursor *Catastrophic Risk: Business Strategy for Managing Turbulence in a World at Risk* has been a privilege.

Two years ago, by chance, I lucked into communication with Tima Bansal, author of the Foreword and Professor of Strategy and Canada Research Chair in Sustainability at Ivey Business School. I had come across Tima's work on sustainability in a commentary published in a high-profile journal and reached out to her to share ideas of mutual interest. What followed was communication about risk and sustainability and an invitation to review and comment on my earlier book on catastrophic risk. Tima is an incisive thinker with a remarkable ability to dive into the heart of a topic, separate centrality and peripherality in its message, and bring its contribution into sharp focus. I have the utmost respect for her acumen and her work, and I am honored that she agreed to craft the Foreword.

This book was two years in development and much in the world changed as it was being written. Given the world we live in, risk is a topic with a long shelf life. Hopefully, this book will repose not on a shelf, but in a reader's hands.

About the Author

Richard L. Alfred is Emeritus Professor of Higher Education at the University of Michigan. Prior to joining the graduate faculty at Michigan, he served as an executive officer in the City University of New York and the Metropolitan Community Colleges in Kansas City. He is the author of numerous books including *Catastrophic Risk: Business Strategy for Managing Turbulence in a World at Risk* (2021), *Developing Tomorrow's Leaders: Context, Challenges and Capabilities* (2015), *Performance: The Dynamic of Results in Postsecondary Organizations* (2012) and an award-winning book on organizational strategy, *Managing the Big Picture in Colleges and Universities: From Tactics to Strategy* (2006). Throughout a 50-year career in academe, he has consulted with hundreds of organizations in the areas of strategy, organizational change and effectiveness, and leadership. His models for strategic planning and performance assessment are widely used by organizations in developing change strategy. Foresight into the future—a hallmark of his books, writing and speaking—is an oft-used resource by leaders to guide strategic decisions through anticipation of challenges and opportunities that lie beyond the horizon.

Dick holds a bachelor of arts degree from Allegheny College and master's and doctoral degrees from Penn State University. He and his wife Pat reside in Ocean Park, Maine.

THE CHANGING FACE OF RISK

Part I

Chapter 1

A Risk Society

"There are tranquil ages, which seem to contain that which will last forever. And there are ages of change, which see upheavals that, in extreme instances, appear to go to the root of humanity itself."

Karl Jaspers, German-Swiss Psychiatrist, 1962

It's 2024. We are sweltering in heat waves caused by climate change and living in a society that has become deeply divided. We are on the cusp of a presidential election involving a choice between candidates neither of whom can claim a clear majority. We are trying to make sense of the overturn of Roe v. Wade and a Supreme Court decision giving immunity to presidents for official acts while in office. War is raging on multiple fronts with thousands killed in Ukraine, Gaza and Lebanon. And there are lingering effects of the pandemic and the advance of artificial intelligence and its implications for life and work going forward. Everything is topsy-turvy, but *these are events of our own making.* We have done this to ourselves, and it brings into question the world we are living in and where it is going.

Ours is a time of upheaval. In the words of political economist Jerome Roos[1]:

> Humanity now faces a confluence of challenges unlike any other in human history. Climate change is rapidly altering the conditions of life on our planet. Tensions over Ukraine and Taiwan have revived the specter of conflict between nuclear superpowers. And breakneck developments in artificial intelligence are raising serious concerns about the risk of an AI-induced global catastrophe. This

DOI: 10.4324/9781003335658-2

troubling situation calls for new perspectives to make sense of a rapidly changing world and where we might be headed.

Instead, we are left with countervailing forces driving our future: one of confidence in our ability to shape the future and the other of risk on a scale potentially beyond our control. These forces challenge our ability to maintain stability in a time of deep change. For organizations, they add form and dimension to risk which gives rise to a conundrum: *The challenge for organizations and leaders lies not in risk itself, but in social dynamics and how they shape behavior in response to risk.* This challenge and its resolution through the effort of organizations and leaders is the raison d'etre of this book.

Five questions are asked and answered in the pages that follow:

- What is modern risk?
- How do people respond to risk?
- What factors shape behavior in response to risk?
- How can organizations manage risk more effectively?
- What skills will leaders need to manage modern risk?

The Social Dynamics of Risk is meant for leaders who want to understand and effectively manage modern risk. Its purpose is to help organizations and leaders see risk in a different way and to achieve success by creating advantage from it.

A Society Divided

Modern risk is both ubiquitous and duplicitous. While scientific and technological advances have provided a measure of control over our destiny, they have also manufactured problems with severe, perhaps even irreversible, consequences. Take, for example, the creation of a vaccine for COVID-19. Weeks after the outbreak of the coronavirus, scientists identified the DNA sequence of the virus and developed a prototype of the protein fueling the virus. A vaccine candidate was designed, manufactured and moved to clinical trials two months later. Twelve months after the outbreak, the Pfizer BioNTech vaccine was authorized for use in the United States by the U.S. Food and Drug Administration, and days later, the Moderna vaccine was approved after testing for 94 percent efficacy.[2]

This was a remarkable scientific achievement—on par with the creation of a polio vaccine in the 1950s. The developer of the vaccine, Jonas Salk, tested the vaccine on himself and his family in the kitchen of his home.[3] Salk's action helped to quell widespread skepticism about the vaccine and mobilized the American public in pursuit of a common goal—the eradication of polio. Our response to the coronavirus vaccine, however, was quite different. Skepticism surrounding the vaccine among parts of the American public continued well beyond its introduction. After a year of disease, death and sheltering in place, vaccination was seen by many as a way out of a once in a lifetime pandemic. Most embraced the prospect of freedom through vaccination, but others weren't as enthusiastic. An antivax movement developed among people buying into false narratives about the vaccine and others hesitant about a vaccine they thought was experimental. Some went as far as to draw comparisons to medical gaslighting and historical abuse of people at the hands of the U.S. government. And then there were those who felt individual liberty was at stake—vaccine promotion was seen as an intrusion on personal choice.

Our response to the COVID-19 vaccine created a new social divide on top of existing divides. As contagious variants emerged following the initial wave of the virus, infections, hospitalizations and deaths rose in regions with low vaccination rates.[4] Those who stepped up and were vaccinated became increasingly intolerant of unvaccinated Americans perceived as not doing their part to stem the virus. Adding to their animus was a fear that as the delta and omicron variants spread, infected people would surround and overwhelm people who were vaccinated through "spillover infection" while continuing to impede herd immunity. For the vaccinated, compromise was neither rational or negotiable. People with different vaccination status steered clear of one another. Friendships were compromised, relationships were dissolved, and we found another way to divide ourselves. A society with two faces came into focus—one an advanced post-industrial culture and the other a primeval culture in which danger, division and risk are an everyday reality.

In the risk society we have become, headlines deliver a daily message of peril. As this book got underway, one day of headlines—September 5, 2021—brought danger into real time: "Nearly 1 in 3 Americans Experienced a Weather Disaster This Summer" (*The Washington Post*), "Hurricane Ida Turns Spotlight on Louisiana Power Grid Issues" (*Associated Press*), "Florida Grapples with COVID-19's Deadliest Phase Yet" (*Associated Press*), "Aerial

Images Show a 'Substantial' Oil Spill Spreading Off Louisiana Coast" (*The New York Times*), and "Hospitalization Rate for Children Soars" (*The New York Times*). Media posts rivet our attention on the everyday reality of danger, and, worse yet, they remind us of ongoing threats we face no matter where we live or wherever we may be.

Manufactured Risk

Sociologist Ulrich Beck attributes elevated attention to risk to "reflexive modernization"—a condition wherein unintended and unforeseen effects of modern life backfire on society.[5] In a risk society, danger and uncertainty are "manufactured" with consequences that are large-scale, not merely individual and personal. Concern is no longer focused principally on economic well-being, but instead on risk and safety and the way they are managed.[6] Development is reflexive rather than progressive with society carrying its own seeds of peril through unwanted side effects of man-made risk. Humanly created tragedies like oil spills in sensitive areas, flooding caused by extreme weather, drought-driven food and water shortages, and nuclear accidents fuel anxiety and mistrust. They are manufactured conditions that have created an environment of far-reaching consequences without historical precedent.

A society preoccupied with man-made risk has a social psychology quite unlike that of a society facing risk that is natural in origin. Manufactured risk impels people to seek safety through avoidance and reinterpretation of conditions and events. Social psychology research is clear that the most reliable way to alleviate discomfort associated with risk is to reframe thinking to fit the threat or to make the threat fit one's way of thinking.[7] We are capable of remarkable mental gymnastics to justify strongly held beliefs. The capacity of cults and mass movements, for instance, to inspire emotional commitment among followers, the ability of a team united by shared belief to overcome a stronger foe, and the ability of movements like Me Too and Black Lives Matter to grow and flourish—all are illustrations of the power of belief over thought and behavior. There is also a dangerous illogic to belief. The resistance of naysayers to scientific evidence of climate change is an example of belief gone awry. Denial and reinterpretation alleviate discomfort by reframing evidence to fit belief—climate change is not real, climate models are unreliable, or climate change is cyclical as Earth moves through heating and cooling cycles.

Habitats of Risk

Scientific models suggest that the likelihood of extinction through naturally occurring events is extremely small. In stark contrast is risk driven by human activity. While scientific and technological developments have expanded our ability to manipulate the environment, their potential consequences have put us at risk. Take, for example, growing concern about artificial intelligence and its use in modern society as reported in *U.S. News and World Report*[8]:

U.S. News and World Report, February 13, 2023

ChatGPT, a fast-growing artificial intelligence program has drawn praise for its ability to write answers quickly to a wide range of queries, and attracted U.S. lawmakers' attention with questions about its impact on national security and education. ChatGPT was estimated to have reached 100 million monthly active users just two months after its launch making it the fastest-growing consumer application in history and a growing target for regulation. It was created by OpenAI, a private company backed by Microsoft Corp, and made available to the public for free. Its ubiquity has generated fear that generative AI such as ChatGPT could be used to spread disinformation while educators worry it will be used by students to cheat.

Representative Ted Lieu, a Democrat on the House of Representatives Science Committee said in a recent opinion piece in the New York Times that he was "excited about AI and the incredible ways it will continue to advance society," but also "freaked out by AI. Specifically, AI that is left unchecked and unregulated."

Andrew Burt, managing partner of BNH, a law firm focused on AI liability, pointed to national security concerns, adding that he has spoken to lawmakers who are studying whether to regulate ChatGPT and similar AI systems such as Google's Bard. "The whole value proposition of these types of AI systems is that they can generate content at scales and speeds that humans simply can't."

Six habitats of risk are described in the pages that follow in terms of their impact on humanity. In the course of reading, consider the risk posed by each habitat and ask yourself: *What is the nature of risk:* Is it a passing threat, a clear and immediate danger, an ongoing threat that must be monitored, or a threat that is irreversible? *What drives response to risk:* our need to avoid or suppress it, our need to reinterpret it to fit our way of thinking, or our need to mitigate it by taking action? *What is most important when facing risk:* ensuring one's personal safety, the safety of others or the safety of community and society? Finally, ask yourself: *As a society, are we capable of timely action in response to risk to avoid its worst effects?*

Climate Change

Climate change has become deadly. It will get worse.

As this book was being written, the nation and world smashed through one all-time heat record after another and sped toward a critical warming threshold. Waves of simultaneously occurring weather events in the United States supercharged by climate change devastated the nation—heat waves across the nation, deep snow and atmospheric rivers in the Western States, stronger and more destructive hurricanes in the South, bomb cyclones in the Midwest and ravaging nor'easters in New England. On the world stage, Cyclone Freddy made landfall in Mozambique on March 11, 2023, for a repeat performance after first walloping the country in February.[9] Freddy lasted more than a month—one of the longest-lived and furthest-traveled tropical cyclones ever, as well as one of Earth's most energetic storms. Freddy killed 400 people, flooded major portions of countryside and disrupted power infrastructure. In the same month:

■ Atmospheric rivers in California brought hurricane force winds and pounding rainfall to the San Francisco Bay area resulting in runoff flooding and mudslides that affected 35 million people.[10] The storm was widely considered to be the worst March storm in California history.
■ Towns and localities were wiped off the map and scores of people left homeless by an EF-4 tornado that ripped through Mississippi and Alabama on March 26.[11] The storm traveled 60 miles on the ground with winds between 160 and 200 miles per hour. It was the deadliest in Mississippi state history in more than a decade.

Human activity has transformed the planet at a pace and scale unmatched in recorded history. In a report released in March 2023, by the United Nations Intergovernmental Panel on Climate Change (IPCC), leading scientists warned that the world's plans to combat climate change are inadequate and far more aggressive action must be taken to avert catastrophic warming.[12] On its current path, the world will default on a crucial goal—limiting warming to 2.7 degrees Fahrenheit above preindustrial temperatures by 2030.[13] Beyond that threshold, climate disasters will become so extreme people will be unable to adapt. Heat waves, famines and infectious diseases will claim millions of lives and basic components of our ecosystem will be irrevocably altered.

Decades of studies on the causes and consequences of rising temperatures have presented irrefutable evidence of the impact of fossil fuels which, when burned, release greenhouse gases into the atmosphere and trap heat. The Earth's average temperature has increased 1.4° F over the past century and without intervention is projected to rise by as much as 11.5° F by the close of the 21st century.[14] Fossil fuels are only part of the problem. Agriculture and deforestation cause land-based ecosystems to release more CO_2 into the air than they absorb thereby increasing the volume of CO_2 in the atmosphere. Warming ocean temperatures release added moisture into the air leading to sea level rise, more frequent and intense weather events and flooding. Heat waves contribute to rising levels of human mortality through drought conditions that cause food shortages and insect-borne disease.

To avoid catastrophe, the relationship between carbon emissions and human behavior will need to be turned upside down. Global warming will need to be limited to 2.7° F above preindustrial temperatures by 2030 and global human-caused emissions of carbon dioxide to "net zero" by 2050.[15] To reach this goal, rapid and unprecedented changes in energy and land use and industry and transportation will be necessary. Our approach to using water and consuming and disposing of food will need to change.

Warfare and Mass Destruction

How could something like this happen in "modern" society?

Images of residential buildings, schools and hospitals in ruins after Russian missile attacks and scores of civilians and soldiers dead in streets brought into our living rooms by media. This must be Armageddon! On February 24, 2022, Russia invaded and occupied parts of Ukraine upon Vladimir Putin's proclamation of a "special military operation."[16] Putin challenged Ukraine's right to statehood and falsely claimed Ukraine was governed by neo-Nazis who persecuted the ethnic Russian minority. Minutes after

Putin's announcement, Russian air strikes and a ground invasion were launched along a northern front from Belarus toward Kyiv, a northeastern front toward Kharkiv, a southern front from Crimea and a southeastern front from Donetsk and Luhansk.[17] In response, Ukraine's president, Volodymyr Zelensky, enacted martial law and a general mobilization. An invasion that in Putin's view was to end with the total occupation of Ukraine in a matter of days, evolved into a grinding war with Western nations joining forces to equip Ukraine with arms. Thousands of lives were lost, refugees streamed out of Ukraine in numbers not seen since World War II, and European nations were brought to the threshold of war.[18]

The worst fears of world leaders became reality when Russia invaded Ukraine. As nations lined up in support of Ukraine and Russia turned toward partners for arms, the possibility of a third world war moved from words to the threshold of reality. War has a beginning and an end. Beyond the act of war, however, are stockpiles of nuclear weapons which pose a continuing threat to humanity. Nine countries—China, India, Israel, France, North Korea, Pakistan, Russia, the United Kingdom and the United States—hold nearly 16,000 nuclear weapons. Enough to destroy the planet several times over.[19] If a nuclear weapon was launched and exploded in a major city, the blast epicenter would be hotter than the surface of the sun, tornado-strength winds would spread flames in every direction, and a million or more people would die.[20] Survivors would have no electricity, transportation or phones, and hospitals would be overwhelmed—if they were still standing.

Until recently, nuclear weapon proliferation had been limited by treaties and agreements among nuclear states. In 1985, Soviet leader Mikhail Gorbachev and U.S. President Ronald Reagan jointly declared "a nuclear war cannot be won and must never be fought."[21] That phrase lived on, evoked by the leaders of both countries, and re-affirmed in January 2022, by Russian President Vladimir Putin, U.S. President Joe Biden, and leaders of China, France and the United Kingdom, all of which have permanent seats on the United Nations Security Council.[22] Everything changed with the invasion of Ukraine and nuclear threats by Russia to block interference from other nations. In March 2022, Russia suspended its participation in New START—the last remaining nuclear weapons treaty between the United States and Russia.[23] New START allows participating nations to verify adherence to the weapons pact by inspecting other nations' nuclear arsenal multiple times each year. It does not, however, stop development of new weapons as nuclear states leapfrog one another to create advantage. Russia has developed a "Skyfall" nuclear cruise missile, a "Poseidon" nuclear-armed unmanned underwater vehicle, an "Avangard" hypersonic glide missile and a "Satan" multiple-warhead intercontinental ballistic missile.[24] China is developing and testing a hypersonic nuclear weapon, and the United States is developing a hypersonic spy plane and advanced nuclear warhead for use with submarine-launched ballistic missiles.[25]

Rogue Technology

We're only in the early stages of AI. Where is it going?

Given the rapid, almost alarming, advance of artificial intelligence, a case can be made that humanity is already on its way to giving up its own dominance. Consider the words of Dan Hendrycks in "Survival of the Fittest" (*Time*, June 12, 2023).[26]

> *Imagine a CEO who acquires an AI assistant. He begins by giving it simple, low-level assignments, like drafting emails and suggesting purchases. As the AI improves over time, it progressively becomes much better at these things, so it gets "promoted." Rather than drafting emails, it now has full control of the inbox. Rather than suggesting purchases, it's eventually allowed to access bank accounts and buy things automatically. At first, the CEO carefully monitors the work, but as months go by without error, the AI receives less oversight and more autonomy in the name of efficiency. It occurs to the CEO that since the AI is so good at these tasks it should take on a wider range of more open-ended goals: "design the next mode in a product line," or "plan a new marketing campaign," or "exploit security flaws in a competitor's computer systems." The CEO observes how businesses with more restricted use of AIs are falling behind, and is incentivized to hand over more power to the AI with less oversight. Companies that resist these trends don't stand a chance. Eventually, even the CEO's role is largely nominal. The economy is run by autonomous AI corporations, and humanity realizes too late that we've lost control.*

Like other revolutions, artificial intelligence comes with promise and peril. It has been suggested that super-intelligent learning computers could become capable of creating unintended results or robots could eventually outperform humans. It has also been suggested that the exceptional organizational capabilities and novel faculties of AI could become matchless and unrivaled—capable of producing almost any outcome and able to foil any attempt to block its path. ChatGPT has challenged the sanctity of everything from college application essays to graduate school tests and medical school licensing exams by producing remarkably clear, long-form answers to complex questions.[27] AI applications have matched or exceeded the performance of experts and professionals in health care, education, transportation, finance and beyond. At their best, AI tools perform tasks at a much greater speed, scale and degree of accuracy than humans—freeing up time and resources for us to solve problems that machines cannot. Chatbots can provide support around the clock; crawlers can scour websites and databases for information; investors can make smarter and better-informed decisions on the market using AI algorithms; and self-driving cars can make travel safer and more convenient.

Despite its many advantages, AI technology is not without perils. Automation of jobs, the spread of fake news and an arms race fueled by AI-powered weaponry are among the dangers posed by AI. A short list of dangers include:[28]

- *Job transformation and losses due to automation.* As AI robots become smarter and more dexterous, the same tasks will require fewer humans. Eighty-five million jobs are expected to be lost to automation between 2020 and 2025, with Black and Latino employees especially vulnerable.[29] AI is projected to create 97 million new jobs by 2025, but workers will need advanced technical skills for these jobs, and many will not have them.[30]
- *Social manipulation through AI algorithms.* Algorithms are not equipped to detect and filter out harmful and inaccurate information. Online media and news are especially prone to deepfakes that have infiltrated social and political spheres—a circumstance facilitating distribution of misinformation and making it nearly impossible to distinguish between credible and faulty information.
- *Biases due to artificial intelligence.* AI can adversely affect individual privacy and security. A prime example occurred in 2019, when researchers found that a predictive algorithm used by UnitedHealth Group was biased against Black patients.[31] Using healthcare spending as a proxy for illness, the algorithm inadvertently perpetuated systemic inequities that have historically kept Black patients from receiving adequate care.

- *Widening social inequality as a result of AI.* AI-driven technologies exacerbate job loss as blue-collar workers performing manual repetitive tasks are replaced by automation while white-collar workers remain largely untouched.
- *Autonomous weapons powered by artificial intelligence.* Technological advancements have a history of being harnessed for the purpose of warfare. Military powers engaged in AI weapons development could change the course of warfare. Autonomous weapons are a threat to civilians, but the threat is amplified when they fall into the wrong hands. If a malicious actor was to infiltrate autonomous weaponry and launch an attack on infrastructure, the result would be catastrophic.
- *Financial crises brought about by AI algorithms.* While AI is a critical tool in the finance industry for market decisions, algorithms don't take context into account, the interconnectedness of markets, and factors like human trust and fear. Algorithms make thousands of trades at a blistering pace with the goal of selling a few seconds later for small profit. Selling off thousands of trades could scare investors into following the same path, leading to sudden crashes and extreme market volatility.

In *Superintelligence: Paths, Dangers, Strategies*, Swedish philosopher Nicholas Bostrom argues that if machines were to surpass humans in general intelligence, superintelligence could replace humans as the dominant life form on Earth.[32] Bostrom is not alone. Physicist Stephen Hawking, Microsoft founder Bill Gates and Space X founder Elon Musk have voiced concerns about the evolution of AI with Hawking theorizing that superintelligence could "spell the end of the human race." AI could run a course from creation of a superintelligent unit to a superintelligence explosion through continuous iteration over its own code in a short period of time. The resulting system would outsmart humans and achieve its own goals through infrastructure profusion—a process wherein AI builds quickly to enhance its cognitive abilities and evolves into an existential threat to mankind.[33]

Outbreak of Disease

Will the world be ready for the next pandemic?

COVID-19 dominated headlines across the world in the third decade of the Millennium. With 65 million cases and 1.5 million deaths worldwide by the close of 2020 and a crippling economic downturn, the short-term impact of

COVID-19 was nothing short of devastating.[34] The coronavirus challenged the boundary between disaster and catastrophe by incorporating elements of each. Similar to a catastrophe, it created wide-ranging impacts at the global level. Unlike catastrophe, however, it did not cause widespread destruction of infrastructure nor did it unravel societal institutions which remained intact. Disease has a beginning and an end and its impact and consequences can be remedied through human intervention—if lessons are learned from it. In the absence of learning, disease can be catastrophic as future generations repeat mistakes of the past.

The immediacy and speed of the pandemic limited the extent to which lessons from the past could be incorporated into planning for the present—a circumstance which doomed the world to repeat history. The response of nations to COVID-19 echoed the 1918–1919 "Spanish Flu" pandemic. One hundred years ago, the Spanish Flu claimed 50 million lives worldwide, after having infected half a billion people—one-third of the world's population at the time.[35] Similar to the COVID-19 pandemic, scientists and public health officials urged the shutdown of public gathering places, supported mandates to wear masks and promoted isolation, quarantine and hygiene as primary weapons in the battle against the virus. Those opposing these measures alluded to their futility, the potential for harm caused by wearing masks and the economic risks of shutting down businesses. People pushed back against the idea that the Spanish Flu was a serious threat irrespective of the fact that there was not a vaccine for influenza, nor antibiotics to treat secondary infections. The media landscape in 1918–1919 was not the encompassing force it is today, but questions linger as to what was learned from the Spanish Flu pandemic leading up to COVID-19 and the extent to which COVID-19 learning will inform planning and treatment of diseases in the future.

Social Inequality

The wealth gap is widening. What does it mean for society?

Despite growth in income and wealth across the globe, variability in economic means has widened and societies are enmeshed in a growing inequality gap. According to the International Monetary Fund, over the past three decades more than half of the world's nations have seen an increase in income inequality with the trend particularly pronounced in advanced economies.[36] Inequality exists in multiple forms, but the common thread is uneven access to goods, resources and opportunity on the basis of race and ethnicity, location, age, gender, and income and occupation.

Social inequality has dramatic consequences which stunt economic growth. Decades of research have documented effects ranging from contraction of growth to reduction of educational attainment. In an essay on the consequences of economic inequality, family activist Mia Birdsong pieced together relationships that illustrate the serial effects of inequality[37]:

> *In the face of rising prices for goods and lower incomes, wealthy citizens maintain disproportionate purchasing power compared to impoverished citizens. As the gap between rich and poor swells, the incentive to commit crimes grows as fewer methods of lawfully obtaining resources are available to indigent citizens. Further complicating the lives of these citizens is a lack of access to education and quality health care. Unequal societies tend to underinvest in programs that provide a financial path for impoverished citizens to access education and health care. Poor nutrition and diminished access to health care make impoverished citizens vulnerable to illness at a higher rate than the general population.*

In January 2020, the United Nations Department of Economic and Social Affairs chronicled historically high levels of inequality exacerbating divisions and retarding economic and social development. According to UN researchers, "more than two-thirds of the world's population reside in countries where inequality has grown." Key findings reveal the social and economic effects of inequality[38]

- Highly unequal societies marginalize opportunity for economic and social development by retaining citizens in cycles of poverty
- Technological innovation, climate change, urbanization and migration exacerbate the effects of inequality
- Inequality erodes trust in government by concentrating influence in the hands of wealthier citizens
- Children in the poorest households and those in disadvantaged ethnic groups evidence lower rates of school attendance and academic performance than children from wealthier families

■ Technology breakthroughs have increased inequality by opening new opportunities for highly skilled workers and diminishing opportunity for workers in routine labor-intensive jobs.

Beyond the numbers, however, is an overarching aspect of social inequality that exacerbates the effects and consequences of risk—the importance of basic individual needs, the role they play in motivation and their effect on behavior in times of crisis. In Maslow's hierarchy of needs, physiological and safety needs must be met before individuals become motivated to pursue higher-level needs.[39] When physiological needs are unmet, personal discomfort rises and incentives to reduce the discrepancy between needs and satisfaction increase. In the world of risk, the cost of inequality is a reduction in capacity for collective mobilization in response to crisis if personal needs are put ahead of societal needs.

Violence and Civil Disorder

A constitutional crisis in a 250-year democracy under attack prompted by a sitting president. How could that be?

On January 6, 2021, following the defeat of President Donald Trump in the 2020 presidential election, a mob of his supporters attacked the United States Capitol Building. The mob sought to keep Trump in power by preventing a joint session of Congress from counting the electoral college votes to formalize the victory of President-Elect Joe Biden. According to the House Select Committee investigating the incident, the attack was part of a seven-part plan by Trump to overturn the election. Five people died, many were injured including 138 police officers, and monetary damages exceeded $1.5 million.[40]

Violence and civil disorder have risen to the top of problems facing America today. Almost half of 5,074 adults surveyed by the Pew Research Center in 2021 about problems facing the nation cited gun violence and violent crime as a "very big problem" superseded only by the affordability of health care and the federal budget deficit.[41] Shortly after the January 2021 rioting in the Capitol, a Pew survey of 5,360 adults found nearly four in ten (37 percent) holding strong negative feelings about the riot and more than one in three (35 percent) expressing shock, anguish and horror that such an event could happen in the United States.[42] These findings are but a small sample of articles and reports on violence and disorder in the United States.

Their overall effect, however, reveals deepening concern about violence and disorder and the threat they pose in American culture.

Violence. There were 163 mass shootings in the United States between January and April 2023, leaving more than 200 people dead, 550 people injured and communities traumatized.[43] Gun violence and mass shootings are no longer localized. They can happen anywhere at any time and their impact is far-reaching as reflected in poll data. In September 2019, 46 percent of 1,250 adults responding to a Gallup poll indicated concern about "being a victim of terrorism" and 45 percent about "becoming a victim of a mass shooting."[44] Twenty years after the 9/11 terror attacks, a record-high 64 percent of U.S. adults indicated they have permanently changed the way they live because of the attacks.[45] In 2022, a Gallup survey of 1,082 adults regarding problems facing the country revealed that four out of five (80 percent) worried a "great deal" or "fair amount" about crime and violence.[46]

Violence is a continuing thread in American life, but time and circumstance condition how people perceive violence and live with fear. Living through the Cold War, with its constant specter of nuclear attack, required an ability to live free of fear in order to function. Jarring instances of violence and a belief that we are left to our own devices to manage threats have brought new meaning to fear. The 9/11 terrorist attack, for example, wasn't as fearsome after the first few months because people believed that government would protect civilians from terrorist attacks on U.S. soil. Loss of faith in government, however, has lowered confidence in the ability of institutions to keep us safe. Part and parcel of declining confidence in institutions is the politics of fear—a strategy employed by leaders to manipulate people's emotions.[47] And let's not overlook the power of media in feeding fear and feelings about government. Searing images of mass shootings appearing instantaneously on television and social media heighten awareness of the potential for violence happening anywhere at any time.

Civil Disorder. A wave of civil unrest triggered by the death of George Floyd in 2020 fueled riots and protests against systemic racism. Since then, hundreds of incidents of unrest and civil disorder have occurred throughout the country. Polls estimate that between 15 million and 26 million people participated in demonstrations between 2020 and 2023 in the United States.[48] The Civil Unrest Index issued by Verisk Maplecroft, a global risk analytics company, uses sociological indicators to gauge civil unrest.[49] In December 2020, six factors were identified as contributing to growing unrest in the United States—dissatisfaction with government, deepening concern about economic security and inflation, protests over racial discrimination, the

Supreme Court ruling on abortion, the rise of populism and the incendiary rhetoric of leaders. Disorder is no longer something that "happens in other places" and that "other people do." It happens here, it crosses demographic and temporal boundaries and it happens with greater frequency. Even from afar, we cannot escape the specter of disorder. It is brought into our homes and minds on a daily basis by the media—disorder has become everyone's business.

Civil disorder has three dimensions which make it a habitat of risk: violence, secondary hazards, and the aftermath of disorder. Consider the dynamics of disorder associated with the death of George Floyd in 2020:

> **Violence.** *Local protests began in the Minneapolis-St. Paul metropolitan area and quickly spread nationwide in more than 2,000 cities and towns as well as internationally in support of the Black Lives Matter movement.[50] In Minneapolis, destruction of property began on May 26, with protests evolving into vandalism and arson. Demonstrations in other cities descended into riots and widespread looting accompanied by claims of police brutality against protestors and journalists. Nineteen people died as a result of rioting.[51]*

> **Secondary Hazards.** *Rioting resulted in insured property losses totaling $2 billion due to arson and fire.[52] Utility and transportation services were disrupted and environmental hazards created by toxic substances. Government operations were affected and businesses lost millions in inventory, sales revenue and economic opportunity.*

> **Aftermath.** *As residents and business owners cleaned up debris, the reality of damage to the communities where violence took place began to sink in. Damage was not only to person and property, but also to the local economy and it would persist long after the last window pane was replaced and burned-out car towed away. Property values and quality-of-life indicators would decline as a result of the riot and communities would face significant economic challenges. Property risk and insurance premiums would rise, taxes would increase for police and fire protection, retail outlets would close or relocate, and higher income households would move away.*

In the early 1990s when Bill Clinton was in the White House, behavioral scientists Jack Goldstone and Peter Turchin were appointed by the Clinton Administration to study how nations fail.[53] In an unpublished paper coming out of their work, Goldstone, a leading authority on the study of revolutions and long-term social change, and Turchin, an expert on mathematical modeling of historical societies, predicted that the United States is "headed for another civil war."[54] The conditions for civil violence, they claimed, were the worst since the period leading up to the Civil War in the 19th century. Crisis indicators were building and crippling the ability of government to deliver policies that would deliver economic relief to citizens.

Goldstone and Turchin developed a two-index model to gauge the potential for violence.[55] The Political Stress Index combined crisis indicators of declining living standards, increasing competition and conflict and weakening of the nation to indicate high potential for violence. A Well-Being Index used indicators of growing equality, greater consensus and a stronger nation to indicate lower potential for violence. When fleshed out with data, the model revealed discord growing out of an era of Post-World War II Prosperity and a Gilded Age between 1960 and 2000.[56] A Boomer generation born in a time of relative peace and plenty fueled population growth after World War II. As this cohort aged and achieved wealth, three conditions evolved that would make the nation vulnerable to political crisis and violence: (1) the path to mobility tightened to favor elites and their children; (2) wage growth diminished for segments of the population enabling elites to claim a greater share of economic gains; and (3) taxation was resisted thereby starving the government of needed revenue.

With the dawn of the new millennium, Goldstone and Turchin's predictions took flight in rising college costs, elevation of skill and credential requirements for higher paying jobs, widening of the wealth divide between rich and poor, and tax policy favoring higher income citizens. The consequences of growing inequality were reflected in the Fragile States Index (FSI)—an annual report published by the non-profit Fund for Peace which examines the vulnerability of nations to internal conflict and societal deterioration and assigns a score indicating their ability to cope with shocks.[57] Two decades of data collected by FSI between 2000 and 2020 revealed a steadily worsening position of the United States on the Index. According to Charles Fiertz, a program manager at FSI, a significant change in the U.S. position on the Index occurred in 2016 following the presidential election and Brexit.[58] The United States and the United Kingdom were among countries in the world experiencing the greatest decline over the preceding years on indicators of economic and material inequality, group injustice and factionalized elites.[59] In periods of stability, nations adapt to worsening conditions through vigilance, social policy and collective action. When the buildup of conditions is long-term and gradual, vulnerable nations cannot readily adapt. Collapse begins slowly and then accelerates rapidly. As conditions worsen, vulnerability grows until a sudden jolt—a war, a climate catastrophe, a pandemic—overwhelms the system.

Exacerbation of Risk

Risk is a corollary of threat, but there is another way to think about it. While a threat is a circumstance or event involving uncertainty and the possibility that something bad could happen, risk is a function of the extent to which an event could inflict damage because of human behavior. The effect and consequences of risk are exacerbated by behavior which impels people to seek safety through avoidance and interpretation of conditions and events. My experience with fear of flying (aerophobia) early in career provides an excellent illustration of the interaction between risk and behavior.

> *I was perfectly comfortable with flight until bad weather and a turbulent flight between Denver and New York in 1978 created anxiety that stayed with me for the better part of a decade. From that point on, in-flight turbulence created anxiety as did dark clouds and rough weather. Days before a flight, I would check the weather forecast for departure and arrival cities. If severe weather was in the forecast, I would change the flight—it relieved my anxiety. After boarding a plane, I used mind games and a simple foot exercise to take my mind off the anxiety of flight. This went on for ten years until air travel associated with work became so frequent and the ratio of bad-weather flights to good-weather flights so low that my anxiety receded.*

I was using safety behavior to cope with an imagined threat and to reduce anxiety. Safety behavior is a common response to risk even if the threat is low. The odds of dying in a plane crash, depending on the form of danger and type of aircraft, are estimated to be as low as one in eleven million.[60] We cope by overestimating the likelihood and severity of threats. We analyze possible risk scenarios, mentally prepare for different outcomes, revisit prior experience good and bad and endlessly debate decisions. Our safety-seeking behavior creates the illusion of control, but it is not enough. We may have reduced the threat by employing protective behavior, but not removed it.

Socially Constructed Behavior

Our conceptions of risk and danger are driven as much by our subjective interpretation of reality as they are by objective reality and personal experience. In the language of behavioral science, *personal conceptions of risk are driven, in large part, by socially determined conceptions of risk.* In this way, risk is not only an objective reality, it is a social construction. We shield ourselves from harm by creating an emotive framework that removes or reinterprets the threat through social construction. In the context of climate change, if one believes climate change is natural and cyclical, information to the contrary will be ignored and the company of others of like mind will be sought. Essentially, we shield ourselves from risk by avoiding the very challenges we need to face to maintain well-being. The cognitive process is social in nature, driven by norms which shape our interaction with events and information, and processes of thought which filter out unwanted information. We are capable of remarkable cognitive gymnastics to spin discomfiting events and circumstances into interpretations which fit our values and beliefs.

Social construction reduces uncertainty and anxiety by narrowing choice to judgments we can make knowing that others will make the same choice. The result is norms for thought and behavior which make plausible views and opinions with which we might otherwise disagree. These norms "order our world" by providing a rationale for what we should do, how we should think and beliefs we should uphold. Opinions, beliefs and values—all are socially constructed. In the world of risk, thought and behavior in response to threats are driven by an innate desire to adhere to norms embraced by people we hold as important or groups to which we belong. Using the example of climate change, individuals with mixed feelings about climate change will avoid discomfort by expressing feelings consistent with the beliefs of important others however inconsistent they may be with personal beliefs.

I can relate to the power of social norms on a personal level:

> *In 2016, I was invited to deliver a keynote address to a national organization comprised of college and university presidents and executive officers. The address was to focus on challenges facing organizations and strategies for action. An obvious challenge was climate change and the evidence was compelling—climate change was a clear and present danger that would affect people, organizations, and society. One would expect leaders to jump onto a topic*

of such importance. At least this was my early thinking about the presentation—thinking that was scuttled when my attention turned to audience appeal. What would be the "best way" to present ideas about climate change to an audience of college and university leaders?

I mulled over different approaches and convention won out. Irrespective of its importance, climate change was and is an "inconvenient truth"—it has elements that depress and deflate. How could one deliver an address touching on catastrophic risk without pulling down the entire room? Further complicating the matter was the circumstantial reality of the occasion. This was a career capstone address to be delivered to an audience of leaders who, for reason of resource limitations, were focused on organizational change and well-being in contrast to the environment. The "norms" surrounding an occasion of this type reduced choice to one option—scrap the content related to climate change and focus on a more upbeat view of the future. What should have been a call-to-arms on disruptive change ended up being a call to leaders to focus on sensemaking as a primary dimension of their work.

A similar circumstance occurred in 2023 when I was asked to address a large gathering of liberal arts college alumni at their Alumni Weekend. The topic was to be catastrophic risk based on my 2021 book *Catastrophic Risk: Business Strategy for Managing Turbulence in a World at Risk.*[61] Alumni weekend is a time of celebration and reconnection with college classmates. Although catastrophic risk is of growing importance given world and national conditions, social norms governing the occasion of a college reunion rendered a presentation on the topic unthinkable. It would have turned a weekend of celebration into a downer. There was nothing to mull over—I declined the invitation.

Social Dynamics of Risk

Human actions have changed the basis of risk in modern society, our sense of danger and our need for safety and security. Risk has objective and socially constructed dimensions. Whether a product of war, climate change, artificial intelligence or social inequality, modern risk is palpable—it can be seen, its impact can be measured, and it has properties that are predictable. It is also imperceptible rising without warning in time and place. Palpable or imperceptible, modern risk is a product of norms that shape thought and behavior. We process risk on the basis of social dynamics which shape cognition—a basis that gives rise to important questions for organizations and leaders:

- Are there multiple dimensions of risk—the risk itself and human behavior in response to risk?
- What are the dynamics of thought and behavior underlying our response to risk?
- What factors individually and collectively condition our response to risk?
- What understanding do organizations and leaders have of modern risk?
- Do organizations and leaders possess the skills necessary to manage modern risk?

In *The Magician and the Prophet*, Charles Mann delved into the controversy surrounding visionaries holding diametrically opposed visions of how humanity can meet existential challenges as our impact on the planet grows.[62] William Vogt, an American ecologist, championed a belief in limits: we should restrict ourselves to what Earth can handle.[63] Norman Borlaug, an American agronomist, subscribed to a belief in innovation: we can invent solutions.[64] These are not binary notions—the road to solution runs through a combination of the two. They are significant in a world of modern risk in which the danger we have created has two dimensions—the experience of danger itself and of human reaction to the experience. Danger manufactured through human activity will, in Vogt's parlance, restrict our potential to reach social maturity. For Borlaug, however, we can innovate our way out of danger by "mining" behavior that mitigates the threat of risk. This can be done through understanding the social dynamics of risk.

In the chapters that follow, modern risk is examined and social dynamics are modeled which drive our response to risk. The human brain—the driving force behind what we think and do—is the starting point for analysis followed by social dynamics which shape response to risk. The closing section of the book turns to organizations and leaders and what they must know and do to effectively manage modern risk.

Notes

1. Roos, J. "We Have Two Visions of the Future and Both Are Wrong." *The New York Times*, April 18, 2023.
2. Park, A. "The First Authorized COVID-19 Vaccine in the U.S. Has Arrived." *Time*, December 11, 2020.
3. Klein, C. "8 Things You May Not Know About Jonas Salk and the Polio Vaccine." *History,* March 25, 2020.
4. Stein, R., Wroth, C., and Fast, A. "Where Are the Newest COVID Hot Spots? Mostly Places with Low Vaccination Rates." *National Public Radio*, July 9, 2021.
5. Beck, U., Giddens, A., and Lash, S. *Reflexive Modernization: Politics, Tradition and Aesthetics in the Modern Social Order.* Cambridge, UK: Polity Press, 1994.
6. Beck, U., Giddens, A., and Lash, S. *Reflexive Modernization: Politics, Tradition and Aesthetics in the Modern Social Order.* Cambridge, UK: Polity Press, 1994.
7. Morin, A. "What Is Cognitive Reframing?" *VeryWellMind*, May 4, 2022.
8. Bartz, D. "As ChatGPT's Popularity Explodes, U.S. Lawmakers Take an Interest." *U.S. News and World Report,* February 13, 2023.
9. BBC Weather. "Freddy: The Deadly Cyclone That Lasted More than a Month." *BBC News*, March 17, 2023.
10. Canon, G. "Atmospheric Rivers Are Inundating California—But What Are They." *The Guardian*, March 15, 2023.
11. Lynch, A., McCarley, G., Gurley, L., Brasch, B., and Shammas, B. "For Some Rolling Fork Residents, Recovery from Mississippi Tornado Is Uncertain." *Washington Post*, March 26, 2023.
12. Kaplan, K. "We Are Not Doing Enough." *Washington Post*, March 21, 2023.
13. Kaplan, K. "We Are Not Doing Enough." *Washington Post*, March 21, 2023.
14. Kaplan, K. "We Are Not Doing Enough." *Washington Post*, March 21, 2023.
15. Kaplan, K. "We Are Not Doing Enough." *Washington Post*, March 21, 2023.
16. Bigg, M. "How Russia's War in Ukraine Has Unfolded, Month by Month." *The New York Times*, February 24, 2023.
17. Bigg, M. "How Russia's War in Ukraine Has Unfolded, Month by Month." *The New York Times*, February 24, 2023.
18. Williamson, H. "Ukraine: Human Cost of the Brutal Russian Invasion." *Church Times*, February 24, 2023.
19. Nuclear Threat Imperative. "The Nuclear Threat: Despite Progress, the Nuclear Threat Is More Complex and Unpredictable than Ever." *NTI Report*, December 31, 2015. http://nti.org/6455A.
20. Bunn, M. and Roth, N. "The Effects of a Single Terrorist Nuclear Bomb." *Bulletin of the Atomic Scientists*, September 28, 2017.
21. European Leadership Network. "The Reagan-Gorbachev Statement: Background to Reaffirm Our Future." November 19, 2021. Press Briefing: January 3, 2022.

22. White House Briefing Room. "Joint Statement by the Leaders of Five Nuclear-Weapon States on Preventing Nuclear War and Avoiding Arms Races." January 3, 2022.

23. Williams, H. "Russia Suspends New START and Increases Nuclear Risks." *Next Generation Nuclear Network*, February 23, 2023.

24. Vikram, A. "Russia's New Nuclear Weapons: Understanding Avangard, Kinzahl and Tsirkon." *Next Generation Nuclear Network*, August 2, 2021.

25. Moore, M. "Leaked Intel Shows China Boosting Hypersonic Missile Program: Report." *New York Post*, April 20, 2023.

26. Hendrycks, D. "Survival of the Fittest." *Time*, June 12, 2023.

27. Wu, G. "6 Big Problems with OpenAI's ChatGPT." *MUOMakeUseOf*, March 21, 2023.

28. Thomas, M. "8 Risks and Dangers of Artificial Intelligence to Know." *Built In*, August 11, 2022.

29. World Economic Forum. "The Future of Jobs Report 2020." October 20, 2020.

30. World Economic Forum. "The Future of Jobs Report 2020." October 20, 2020.

31. Obermeyer, Z., Powers, B., Vogeli, C., and Mullainathan, S. "Dissecting Racial Bias in an Algorithm Used to Manage the Health of Populations." *Science*, 366(6464), October 2019.

32. Bostrom, N. *Superintelligence: Paths, Dangers and Strategies*. Oxford, UK: Oxford University Press, 2014.

33. Bostrom, N. *Superintelligence: Paths, Dangers and Strategies*. Oxford, UK: Oxford University Press, 2014.

34. United Nations. "With More than 1.5 Million Lives Lost to COVID-19, World Leaders in General Assembly Demand Urgent Action to Guarantee Equitable Distribution of Life-Saving Vaccines." *Thirty-First Special Session of the United Nations General Assembly*, December 3, 2020.

35. Hagemann, H. "The 1918 Flu Pandemic Was Brutal, Killing More than 50-Million People Worldwide." *National Public Radio*, April 2, 2020.

36. International Monetary Fund. "Build Forward Better." *IMF Annual Report 2021*, June 20, 2022.

37. Birdsong, M. "The Stark Relationship Between Income Inequality and Crime." June 7, 2018. https://wwweconomist.com/graphic-detail/2018/06/.

38. United Nations. "Rising Inequality Affecting More than Two-Thirds of the Globe, But It's Not Inevitable: New Report." *UN News*, January 21, 2020.

39. Maslow, A. *Motivation and Personality*. New York, NY: Harper & Brothers, 1954.

40. Swalec, A. "January 6 by the Numbers: 775 Arrested, $1.5M in Damage to the Capitol." *NBC News Washington*, March 13, 2022.

41. Pew Research Center. "Americans' Views of Problems Facing the Nation." April 15, 2021. Retrieved: November 1, 2022.

42. Gramlich, J. "A Look Back at Americans' Reactions to the Jan. 6 Riot at the U.S. Capitol." *Pew Research Center*, January 4, 2022.

43. Alfonseca, K. "There Have Been More Mass Shootings than Days in 2023, Database Shows." *ABC News*, April 17, 2023.

44. Brenan, M. "Americans Equally Worried About Mass Shooting and Terrorism." *Gallup*, October 11, 2019.

45. Jones. J. "More in U.S. Say American Lives Permanently Changed by 9/11." *Gallup*, September 2, 2021.

46. Brenan, M. "Worry About Crime in U.S. at Highest Level Since 2016." *Gallup*, April 7, 2022.

47. Rothman, L. "Why Americans Are More Afraid than They Used to Be." *Time*, January 6, 2016.

48. Buchanan, L., Bui, Q., and Patel, J. "Black Lives Matter May Be the Largest Movement in U.S. History." *The New York Times*, January 11, 2021.

49. DeLuco, R., Burke, K., and Pillai-Essex, A. "Civil Unrest 2021: Learning from Last Year's Record Losses." *Verisk*, December 29, 2021.

50. Smerconish, M. "How George Floyd's Death Reignited a Movement." *CNN News*, May 5, 2021.

51. McEvoy, J. "14 Days of Protests, 19 Dead." *Forbes*, June 8, 2020.

52. Polumbo, B. "George Floyd Riots Caused Record-Setting $2 Billion in Damage, New Report Says. Here's Why the True Cost Is Even Higher." *FEE Stories*, September 16, 2020.

53. Purtill, J. "This Model Forecast the US's Current Unrest a Decade Ago. It Now Says 'Civil War'." *ABC Triple Hack*, June 17, 2020.

54. Purtill, J. "This Model Forecast the US's Current Unrest a Decade Ago. It Now Says 'Civil War'." *ABC Triple Hack*, June 17, 2020.

55. Purtill, J. "This Model Forecast the US's Current Unrest a Decade Ago. It Now Says 'Civil War'." *ABC Triple Hack*, June 17, 2020.

56. Purtill, J. "This Model Forecast the US's Current Unrest a Decade Ago. It Now Says 'Civil War'." *ABC Triple Hack*, June 17, 2020.

57. Hartigan, R., Parker, L., Nowakowski, K., and Marques, D. "An Index Measuring Country Stability Finds the U.S. Dropping." *National Geographic*, January 15, 2021.

58. Purtill, J. "This Model Forecast the US's Current Unrest a Decade Ago. It Now Says 'Civil War'." *ABC Triple Hack*, June 17, 2020.

59. Purtill, J. "This Model Forecast the US's Current Unrest a Decade Ago. It Now Says 'Civil War'." *ABC Triple Hack*, June 17, 2020.

60. Davis, R. "What Are the Chances of Surviving a Plane Crash?" *Executive Flyers*, April 3, 2023.

61. Alfred, R. *CATASTROPHIC RISK: Business Strategy for Managing Turbulence in a World at Risk*. New York, NY: Routledge, 2001.

62. Oury, J-P. "Borlaug vs Vogt: Limiting Population or Developing Precision Agriculture." *European Scientist*, January 6, 2019.

63. Oury, J-P. "Borlaug vs Vogt: Limiting Population or Developing Precision Agriculture." *European Scientist*, January 6, 2019.

64. Oury, J-P. "Borlaug vs Vogt: Limiting Population or Developing Precision Agriculture." *European Scientist*, January 6, 2019.

Chapter 2

Risk and Response

We now exercise such control over the planet that we have cata-
pulted it and ourselves into a new geological era known as the
Anthropocene: the human-shaped epoch, in which the pen of his-
tory has been passed from nature to humanity, and we are the ones
determining what will be written.

Christiana Figueres, Executive Secretary, U.N.
Framework Convention on Climate Change, 2010

In the July 12, 2022, issue of the *New York Times*, columnist Max Fisher put
the seeming chaos of our world into perspective with a question: "Has the
world entered a time of unusual turbulence or does it just feel that way?"[1]

If you scan the headlines, it's easy to conclude that something has
broken. The pandemic. Accelerating crises from climate change.
Global grain shortage. Russia's war on Ukraine. Political and eco-
nomic meltdown in Sri Lanka. A former prime minister's assassina-
tion in Japan. And, in the United States, inflation, mass shootings,
a reckoning over January 6, and collapsing abortion rights...This
sense of chaos can be difficult to square with longer term data
showing that, on many metrics, the world is generally becoming
better off. War is rarer today, by some measures, than it has been
for most of the past 50 years—and when it does occur it is signifi-
cantly less deadly. Genocides and mass atrocities are less common,
too. Life expectancy, literacy, and standards of living have all risen
to historic heights. Also, steadily declining in recent decades are

DOI: 10.4324/9781003335658-3

hunger, child mortality, and extreme poverty, liberating hundreds of
millions from what are, by sheer numbers, among the pre-eminent
threats facing humanity. So why does it often feel like, despite all the
data, things are only getting worse?

Fisher answered his own question. Subtle gains in well-being unfolding over
generations have given way to obvious crises.[2] Our attention is directed
to the urgency of the immediate, not progress decades in the making.
Hundreds of millions might live healthier and safer lives than their parents
did, but subtle change benefits entire societies over time, making it harder
for individuals to notice the change. Even more telling is our tendency to
overlook positive change because it is about prevention. No one notices the
wars that don't happen, the family members who are not claimed by disease, the children who don't die in infancy. When we feel as if the world is
falling apart, we're not thinking about long-view metrics like life expectancy.
Rather, we are feeling that humanity is facing upheaval and risk to a degree
it has never before experienced.

The disparity between chaos and progress described by Fisher and
human response to it prompts one to delve into and understand the basis
of risk in modern society. Is it a state of danger capable of inflicting great
harm, a socially constructed reality, a human response to instability or something else? Much would depend on time and place. A visit to Ukraine amidst
the Russian invasion would yield one answer; a discussion about civic
unrest with a social scientist another; and an analysis of climate change by a
meteorologist yet another. The unending flow of information through social
media has made risk personal. Time and place do not separate us from risk
as even those far from a crisis live with it. In the pages that follow, modern
risk is described in terms of its unique characteristics and considered in relationship to contextual factors that influence our behavior in response to it.

A Uniquely Human Creation

Arguably, we live in a world which is risk-free when compared to the past.
Many of us would not be alive today were it not for advances in science and
technology. Life expectancy has been extended through safe drinking water,
sanitary sewage disposal, hygienic food preparation, refrigeration, eradication of major parasitic diseases, central heating and cooling and a host of
scientific advances. On the surface, our lives would appear to have changed

for the better. But, have they? In a world scourged by a global pandemic, on the edge of nuclear war, and facing the relentless march of climate change, are we better off than earlier times when life was simpler? Are we living in a present with risks that exceed those of the past?

Self Induced Peril

Climate change was a major contributing factor to the windswept fire that destroyed the historic town of Lahaina in August 2023. It is an exemplar of *manufactured risk*—peril created by the impact of human behavior on the environment.[3] Lahaina was rendered vulnerable to risk through two centuries of human activity:

■ A flammable landscape of non-native grasses brought to Hawaii to feed cattle when people of European ancestry arrived on the islands. Non-native grasses spread quickly over abandoned farm and ranchland and built high amounts of biomass that rendered land vulnerable to wildfires.

■ Increasingly frequent and longer duration climate events fueled by rising CO_2 levels in the atmosphere created temperature and drought conditions that dried out grasses and trees and increased the likelihood of ignition.

■ Grass growth and desiccation fueled by cycles of bountiful rain and extreme drought contributed fuel load for fires.

■ Irreversible changes in forestland caused by frequently occurring wildfires resulted in permanent eradication of forests and replacement by fire-prone invasive grasses.

■ Inhabitants left with little or no warning before a wall of flames bore down on their homes because of lack of a contingency plan.

Science and technology have brought us to risk that is qualitatively different than earlier times. Our safety and security are imperiled by carbon-based power generation, nuclear weapons, petroleum and petrochemicals, technological failures and toxic by-products of industrial processes. Pollution and toxic waste are preventable and treatable—a stark contrast to hazards in the past which were viewed as natural and unpredictable.[4] Diseases would spread, bad weather would damage crops, and fires would consume large tracts of land under the influence of natural forces. Natural hazards could be exacerbated by human activity, to be sure, but the prevailing view was that they were outside of human control.

Dual Effect

Modern risk is not bound by time and space. Future generations are affected, geographic boundaries are crossed, and life is interpreted in terms of danger and risk as much as by growth and progress. Scientific and technological advances have enhanced how we live and work but have also brought concerns about safety and security to the forefront of consciousness. Consider:

- Automotive and aviation technologies which have contributed in important ways to economic development but accelerated the pace of climate change through rising CO_2 emissions associated with growing transportation demand.
- Research on deadly pathogens for the purpose of developing life-saving antibiotics which could threaten life if released through a laboratory accident or an act of terror.
- Agricultural herbicides which increase crop yield but become a weapon of mass destruction when used as an agent in the production of biological and chemical weapons.
- Nuclear energy which generates electricity to power homes, schools, businesses and hospitals but becomes a threat to civilization when used to create weapons of mass destruction.
- Artificial intelligence which makes life and work easier by automating critical processes but could endanger life if it was to go rogue and outstrip human capabilities.

Uncertanty and Confusion

In a world in which science and technology have dual meaning, risk is an anomaly that prompts questions about our ability to protect ourselves from hazards of our own making. We face danger in everyday aspects of life heretofore considered safe.

> **New York Times, July 9, 2022:** *Jolanda Wielenga was checking documents accompanying containers bound for Russia when her heart skipped a beat: One held a substance that could be used*

to make a chemical weapon. The substance could be used for both civilian and military purposes. Exporting it to Russia would have been legal before the invasion of Ukraine. But the E.U. sanctions imposed on Russia in recent months changed that. Ms. Wielenga, a two-decade veteran customs investigator at Europe's largest port, blocked the shipment.[5]

Modern risk has little historical reference, its potential for harm is significant, and its effects and consequences are uncertain. We cannot be certain, for example, of the full range of effects that modifying the genetic structure of food will have, and we do not know the long-term effects of newly developed vaccines. Scientists working with genetic modification of food extoll the virtues of designing a plant with an insecticide gene that eliminates unwanted bugs but simultaneously caution that stronger insects may survive resulting in a new class of superbugs. Supplemental drugs such as beta-carotene once advanced as protection against cancer were later proven to put people at greater risk for cancer. Hormone replacement therapy recommended for use by postmenopausal women as a means for reducing risk of heart disease was later shown to increase the risk of breast cancer. COVID-19 was accompanied by an "infodemic"—a state of confusion caused by a global spread of misinformation through news, public health guidance, "fact" sheets, infographics and research opinions. Confusion reigns when the danger we are facing is unclear and its consequences are uncertain.

Ambiguity and Uncertainty

The *Columbia* space shuttle disaster is a prime example of the ambiguous and uncertain nature of modern risk. On February 1, 2003, the world watched in horror as the *Columbia* space shuttle broke apart while reentering the Earth's atmosphere. An investigation revealed that a large piece of insulating foam had dislodged from the shuttle's external tank during the launch, damaging the leading edge of a wing and causing the disaster 16 days later.

NASA's failure to respond proactively to the foam strike during *Columbia*'s mission was construed by many as evidence of irresponsible and incompetent management. Research by Roberto, Bohmer and Edmondson (2006), however, suggests otherwise.[6] NASA exhibited a pattern of behavior common to people and organizations in a risk environment—the tendency to downplay threats on the basis of previous experience. When the foam strike occurred, NASA officials did not have a clear line of sight to the extent of damage and what would happen as a result. Engineers had noticed the foam strike during routine reviews of videos taken at launch, but senior managers downplayed the threat, noting that foam strikes had caused minor damage to shuttles in the past but never resulted in a major accident. Engineers described the foam strike as "the largest ever" and asked that additional satellite images of the strike area be taken, but top managers rejected this request on the basis of prior experience.

Disasters stemming from manufactured risk strike with and without warning, from inside and outside of organizational walls, and as a result of happenstance and individual behavior.[7] The 2010 Deepwater Horizon oil platform explosion and 9/11 terrorist strikes on New York City and Washington, D.C., occurred without warning. Wells Fargo Bank suffered enormous losses from improper lending practices, Volkswagen tarnished its reputation by falsifying auto emissions data and Boeing by introducing a fatal flaw into its 737-MAX aircraft—occurrences inside company walls with warning signs and insider knowledge. Leaders exacerbate risk by ignoring or failing to heed signs of looming calamity:

- Missed warnings by bank executives that signaled the financial meltdown of 2008–2009[8];
- Shell Oil leaders misreading intent and mismanaging company response to Greenpeace activists boarding and occupying an obsolete oil-storage platform in the North Sea[9];
- Merck executives misjudging the threat to company reputation when early data linked its painkiller Vioxx with cardiovascular risks[10];
- Radio Shack filing for bankruptcy and closing stores by failing to implement any form of e-commerce when electronic online sales moved into high gear[11];
- Schwinn executives discounting the threat from mountain bikes which eventually eclipsed the company's road bikes in popularity[12];
- Kodak executives' dismissal of early signals portending a major decline in its film business when digital photography came along and the company failed to move quickly.[13]

These examples illustrate the consuming nature of modern risk. Threats can take many forms as can their onset, consequences and resolution—a conundrum leading to the obvious conclusion that organizations that develop systematic capabilities for identifying, evaluating and responding to threats are better equipped to head off disaster than those that don't.

Known, Ambiguous and Unforeseen Threats

Some risks are obvious in onset and consequences (the onset and impact of climate change, for example) and the response is clear (curtail CO_2 emissions). In other instances, risk is unforeseen although its consequences and response are clear once a threat is confirmed. COVID-19 was not anticipated or predicted and its onset prompted intensive research leading to development of a vaccine. The most dangerous situations involving risk arise when warning signs are ambiguous, consequences are unpredictable, and the potential for harm is great.[14] In these situations, judgment can be clouded and risk minimized or ignored with potentially catastrophic results.

Known threats are exactly what the name implies—dangers signaled by early warning with a predictable outcome and clear path to resolution. The Great Pacific Garbage Patch, a humanly created scourge with a devastating impact on marine life, is a 600,000 square mile collection of floating trash halfway between Hawaii and California.[15] Discovered in the early 1990s, much of its mass is comprised of individual pieces of plastic with a cumulative weight of 88,000 tons. The Patch impacts health through the destruction of marine life and the release of greenhouse gases into the atmosphere when plastic is exposed to sunlight. Its impact can be assessed using modern technology to measure the volume of CO_2 released into the atmosphere. The path to resolution is clear: remove large quantities of plastic from the ocean.

The world food crisis, the Flint water crisis and the Southwestern water shortage are contemporary threats with a known development path, predictable consequences and a clear response. The world has been on a collision course with *food security* for years as a result of climate-related shortfalls in crop output, the economic impact of the pandemic, supply chain problems and ongoing conflict worldwide—most recently, the war in Ukraine.[16] Food insecurity has documented negative impacts including malnutrition, mortality and political upheaval. Currently 2.4 billion people worldwide and over 150 million children under age five experience chronic malnutrition.[17] The road to resolution is clear: grow additional foodstuffs and make them available in greater volume to vulnerable populations.

The *Flint water crisis* was created in 2014 when Flint contaminated its drinking water with lead by changing its water source from treated Detroit water to the Flint River.[18] City officials failed to apply corrosion inhibitors to the water, which resulted in lead from aging pipes leaching into the water supply, exposing 100,000 residents to elevated lead levels.[19] Children are particularly at risk from lead poisoning as documented in research revealing long-term effects of a reduction in intellectual functioning and IQ, and an increased chance of Alzheimer's disease. The obvious solution: switch the water supply back to the Detroit River and replace lead water service pipes.

The *Southwestern water shortage* was created by dropping water levels in Lake Mead. The Colorado River serves 40 million people in the West.[20] Water levels in its largest reservoir—Lake Mead—have been dropping since the 1980s, reaching a record low of 1059 feet in 2022.[21] The cause, consequences and solution are clear: global warming has reduced the size of mountain snowpacks feeding the Colorado River, and developing communities have consumed ever-larger quantities of water. The short-term solution: curtail water allotments to Southwestern farms and cities and reduce availability to homes and businesses.

Ambiguous Threats are characterized by warning signs that are imprecise and potential for harm that is indeterminate. Hurricane Katrina—an Atlantic hurricane that caused over 1,800 fatalities and $108 billion in damage in August 2005—developed slowly as a tropical depression, gained strength over the warm waters of the Gulf after weakening over southern Florida and roared into Louisiana and Mississippi as a Category 5 hurricane.[22] Its irregular pattern of development and unpredictable consequences made it an ambiguous threat with the potential for great harm. Unknown at the time the hurricane made landfall and magnifying its impact, were fatal engineering flaws in the flood protection system around New Orleans. At the storm's end, 80 percent of the city and large tracts of neighboring parishes were under water.[23] Transportation and communication facilities were destroyed leaving tens of thousands of people stranded with limited access to food, shelter and basic necessities. The scale of the storm completely overwhelmed government agencies and emergency responders. Multiple investigations in the aftermath of the catastrophe identified failures in engineering and disaster response in place before the catastrophe.[24] The U.S. Army Corps of Engineers, which had designed and built the region's levees decades earlier, bore responsibility for the failure of flood control systems. Government agencies were responsible for mismanagement of emergency response.

Unforeseen Threats arise without warning and with devastating effect. Their impact and potential consequences are known at onset and immediate action is required to mitigate the threat. The Three Mile Island Accident is a prime example of an unforeseen threat with great potential for harm.[25] At 4 am on March 28, 1979, Three Mile's Unit 2 non-nuclear secondary system failed followed by a jammed pilot-operated relief valve in the primary system which allowed large amounts of nuclear reactor coolant to escape.[26] Mechanical failures were compounded by a failure of plant operators to recognize the situation as a loss of coolant accident. Malfunctioning equipment was only part of the problem. Post-disaster investigations revealed flaws in the design of instruments and controls and inadequate training protocols that left operators ill-prepared to manage the deteriorating situation.[27] The accident crystallized anti-nuclear safety concerns among activists and the general public and resulted in new regulations for the nuclear industry.

Irrespective of their onset, known, ambiguous and unforeseen threats imperil our security and safety. They are a departure from earlier times when threats were manifested through the senses. We could see a tornado or tsunami with the naked eye; we could smell polluted water; we could feel the vibration of an earthquake. The threats we experience today are embedded in scientific and technological advances not readily subject to sensory perception. A malfunction in a nuclear plant is not visible to the average citizen, yet it can kill or harm millions. A gas leak can kill thousands within hours if not detected. An insidious process of long-term change like global warming can impact human life decades into the future unless efforts are made to mitigate its march. We are the architects of a society which, unlike earlier societies, lives under the continuing threat of risk it has created.

Illustration 2.1   Threats Manufactured Through Human Activity

Known Threats	Ambiguous Threats	Unforeseen Threats
Early Warning	*Unclear Warning*	*No Warning*
Predictable Consequences	*Unpredictable Consequences*	*Predictable Consequences*
Clear Response	*Unsystematic Response*	*Clear Response*
Climate change	Columbia shuttle disaster	COVID-19 pandemic
World food crisis	Love Canal toxic landfill	Chernobyl nuclear meltdown
Gulf of Mexico dead zone	DuPont Teflon crisis	Deepwater Horizon oil spill
Pacific garbage patch	Hurricane Katrina	Exxon Valdez oil spill
Coastal flooding	2007 MPL bridge collapse	Bhopal gas leak
Flint water crisis	Iraq invasion of Kuwait	Al Qaeda terrorist strike
Western water shortage	Challenger shuttle disaster	Three Mile Island accident

Risk Response

We have a complex relationship with risk. While we have an instinct for self-preservation, we are hardwired to misinterpret or ignore warnings embedded in risk events, and, all too often, they go unheeded or, perversely, they are seen as signs that our systems are resilient and will protect us from harm. Evolutionary psychology holds that we adhere to traits over time that have made survival possible—for instance, the instinct to fight or flee when threatened. Behavioral models suggest that our feelings and beliefs about risk influence our readiness to act as do social factors such as pressure to conform. Group studies postulate that much of our behavior in response to risk is dictated by norms that reflect expectations of how people should act and interact. Taking everything into account, four factors loom large as influences on our behavior in response to risk: *cognition and affect, social forces, group dynamics* and the *influence of institutions.*

Cognition and Affect

Cognition and affect are mental processing systems operating side-by-side which convert information from the environment into judgments that shape thought and behavior. The affective system operates outside of conscious thought and is automatically initiated in response to sensory information. In contrast, cognitive processing is deliberate and involves conscious analysis of sensory information. Affective and cognitive systems operate in tandem in response to threats. Think about your state of mind as you prepare to deliver a speech to a room full of people. Emotion and affect are probably running high as hormones beyond your control are released in response to the situation. Your anxiety is counterbalanced by the calming force of cognition as you steady yourself by focusing on speech content and key points you want to get across.

> ***Affect.*** *You are scheduled to travel coast-to-coast by air in the next day. You have learned that the aircraft you will be traveling on is a Boeing 737 MAX. It is an aircraft with a troubled history—fatal crashes in 2018 and 2019 that killed 346 people and grounded the airliner.[28] It was pulled from service and restored to service 22 months later and you are on one of its first flights. As you think about the flight, your heart begins to race, your blood pressure elevates, and you break into a cold sweat as you imagine what could happen. Is the aircraft safe? Has it been tested with sufficient*

rigor to ensure it is fail-safe? Has the aircraft been returned to service prematurely? Are the pilots trained to deal with any emergency? You consider your options and decide to book a flight on a different aircraft.

You are experiencing *fear*—an instinctive response to real or perceived danger caused by a belief that someone or something could be capable of harm. A natural instinct when facing danger is to get out of the situation as quickly as possible—a response triggered by hormonal and physiological changes designed to shield us from harm. The amygdala, an almond-shaped mass of gray matter inside each cerebral hemisphere, signals danger to the hypothalamus which, in turn, stimulates the autonomic nervous system to release adrenaline and cortisol—stress hormones which quicken heart rate and delivery of oxygen to muscles.[29] As your heart rate accelerates, your blood pressure and respiration elevate, your muscles become tense, your pupils dilate to improve vision by letting in more light, and your hearing sharpens. You are ready to run from danger or stand and fight.[30]

Not everyone reacts to danger in the same way. Aggression and flight are common reactions, but fear response varies from individual to individual. Depending on temperament and the immediacy and severity of a threat, response may be different. If escape or avoidance is perceived as unfeasible or a threat is seen as stationary, the response may be one of immobility.[31] The autonomic nervous system is involved, but this time in reverse. Attentiveness to the environment and the potential threat intensifies, heart rate and breathing attenuate, and peripheral vision sharpens. If the threat changes from stationary to imminent or is perceived to be active, the sympathetic branch of the autonomous nervous system is activated and stress response kicks into active mode with accompanying physiological changes.[32] Stress reaction doesn't last long. Once a fight, flee or freeze signal ceases, the brain releases hormones that slow heart rate and breathing and provide a sense of cognitive relief.[33] Generally, the human body returns to a natural state within 20–30 minutes after encountering a threat.[34]

Cognition. *You have strong negative feelings about a gubernatorial candidate in your state because of his naysaying position on climate change at an earlier point in his political career—a position in sharp contrast to your own. Five years have passed and the candidate's position appears to have softened, but you cannot bring yourself to vote for him. Your memory is rooted in the past and once a naysayer, always a naysayer.*

Cognition starts with perception in response to stimuli. The senses serve as the interface between the mind and stimuli, receiving and translating stimuli into impulses that are transmitted to the brain. The brain processes this information to create thoughts expressed in language and action or stored in memory. Our memory bank would explain why we interpret events in terms of prior experience and commit to known courses of action.[35] With the 737 MAX, for example, searing media images of downed commercial aircraft and prior personal experience with jet engine failure could trigger anxiety for a passenger traveling on an aircraft with a questionable safety record. Memory in combination with personal experience would play a critical role in a decision on whether or not to fly the MAX.

On a broad societal scale, the invasion of Ukraine offers an excellent illustration of cognitive dynamics at work. The Cold War relationship between the United States and Russia was in stasis when Russia invaded Ukraine in February 2022. Vladimir Putin opened the invasion with a declaration that Russia's nuclear capabilities were being put on heightened alert—a clear message to U.S. leaders and allied NATO nations to back off or risk massive destruction. It was a stark reminder of Russia's nuclear power and of the capacity of one person, Putin, to end life as we know it. For U.S. leaders, a sequence of cognitive events unfolded[36]:

■ *a threat was received* (Putin's declaration that nuclear weapons were being put on heightened alert)
■ *the threat was evaluated against a backdrop of prior experience* (a 75-year history of political hostility and nuclear impasse between the United States and Russia)
■ *the threat was interpreted in the context of modern-day sociopolitical realities* (heightened public awareness of growing hostility between nuclear powers edging toward war with weapons thousands of times more powerful than the atom bomb)
■ *the threat's impact was calculated* (parts of the United States would be turned into a radioactive desert by a nuclear warhead 6000 times more powerful than the atom bomb)
■ *prior experience with nuclear weapons affirmed commitment to an existing course of action* (nuclear impasse was maintained with Russia by withholding long-range weapons from Ukraine)

Manufactured risk emerges from environmental, technological and sociopolitical conditions which are interconnected and, at an early stage, may be beyond human comprehension. Every so often, however, an event occurs that personalizes risk to the point that it galvanizes public fear and attention. Aviation failure caused by a design flaw, hyperbolic rhetoric of world leaders and a pandemic killing millions in the short space of months—all are episodes of risk of our own making, yet they may not enter our field of vision until they are right upon us.

Social Forces

Thought and behavior are influenced by changing conditions in society. Examples include the Great Recession, the consequences of technological advance and the condition of polarization. Thought and behavior are also influenced by inertia—a need to maintain consistency and continuity in the face of change.[37] Examples include normalization of behavior falling outside of social norms and altering behavior to fit new norms.

> **Social Change**. *A process involving transformation of the social order including change in social institutions, behavior and social relations affecting all aspects of life.*

Irrespective of the lens through which change is viewed, disruption is a common thread. People are troubled by inconsistency between evidence and belief. When encountering information contrary to deeply held beliefs— for example, approval of previously objectionable behavior—a natural tendency is to resolve the discrepancy through acceptance, avoidance or reinterpretation.

- *Cognitive dissonance.* A defensive tactic people use to relieve anxiety when confronted with evidence that contradicts personal belief.[38] For example, when confronted with evidence of climate change, naysayers may alleviate tension by refusing to accept the evidence, reinterpreting the evidence or seeking out fellow naysayers to garner support. No matter which path is taken, the objective is the same: eliminate or reduce the difference between evidence and belief.
- *Intuitive thinking.* Quick thinking in response to circumstances or occurrences of an uncertain nature.[39] Intuition comes first in emotionally charged circumstances and dominates reasoned judgment unless an effort is made to override feelings and emotion.

■ *Categorical thinking.* A tendency to use categories to simplify and structure information to facilitate quick decisions about events and conditions.[40]

Intuitive and categorical thinking are functional in simple circumstances where reasoning is not required. In more complex circumstances, especially those involving risk, categories and quick thinking can distort perception and lead to erroneous decisions. For example, when listening to weather reports of a hurricane approaching the Florida coast, your mind might kick into fast mode and lead you to think that you are not in imminent danger. Your home is inland in the northern part of the state, hurricanes generally do not travel that far north, and they weaken when they travel over land. Your assessment of the danger posed by the hurricane has been based upon intuition (quick recall of prior instances of the event) and categorization (structuring and processing information in categories to facilitate decision-making).

Inertia. *Stasis that is part of resistance to change and commitment to the status quo.*

Research on inertia is limited, particularly into its causes, but it has a clear effect on decision-making by impelling individuals to choose the default option when grappling with change.[41] It is most commonly experienced as a preference for the certainty of the status quo in contrast to the uncertainty of change. Key constructs in inertia theory are status-quo bias, satisfice and normalization.

■ *Status-quo bias.* An outlook on change with status taken as a reference point and any shift from that outlook perceived as harmful. Status-quo bias is distinguished from rational thought inasmuch as it involves a preference for one's current state even if a superior alternative is available.[42] One would prefer to avoid the discomfort of change by maintaining one's current position rather than adopting an alternative which may yield greater benefit.
■ *Satisfice.* Introduced by economist Herbert Simon in 1956, satisfice is the tendency to choose solutions which are acceptable over those that are optimal because achieving the optimal solution would cost more in effort and resources.[43] Simon blended "satisfy" and "suffice" to explain how and why people make decisions that favor stasis over change. Optimal solutions require consideration of wide-ranging

alternatives—choices that may be neither realistic or cognitively possible when facing the pressure of change.

■ *Normalization.* Perceptions of "normal" can change over time as people become accustomed to deviations from routine that are no longer considered deviant despite the fact that they exceed prevailing norms.[44] Normalization occurs through an intuitive process of accommodation and adjustment. In the domain of climate change, for instance, extreme temperatures can become part of an undifferentiated normality of "hot" or "cold" irrespective of how extreme they are. People adjust their behavior to fit prevailing conditions by wearing warmer or cooler clothing but do not delve into the root cause of extreme temperatures.

Unquestionably cognition and affect, in tandem with social forces, play an important role in shaping behavior in response to risk. Psychological factors fuel inertia by focusing attention on personal safety. Social forces influence judgment and reasoning. When people are unable or unwilling to face the threat and consequences of risk, default may be the only option. A circumstance that may put lives in danger.

Group Dynamics

Group dynamics have much to do with how we see the world and respond to risk. Sociologists Peter Berger and Thomas Luckmann coined the term *socially constructed reality* to describe the process by which conceptions of what is "real" are determined by subjective construction of reality through interaction with others rather than objective reality—how things really are.[45] Social construction reduces anxiety and uncertainty by narrowing choice about circumstances and events to judgments individuals can make knowing that others will judge them in the same way.[46] Opinions, perceptions, values and beliefs are socially constructed as thought and behavior are channeled into patterns that comply with social conceptions. In the world of risk, feelings and beliefs about risk are driven, in large part, by a desire to be sympatico with the feelings of others toward risk.

I can relate to the power of socially constructed reality on a personal level. In the 1990s, I was part of a consulting team charged with developing a strategic plan for a large college with a sterling reputation. The college—I'll call it Southeastern College (SC)—had achieved national recognition for its innovative teaching, student-centered instruction and progressive leadership. Reinforced by its early success and buttressed by media trumpeting its accomplishments, SC's faculty adopted a credo of excellence which over time came to symbolize the college as a whole. Behavior and attitudes were aligned with belief and a "culture of excellence" became the face of the college.

> *Early findings in the strategic planning process brought a different picture of SC into focus. Conversations with groups and organizations in the community and interviews with civic and private-sector leaders described an institution providing inadequate service to the community, slow to respond to expressed needs, and delivering outdated programs and services. College personnel were viewed as mired in an illusion of excellence—a circumstance that stifled creativity and innovation. The consulting team had come upon a reality warp—a disjuncture between internally held belief and external perception.[47] This discovery became the central point of a progress report to college faculty and administrators at the midpoint of the project.*
>
> *Two reporting options were available to the consulting team: (1) narrow the gap between internal belief and external perception by balancing critical findings with college strengths and achievements or (2) deliver an unvarnished picture of objective reality through full disclosure of community perceptions. The second option was chosen, and the result was one that would not be unexpected. College faculty and staff reacted vehemently to the report, and the planning project was put on hold to provide time for faculty and staff to reconcile belief with external reality. The consultants returned to the college after a three-month hiatus with marching orders from college leaders to factor faculty values and beliefs into planning findings through added emphasis on achievement rather than problems and to provide documentary evidence in support of critical findings. Toward the close of the project, two views of reality stood side-by-side: socially constructed reality and objective reality.*

Socially Consructed Reality. Reality is not an objective state; it is humanly created. The interpretation of a situation or event depends on an individual's subjective perception of it, and not entirely on the situation itself.[48] In a group context, the cognitive cycle begins with construction of a personal framework to understand and comprehend characteristics of a social situation. The opinion of others is sought to gauge the veracity of one's personal framework. When a situation is interpreted by others in a way that concurs with one's personal judgment, perception is reinforced and one is in harmony with the group. When group and individual perception differ, conflict ensues which triggers a need to either reframe one's thinking or make the interpretation fit one's way of thinking. Interpretation is a personal matter, but irrespective of situation a natural tendency is to relieve anxiety by interpretating situations in ways that facilitate social cohesion.[49]

This would explain the adherence of faculty, in the foregoing example, to a shared interpretation of excellence irrespective of the objective reality of external perception. It would also explain panic buying and hoarding behavior during the pandemic:

> *Objective reality:* COVID-19 spreads primarily between people who are in close contact. The virus is contracted when infectious particles pass through the air from one person to another and are inhaled at short range or if infectious particles come in direct contact with eyes, nose or mouth.[50] To control spread of the virus, localities and states across the nation issued shelter-in-place orders and created communication channels to share evolving public health information. Consumers flocked to stores, purchased large amounts of household goods—particularly toilet paper—and depleted retailers of inventory. The supply chain for toilet paper, however, remained consistently strong throughout the pandemic. From a public health standpoint, there was no evidence of a correlation between toilet paper use and resistance to COVID-19.[51]

> *Socially constructed reality:* Rumor of a toilet paper shortage floated early on during the pandemic.[52] A zero-sum mentality kicked in—someone else's gain is my loss. People rushed to stores, bought out toilet paper supplies and hoarded toilet paper. The demand for toilet paper became greater than the supply leading to a shortage as stocks ran out. Panic buying and hoarding turned subjective interpretation of a situation into a real-time circumstance.

Institutional Influence

In an environment of uncertainty and change, organizations and media shape behavior through culture and information. Organizations through shared values, beliefs and norms embedded in culture that shape the way employees interact and approach their work.[53] Media through information influencing opinions and promoting cultural norms that impact beliefs, attitudes and behavior. Social media is capable of distributing content to a global audience instantly by technology designed to keep people engaged. It influences what we think and do by distributing information that supports or challenges personal views, builds understanding of different topics and shapes self-perception.

Organizational Leverage. Organizations with robust cultures build *shared values* and bind employees to those values. Presumably this would reduce vulnerability to risk, particularly in organizations where management is a shared responsibility. A deeper look, however, reveals a shortcoming rooted in organizational culture that could impede risk response. *Norms* can bind individuals to a belief that an organization's culture is sound and its vulnerability to risk minimal.[54] When threats appear, norms may take over leaving no place for intuition or impromptu response. Take, for instance, a tightly coupled organization, in which decision-making is top down. Rank and file employees may have authority that they feel unable to use because organizational norms preclude downstream decision-making. The opposite would be true in a loosely coupled organization where front-line employees are empowered to make decisions in response to a threat. At Toyota, for example, the Andon cord permits assembly line employees to immediately stop production when a problem or a defect is noticed.[55]

Beyond the binding power of culture and norms are issues related to *comprehension* among leaders, managers and workers who view and process risk differently. Executives looking at risk from 20,000 feet would naturally see and react to it as a threat to the total organization. Their job is to shield the organization from threats. Employees, however, would be more likely to view threats as the responsibility of management—not something within their purview. Employee resistance is frequently cited by leaders as a barrier to risk management.[56] The reasons are many: employees may see responsibility for risk as getting in the way of job performance; compliance mandates may add an unnecessary burden to meeting performance targets; and a feeling that risk involves bad news that leaders may not want to receive. Organizations which place more value on "good news" than on information about problems are especially vulnerable to risk.

Picture this:

> *Senior leaders and division managers are seated at a round table*
> *brainstorming ways to build an organization-wide risk culture.*
> *The objective is to enhance the organization's ability to manage*
> *risk by instilling values, knowledge and an understanding of risk*
> *in employees throughout the organization. Senior executives believe*
> *that managers are responsible for building and maintaining risk*
> *protocols and ensuring employee compliance. Managers believe*
> *they are caught between executives and employees and tasked with*
> *the difficult job of engaging employees who have no interest in risk.*
> *Employees see risk as a leadership responsibility of executives and a*
> *performance mandate for managers. It is not their business, nor is*
> *it part of their job.*

The disconnect between executives, managers and employees has important implications for the risk culture of an organization. Leaders and managers can set all the risk targets they want, put needed protocols in place and enforce compliance, but engagement with risk is not going to happen in the absence of insight into employee attitudes and motivation. An organization's risk culture is, in large part, a product of employee behavior—its first line of defense against risk.

Organizations help or hurt themselves by choice and *decision-making* in response to threats. A simple dichotomy can be used to illustrate the consequence of choice. Threats can be approached operationally as a functional process supported by standardized systems and procedures and tightly coupled relationships among personnel. Alternatively, they can be approached organically as a dynamic process managed through broadly defined protocols, multi-directional communication and shared responsibility. Dichotomies are, of course, blind alleys in an organization. Put yourself, however, in the position of an executive leading a company facing the challenge of elevated risk. Would your company be better equipped to respond on the basis of top-down authority or shared responsibility using all of its human resources? The answer is self-evident—savvy leaders use all available resources to manage risk.

Interestingly, many organizations, particularly large-scale enterprises, continue to employ rational decision-making as a basis for validation of a course of action before committing to it. For decades, rationality has been a basis of management. Weber (1972) spoke of a rational organization or bureaucracy, Daft (1983) of rational processes, Simon (1997) of rational decision-making and Scott (2003) of a balance between rational, natural and open systems.[57] Rationality is systematic and structured—a time-consuming process not always appropriate in periods of fast change.[58] Its antithesis, intuition, offers the advantage of speed through rapid and unstructured decision-making that does not follow a linear reasoning process or involve methodical calculation.[59] By itself, intuition is a gamble that leaders are often reluctant to take in situations involving uncertainty. It offers the advantage of speed, but poorly made decisions can result in devastating outcomes for a company. Rational decision processes provide safe passage to a decision outcome because leaders can document and provide evidence of the process used to make a decision.

Writing about organizational improvisation in the metaphor of jazz, Eisenhardt (1997) argued that intuitive, well-executed performance analogous to that of expert jazz musicians is critical for effective decision-making in organizations.[60] Intuition becomes less random and more likely to culminate in a successful decision outcome as the breadth of the decision-maker's expertise increases. Leaders with broad experience and a wide latitude of expertise are not bound by rules and maxims in the same way as employees with limited latitude. When encountering complex situations that challenge the limits of cognitive processing, leaders can rely on deductive logic to make difficult decisions. The decision experience of front-line employees carried out in job-specific protocols enforced by managers is markedly different.

Media Leverage. Media has a profound influence on risk perception and behavior by amplifying its visibility and evoking emotions which heighten its effect. It can make risk feel more personal through the influence of others discussing their experience with risk. It can distort perception through misinformation leading to overestimation or underestimation of actual risk. And it can shape perception through frames used to describe risk. A considerable amount of research has evidenced the role that media plays during crisis periods, for example, in arousing affect in response to emotional content framing risk (Seo, 2021), disseminating misinformation (Somma et.al., 2020), promoting collective identity among groups (Waeterlose et. al. 2021), raising public awareness and knowledge about risk (Re et. al. 2022) and changing beliefs about risk (Domnich et. al. 2021).[61]

A notable example of media impact on risk perception and behavior is the spread of misinformation during the COVID-19 pandemic. Social media platforms like Facebook, Instagram and Twitter were flooded with accurate information and misinformation about the virus, vaccines and treatment. This fueled confusion and fear in the public. False claims about the danger of the vaccines spread rapidly causing segments of the public to perceive the risk of vaccination as higher than the risk of contracting COVID-19—an occurrence which negatively impacted public health efforts to control the pandemic. Another example is the influence of media on health risk behavior among adolescents. Studies disclosed that frequent social media use is associated with changing attitudes toward risk evidenced in behaviors such as alcohol and drug use, smoking and unhealthy dietary habits. Exposure to content showcasing risk behavior was evidenced to alter perception of prevalence and acceptability of risk behavior thereby leading to underestimation of actual risk.

The Challenge of Modern Risk

Modern risk has changed how we live through developments in science and technology that play out over time with consequences that are not always predictable. It is met by cognitive processes that shield us from harm, social forces and group dynamics that influence how we think and act in response to risk, and organizational and media influence that shapes our attitude toward risk. The relationship between risk and behavior can be expressed in a conundrum:

> *Risk is amplified when people frame threats in ways that are out of proportion to their consequences*

When threats are interpreted inappropriately, they become difficult to manage. Our engagement with risk does not happen in a vacuum. It is mediated by social dynamics—the interplay of cognitive, social, group and organizational factors that shape our inrterpretation of risk and how we respond to it. In the chapter that follows, the social dynamics of risk are modeled in four dimensions: triggers or events leading up to behavior (*antecedents*), our response to the event (*behavior*), factors that mediate our response (*intervening factors*) and outcomes of our behavior (*consequences*). Critical factors mediating our response to risk are described in Chapters 4 through 7 beginning with cognition and affect, extending through social forces and group dynamics and closing with organizational and media influence. In combination, these factors create a "perfect storm" augmenting the effect and consequences of risk—the subject of Chapter 8.

Notes

1. Fisher, M. "In Many Ways, the World Is Getting Better. It Also Feels Broken." *The New York Times*, July 13, 2022.
2. Fisher, M. "In Many Ways, the World Is Getting Better. It Also Feels Broken." *The New York Times*, July 13, 2022.
3. Lin, R-G. Petri, A., and Winton, R. "Failed Communications Left Maui Residents Trapped." *Los Angeles Times*, August 12, 2023.
4. Beck, U. *Risk Society: Towards a New Modernity*. New York, NY: SAGE Publications, 1992.
5. Frost, N. "Europe's Largest Port Shoulders Burden of Fulfilling a United Front Against Russia." *The New York Times*, July 8, 2022.
6. Roberto, M., Bohmer, R., and Edmondson, A. "Facing Ambiguous Threats." *Harvard Business Review*, 84(11) (November 2006), pp. 106–113.
7. Roberto, M., Bohmer, R., and Edmondson, A. "Facing Ambiguous Threats." *Harvard Business Review*, 84(11) (November 2006), pp. 106–113.
8. Schwartz, N. and Bajaj, V. "How Missed Signals Contributed to a Mortgage Meltdown." *The NewYork Times*, August 19, 2007.
9. Rabin, R. "What Matters Most: Shell Oil's CSR Crisis in the North Sea." *GreenBiz*, May 16, 2004.
10. Loftus, P. "Merck to Pay $830 Million to Settle Vioxx Shareholder Suit." *Wall Street Journal*, January 15, 2016.
11. Rashid, B. "The Complications That Led to Radio Shack Filing for Bankruptcy for a Second Time in Two Years." *Forbes*, August 8, 2017.
12. Essay. "Situation Analysis: Schwinn Bicycles." *Study Mode Research*, November 21, 2018.
13. Zhang, M. "What Kodak Said About Digital Photography in 1975." *PetaPixel*, September 21, 2017.
14. Roberto, M., Bohmer, R., and Edmondson, A. "Facing Ambiguous Threats." *Harvard Business Review*, 84(11) (November 2006), pp. 106–113.
15. Albeck-Ripka, L. "The Great Pacific Garbage Patch Is Ballooning, 87,000,000,000 Tons of Plastic and Counting." *The New York Times*, March 22, 2018.
16. Dasgupta, S. and Robinson, E. "Attributing Changes in Food Insecurity to a Changing Climate." *National Library of Medicine*, March 18, 2022.
17. FAO, IFAD, UNICEF, WFP, and WHO. *The State of Food Security and Nutrition in the World 2021. Transforming Food Systems for Food Security, Improved Nutrition and Affordable Diets for All*. Rome: FAO, 2021.
18. Denchak, M. "Flint Water Crisis: Everything You Need to Know." *National Resources Defense Council*, November 8, 2018.

19. Denchak, M. "Flint Water Crisis: Everything You Need to Know." *National Resources Defense Council*, November 8, 2018.
20. Findijs, A. "Federal Officials Warn of Impending Water Crisis in the American Southwest." *World Socialist Web Site*, June 23, 2022.
21. Taylor, A. "Water Levels in Lake Mead Reach Record Lows." *The Atlantic*, May 18, 2022.
22. Zimmerman, K. "Hurricane Katrina: Facts, Damage & Aftermath." *LiveScience*, August 27, 2015.
23. Zimmerman, K. "Hurricane Katrina: Facts, Damage & Aftermath." *LiveScience*, August 27, 2015.
24. Zimmerman, K. "Hurricane Katrina: Facts, Damage & Aftermath." *LiveScience*, August 27, 2015.
25. Wikipedia. "Three Mile Island Accident." https://wikipedia.org/wiki/Three _Mile_Island_accident. Retrieved: May 12, 2022.
26. Wikipedia. "Three Mile Island Accident." https://wikipedia.org/wiki/Three _Mile_Island_accident. Retrieved: May 12, 2022.
27. Wikipedia. "Three Mile Island Accident." https://wikipedia.org/wiki/Three _Mile_Island_accident. Retrieved: May 12, 2022.
28. Hawkins, A. "Everything You Need to Know About the Boeing 737 Max Airplane Crashes." *The Verge*, March 22, 2019.
29. Caldwell, A. "The Neuroscience of Stress." *BrainFacts.org*, June 19, 2018.
30. Caldwell, A. "The Neuroscience of Stress." *BrainFacts.org*, June 19, 2018.
31. Nunez, K. "Fight, Flight or Freeze: How We Respond to Threats." *Healthline*, February 21, 2020.
32. Nunez, K. "Fight, Flight or Freeze: How We Respond to Threats." *Healthline*, February 21, 2020.
33. Nunez, K. "Fight, Flight or Freeze: How We Respond to Threats." *Healthline*, February 21, 2020.
34. Nunez, K. "Fight, Flight or Freeze: How We Respond to Threats." *Healthline*, February 21, 2020.
35. Roberto, M., Bohmer, R., and Edmondson, A. "Facing Ambiguous Threats." *Harvard Business Review*, 84(11) (November 2006), pp. 106–113.
36. Roth, A., Walker, S., Rankin, J., and Borger, J. "Putin Signals Escalation as He Puts Nuclear Force on High Alert." *The Guardian*, February 27, 2022. The social dynamic illustrated by the construction of events following Putin's declaration of nuclear force was derived from analysis of the behavioral patterns associated with the Columbia space shuttle disaster by Roberto, Bohmer, and Edmondson in "Facing Ambiguous Threats." *Harvard Business Review*, 84(11) (November 2006), pp. 106–113.
37. Berger, P. and Luckmann, T. *The Social Construction of Reality*. Palatine, IL: Anchor Books, 1966.
38. Hopper, E. "Cognitive Dissonance Theory: Definition and Examples." *ThoughtCo*, February 28, 2020.

39. Kunreuther, H., Slovic, P., and Olson, K. "Fast and Slow Thinking in the Face of Catastrophic Risk." *SSRN Electronic Journal*, August 19, 2014. https://ssrn.com/abstract=2488653.
40. de Langhe, B. and Fernbach, P. "The Dangers of Categorical Thinking." *Harvard Business Review*, 97(5) (2019), pp. 81–91.
41. Herbert, W. "When Patients Do Nothing: Illness and Inertia." *HuffPost*. February 6, 2013.
42. Vinney, C. "Status Quo Bias: What It Means and How It Affects Your Behavior." *ThoughtCo*, December 11, 2019.
43. Simon, H. "Rational Choice and the Structure of the Environment." *Psychological Review*, 63(2) (1956), pp. 129–138.
44. https://en.wikipedia.org/w/index.php?title=Normalization_(sociology)&oldid=892692859. Retrieved: June 15, 2022.
45. Berger, P. and Luckmann, T. *The Social Construction of Reality*. Palatine, IL: Anchor Books, 1966.
46. Berger, P. and Luckmann, T. *The Social Construction of Reality*. Palatine, IL: Anchor Books, 1966.
47. Williams, P. "Emotions and Consumer Behavior." *Journal of Consumer Research*, 40(5) (February 2014), pp. vii–xi.
48. Thomas, W. "The Definition of the Situation." In *Self, Symbols, and Society: Classic Readings in Social Psychology*, ed. Nathan Rousseau. Lanham, MD: Rowman & Littlefield, Inc., 2002.
49. Thomas, W. "The Definition of the Situation." In *Self, Symbols, and Society: Classic Readings in Social Psychology*, ed. Nathan Rousseau. Lanham, MD: Rowman & Littlefield, Inc., 2002.
50. Centers for Disease Control and Prevention. "How COVID-19 Spreads." August 11, 2022.
51. Moore, A. "How the Coronavirus Created a Toilet Paper Shortage." *North Carolina State University, College of Natural Resources News*, May 19, 2020.
52. Moore, A. "How the Coronavirus Created a Toilet Paper Shortage." *North Carolina State University, College of Natural Resources News*, May 19, 2020.
53. He, G. "Organizational Culture: Definition, Examples, & Best Practices." *Teambuilding.com*, December 10, 2023.
54. Qian, J. "Risk Culture." *Institute of Risk Management*, July 7, 2022.
55. Novkov, A. "Stop the Line: No Compromise on Quality." *Lean Product Development, Lean Agile*, April 17, 2018.
56. Maurer, B. "Workers' Attitudes Cited as Biggest Barrier to Safety." *Society for Human Resource Management*, August 23, 2015.
57. Calabretta, G., Gemser, G., and Wijnberg, N. "The Interplay Between Intuition and Rationality in Strategic Decision Making: A Paradox Perspective." *Organization Studies*, 38(3–4) (2017), pp. 365–401.
58. Calabretta, G., Gemser, G., and Wijnberg, N. "The Interplay Between Intuition and Rationality in Strategic Decision Making: A Paradox Perspective." *Organization Studies*, 38(3–4) (2017), pp. 365–401.

59. Calabretta, G., Gemser, G., and Wijnberg, N. "The Interplay Between Intuition and Rationality in Strategic Decision Making: A Paradox Perspective." *Organization Studies*, 38(3–4) (2017), pp. 365–401.
60. Eisenhardt, K. "Strategic Decisions and All That Jazz." *Wiley Online Library*, 1997. https://doi.org/10.1111/1467-8616.00031. Retrieved: July 25, 2022.
61. Purba, A., Thomson, R., Henery, P., Pearce, A., Henderson, M., and Katikireddi, S. "Social Media Use and Heath Risk Behaviours in Young People: Systematic Review and Meta-Analysis." *PubMed*, National Institute of Health, November 29, 2023.

Chapter 3

Modeling Social Dynamics

The social sciences, unlike most fields of the physical sciences, have to deal with structures of essential complexity—structures whose characteristic properties can be exhibited only by models made up of relatively large numbers of variables.

Friedrich August von Hayek, Economist, 1942

The study of how people interact with others—one-on-one and within groups—is known as social dynamics.[1] Social dynamics help us understand behavior by structuring variables that underlie how we interact with one another and how these interactions influence what we see, think and do. In the world of risk, behavior is in large part a result of an interactive process which can be as simple as expressing a feeling about risk or as complex as deciding what to do during a disaster. Irrespective of circumstance, the behavior and attitudes of others are a powerful force shaping how we perceive and respond to risk.

Risk: A Social Dynamic

Most of us have heard about instinctive reactions in response to danger—for instance, survival reactions such as fight or flight when facing someone or something that may cause injury or harm. We know comparatively little, however, about sociopsychological factors and their effect on how we respond to risk. The connection between social factors and risk has been a long-standing interest of social scientists. Early work consisted primarily

DOI: 10.4324/9781003335658-4

of essays and anecdotal evidence which piqued interest in the topic but did little to explain dynamics of the relationship. In *Risk and Culture* (1982), for example, Douglas and Wildawsky described risk response as a reflection of social context—our perception of risk is shaped by norms of the group or community we are part of.[2]

More recently, however, our understanding of the relationship between social factors and risk has been furthered through empirical research on behavior in high-risk settings. In research on risk perception among fishermen in the Norwegian commercial fishing industry, for example, Bye and Lamvik (2007) found behavior to be governed by factors beyond instinct.[3] Accident statistics, survey and interview data, and observation revealed collective mindsets and behavior within an industry-wide culture to be a prime determinant of risk perception and behavior.[4]

The Norwegian Commercial Fishing Industry

Commercial fishing is one of the most dangerous industries in the world with a global fatality rate exceeding that of almost all occupational sectors.[5] Commercial fishermen "race to catch"—a practice prompting crews to ply their trade in dangerous waters. Safety boundaries are breached by fishermen working in waters that are a great distance from land and subject to rapidly changing conditions. Rising sea surface temperatures and extreme weather associated with climate change have made ocean waters more turbulent. Economics are also at work as commercial fishing is an irresolute industry. Lack of a minimum wage, uncertainty of income and the need to maximize catch place economic considerations above safety.[6] Safety training is minimal, and many boats lack state-of-the-art life-saving equipment.

Social Forces. Domestic consumption of fishery products in Norway is among the highest in the world, and demand is growing.[7] The combination of rising demand and shrinking fish stocks has placed added pressure on commercial fisherman to locate new fishing grounds and take on added risk. The economic and physical circumstances of fishermen, whether working on company-operated vessels or small independent vessels, are common across the industry. All face dangers of the open sea in their everyday work; lack predictability because they cannot predetermine the outcome of their work; and are subject to a work medium where the relationship between labor and reward is uncertain.[8] The catch is entirely dependent on effort, and land-based operators must be satisfied for contracts to remain in force.

Institutional Culture. A common culture is at work in the Norwegian commercial fishing industry. Crewmen working on vessels operated by large companies and those working independently on small boats avoid discussion of risk.[9] Safety is not an active concern, and the hazards of work are not a subject of discussion. Fishermen do not feel at risk or express concerns about safety because of industry-wide "cultural conventions." Norms learned in different work settings—land-based fish processing operations, merchant fleet operations and offshore fishing operations—are part of an industry-wide culture that binds fishermen to a common codex.[10]

Group Dynamics. In group interviews, company-employed fishermen described risk as a topic of marginal importance in dialogue among crew members.[11] Crewmen shared stories with one another about accidents and near misses but did not link stories to explicit discussion of danger. Stories were presented as "entertainment" for fellow crewmen. When the issue of safety arose among crew members, negative comments such as "weakling," "chicken" or "fraidy cat" were directed to individuals expressing concern. Individual interviews yielded a different pattern of results. Fishermen willingly described their work as dangerous including examples of accidents resulting in death or serious injury.[12]

Behavior. Aversion of risk was part of an industry-wide credo in which personal safety is subordinated to the catch.[13] This behavioral pattern flies in the face of conventional wisdom which would suggest that fishermen working side-by-side with crew members on large company-owned boats would adopt a different credo from fishermen working alone on small boats. This was not the case. Aversion of risk was an industry-wide adaptation to dangerous work. Irrespective of the type of vessel or context for work, fishermen did not express fear or concern about personal safety. Danger is inherent in the industry, and risks must be taken to successfully carry out work.

Interpretation

The Norwegian commercial fishing industry is a hazardous industry. Risk is inherent in the work, and it is managed by avoidance behavior driven by ***cognition***—the mental proocess of learning and understanding norms of the industry; ***social forces***—fishermen put themselves at greater risk as a function of rising demand for diminishing fish stocks; ***institutional culture***—an industry-wide credo constraining discourse about risk; and ***group***

dynamics—norms guiding interaction among group members limiting discourse about risk.

Modeling Social Dynamics

The relationship between risk and behavior is complex and best understood in a framework incorporating forces that drive and influence how people respond to threats. The notion of offsetting forces is a core element of *force-field analysis*—a sociological principle developed by Kurt Lewin in which behavior is a function of the interplay between person, group and environment.[14] The "field" or "life space" is the psychological makeup of an individual or group at a given point in time. When fully constructed, it is a gestalt of motives, needs, goals and ideals that drive behavior. In Lewin's force field, behavior unfolds in a "boundary zone" of competing forces formed by the intersection of stimuli from the physical and social environment and life space.[15] In the world of risk, the interplay of personal, group and environmental factors at a given point in time shapes behavior in response to threats.

Modeling Risk and Behavior

Human behavior is a gestalt of countless variables many of which are interrelated. This introduces a dilemma in modeling—attribution. How to take into account the many and varied factors that drive behavior. It is impossible to include all relevant variables. Therefore, choices must be made about what to include and what to omit and a basis provided for inclusion.

The social sciences provide a basis for inclusion. Psychologists claim that the primary determinant of human behavior is cognitive programming of the human mind.[16] Sociologists maintain that it is society, or the social system, which can be divided into four categories: *situational factors*—environmental challenges people face; *cultural factors*—the culture people belong to; *social factors*—how people interact with one another; and *institutional* factors—organizations with rules and norms that influence how people and society function.[17] Both perspectives contribute in important ways to our understanding of risk behavior. Combining them brings four sets of variables together in a relationship between risk and behavior:

Antecedent Conditions: situational factors preceding the onset of risk. *Dynamic Conditions:* rapidly developing conditions leading to the onset of risk (e.g., mechanical failure resulting in a nuclear meltdown). *Progressive Conditions:* Gradually developing conditions that threaten people over time (e.g., continuous release of CO_2 into the atmosphere leading to climate conditions that threaten human life).

Cognition and Affect: the mental process of learning through thought, experience and the senses that shapes response to danger (e.g., the way our brain makes a connection with prior experience in response to danger).

Intervening Factors: social, institutional and group factors which mediate the interaction between threat and behavior (e.g., the impact of group dynamics on individual behavior in response to danger).

Behavior: the response of individuals to threats.

Simplicity is a virtue in modeling. This is particularly true in the domain of risk where behavior is vastly more complex than instinctive physiological and psychological changes in response to danger. Contextual factors intervene. Among them are *social forces* creating conditions of stability and change, *group dynamics* influencing individual thought and behavior in social situations and *institutions* influencing behavior in times of crisis.

The intersection of these factors and their influence on behavior can be represented in a model positing cause-and-effect relationships among variables as depicted in Figure 3.1.

Implicit in the model is the understanding that behavior in response to risk is a product of the combined effect of social forces, group dynamics and institutions which *mediate* the relationship between cognition and risk.

Hurricane Katrina

Hurricane Katrina provides an excellent example of the mediating effect of sociopsychological factors on cognition and risk behavior. Katrina was one of the worst disasters in U.S. history. It made landfall on August 29, 2005, as a Category 5 hurricane 30 miles east of New Orleans with sustained

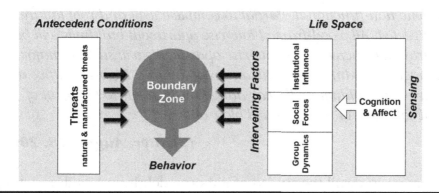

Figure 3.1 Social Dynamics Model

winds of 175 mph.[18] Although not the strongest recorded hurricane in history, Katrina impacted 90,000 square miles of land along the Louisiana and Mississippi coastline.[19] Breached levees in New Orleans flooded 80 percent of the city with poor neighborhoods and people of color most vulnerable to the storm's damaging water and winds.[20] Katrina caused 1,800 deaths, 400,000 people were left homeless, and hundreds of thousands lost access to homes and jobs.[21]

Antecedent Conditions

Katrina was initially spotted in Caribbean waters as a tropical depression over the southeastern Bahamas. The depression strengthened, and its circular motion intensified into a tropical storm with wind speeds between 39 and 75 mph. The storm first made landfall in Florida on August 25, weakened into a tropical storm as it passed over land and gained strength as its path turned northwest.[22] The storm traversed the Gulf of Mexico eventually making landfall on the Louisiana coast on August 29 with storm-force winds 200 miles in each direction from its center.

 Meteorological Forecast. As Katrina gathered strength in the Gulf of Mexico, National Weather Service meteorologist Robert Ricks of Slidell, Louisiana, predicted that it would be "a powerful hurricane with unprecedented strength rivaling the intensity of Hurricane Camille of 1969."[23]

> *Most of the area will be uninhabitable for weeks—perhaps longer. At least one-half of well-constructed homes will have roof and wall failure. All gabled roofs will fail leaving those homes severely damaged or destroyed...The majority of industrial buildings will*

*become non-functional. Partial to complete wall and roof failure
is expected. All wood-framed low-rise apartment buildings will be
destroyed. Concrete block low-rise apartments will sustain major
damage, including some wall and roof failure…High-rise office and
apartment buildings will sway dangerously, a few to the point of
total collapse. All windows will blow out.*

(Twitter, August 28, 2005)

Ricks went on to detail the spread of airborne debris and its devastating
effects—a power outage that would last for weeks and water shortages that
would make human suffering incredible by modern standards.[24] The upshot:
Ricks' prediction was largely ignored in the run-up to the storm.

Faulty Engineering. Post-mortem studies revealed that the greatest
amount of destruction associated with Katrina was not caused by the storm
itself but the storm's exposure of construction and engineering failures.[25]
Floodwalls and levees failed because of the compound effect of misinformed
decisions of engineers and officials at all levels of government. Levees with
concrete floodwalls collapsed as a result of overtopping and the way they
were designed. Water eroded structures as it poured over floodwalls and
levees. Pump stations that would have been helpful in eliminating floodwa-
ters were not functioning at the time of the storm.[26]

The engineering design failed to address inconsistency in strength of the
soft soils beneath and adjacent to floodwalls.[27] Engineers erred by failing to
design a model that would account for a water-filled gap that would form
behind concrete floodwalls as a result of flood waves. Incorrect data was
used to measure levee elevations; most levees were constructed at a height
that would not withstand flood waters.[28] In some cases, levees were erected
1–2 feet lower than the design elevation required to withstand flood waters.

Regulatory/Management Failure. Federal funding for the hurricane
protection system around New Orleans was periodic and discontinuous.
Construction was completed in sections rather than as an interconnected
system.[29] Oversight was minimal, and decisions were based on low-cost
solutions and tradeoffs which compromised project quality and reliability.
No single agency was tasked with overall responsibility for hurricane protection, especially in New Orleans. Responsibility for managing and monitoring
pump stations and levees was shared among federal, state and local agencies.[30] Inter-agency coordination fell short of the level needed to maintain
the hurricane protection system leaving elements of the system poorly maintained and, in some cases, abandoned.

Ethical Oversight. Early on, government authorities and contractors were unaware of the risk facing inhabitants of New Orleans even though the region had faced hurricane disasters before. Little attention was paid to weather-related risk, and stakeholders failed to account for the possibility of system failure and consequences thereof for health and safety.[31] The importance of evacuating people and safeguarding property was underestimated. Post-mortem analysis revealed a breach of engineering standards and deficiencies in the management and maintenance of the hurricane protection system.[32] Senior engineers did not subject the design of the protection model to external evaluation—a process routinely conducted on life-saving systems and structures. Government authorities failed to monitor the project during and after construction even though they were obligated to do so as standard procedure on projects that are of safety concern to the public.

Cognition and Affect

The cognitive impact of Hurricane Katrina on people during the storm varied as a function of proximity to the storm and the personal experience and coping behavior of individuals. Brandi Wagner, a survivor of Hurricane Katrina, thought she had escaped the wrath of the storm. She hung tough while the storm's 125-mph winds pummeled her home and endured two months of sleeping in a sweltering camper outside the city with her boyfriend's mother. It was later, after storm waters had receded and Wagner went back to New Orleans to rebuild her home, that she fell apart.

> *I didn't think it was the storm at first. I didn't really know what was happening to me. We could see the waterline on houses, and rooftop signs with "please help us," and that big X where dead bodies were found. I started sobbing and couldn't stop. I was crying all the time, just really losing it.*

Twelve years later, Wagner fell victim to disability because of depression and anxiety she developed in the wake of the storm. She continues in treatment for an opioid addiction that developed after she started popping prescription painkillers and drinking heavily to blunt the day-to-day reality of recovering from Katrina.[33]

People had difficulty coping with the effects of Katrina—not only the storm itself but also the new normal after the storm including mental illness. Survivors struggled with short-term memory loss and cognitive impairment, a syndrome dubbed "Katrina Brain."[34] Psychiatric helpline calls increased 61 percent in the months after Katrina compared with the same period before the storm, death notices increased 25 percent, and the city's murder rate rose 37 percent. People not directly impacted by Katrina, but seeing its effect on others, were just as likely to seek psychiatric help as those directly impacted. They may not have known where the anxiety was coming from, but Katrina's cognitive impact extended beyond the storm itself to a populace caught in the grip of enduring trauma.

Intervening Factors

Katrina's destructive power was intensified by economic, social and political conditions in New Orleans and the surrounding area. The high poverty rate of New Orleans, racial dimensions of its poverty, and funding cuts for levee construction and maintenance made New Orleans vulnerable to the worst effects of the storm. Beyond socioeconomics, however, were group dynamics and cultural conventions which heightened Katrina's devastation. Response and recovery efforts were hampered by government authorities hunkered down in enclaves of self-reinforcement casting blame at one another. Relief efforts were delayed by a president detached from the devastation in New Orleans. Coordination efforts were stifled by government agencies and local authorities using policy statements and protocols to locate responsibility for storm response elsewhere. Group behavior and cultural conventions turned a natural disaster into a human disaster.

Social Forces. Thousands chose not to evacuate in spite of the danger posed by Katrina. As the storm approached landfall, a collective sigh of relief rippled across the Gulf Coast. Katrina was weakening and projections called for it to make landfall east of New Orleans. Evacuation would be unnecessary because previous storms changed direction before making landfall and turned out to be less severe than predicted. A storm etched in local memory was Hurricane Georges—a Category 3 storm bearing down on New Orleans in 1998. Georges prompted an evacuation but changed direction hours before making landfall. Georges and near misses like it encouraged many New Orleanians to wait before taking action.[35] By the time Katrina's power became evident, it was too late to leave.

Beyond prior storm experience, socioeconomics played a role in evacuation decision-making. Many did not evacuate because they lacked access to information, did not have means of transportation, or could not afford alternative housing.[36] For low-income families, the cost of fuel, alternative housing and lost wages put evacuation beyond reach. Families without financial means were also more likely to reside in low-lying flood plains or mobile homes and lack awareness of the storm's power because electronic communication devices were beyond their budget.

Group Dynamics. Group dynamics were in play throughout all phases of Katrina—from planning to response to recovery. Residents with financial means and access to transportation did not always evacuate. Family ties and strong support networks impelled many to wait out the storm. Residents with economic means and social support who chose to stay did so on the basis of group dynamics—shared norms and customs that led them to trust their social networks rather than instructions from authorities.[37]

Group dynamics were also at play in government agencies over response to Katrina. The September 18, 2005, issue of *Newsweek* described the response of federal government leaders to Katrina as a "disaster within a disaster."[38]

A standing joke among top aides to President George W. Bush was who would deliver bad news to a president who did not like bad news. The bad news 24 hours after Katrina ripped through New Orleans was that the president would have to cut short his 5-week vacation by a couple of days and return to Washington. Bush knew the storm and its consequences had been bad, but he didn't realize how bad....

Bush has always trusted his gut—he prided himself on ignoring distracting chatter, the caterwauling of media elites, and the Washington political buzz machine. He has boasted that he doesn't read the newspapers. But it is not clear what Bush does read or watch. He can be petulant about dissent; he equates disagreement with disloyalty. After five years in office he is surrounded largely by people who agree with him....

Most presidents keep a devil's advocate around. When Katrina struck, there was no one to tell President Bush the plain truth: that state and local governments had been overwhelmed, that the Federal Emergency Management Agency (FEMA) was not up to the job, and that the military—the only institution with the resources to cope—couldn't act without a declaration from the president overriding all other authority....

The inner thoughts and motivations of Bush and his top advisors are impossible to know for certain. Though it seems abstract at a time of suffering, high-minded considerations about the balance

*of power between state and federal government were clearly at play.
It's possible, as well, that after four years of more or less constant
crisis, Bush and his team are numb....
The failure of the government's response to Katrina worked like a
power blackout. Problems cascaded and compounded; each mistake
made the next mistake worse. The foe in this battle was a monster;
Katrina flattened the Gulf Coast with the strength of a vengeful god.
Bush's leadership style, group dynamics within a coterie of advisors,
and bureaucratic culture combined to delay response and produce
a disaster within a disaster.*

Institutional Influence. Organizations and the media are power players
that shape behavior in times of crisis. In the aftermath of Katrina, government
agencies played a prominent role in response to the storm—a response that
was widely criticized for inadequacy and lack of preparedness. The media
also played a critical role in Katrina's aftermath—a role that was both praised
and criticized for the way narrative of the disaster was framed to the public.

Organizations. Avoidance of blame is a survival tactic in organizations.
In 1986, political scientist R. Kent Weaver published a famous article entitled
"The Politics of Blame Avoidance."[39] Bureaucratic and political cultures are
more likely to avoid blame for unfavorable actions than claim credit for
favorable ones. Within days after Katrina's landfall, public debate arose
about the role of local, state and federal government in preparation for and
response to the storm. Government officials blamed each other for the disastrous response to Katrina.

- *New Orleans Mayor Ray Nagin and Louisiana Governor Kathleen
  Blanco* blamed the federal government, particularly the Federal
  Emergency Management Agency, for the slow response.[40] Federal agencies were criticized for a lack of flexibility, bureaucratic logjams and
  insufficient resources to meet demands on the ground.
- *Federal government officials* blamed local and state government.
  Evacuation and hurricane protection plans were the responsibility of
  city and state officials, and these officials did not ask for federal assistance soon enough nor were they specific when they did request help.[41]
  Mayor Nagin was criticized for failing to implement a flood plan, for
  delaying an emergency evacuation order until less than a day before
  landfall and for ordering residents to seek public shelter without provi-
  sions for food, water, security or sanitary conditions.

Blame must not only be avoided in bureaucratic cultures—it must also be managed. In the first days of the Katrina disaster, government agencies toiled to defuse blame in enclaves of self-reinforcement.

- *President Bush* used performance metrics to show what the Feds were doing in disaster relief—400 trucks transporting 5.4 million meals and 13.4 million liters of water along with 3.4 million pounds of ice.[42] These statistics were rattled off in press briefings ostensibly to assure the nation that federal officials were performing responsibly, but inwardly to convince themselves that POTUS was on top of the disaster and taking the right steps.
- *New Orleans Mayor Ray Nagin* became the lightning rod of local government officials seeking help and trying to distance themselves from blame. In an on-air call to a local radio station three days into the disaster Nagin assailed the federal government: "Don't tell me 40,000 people are coming here. They're not here. It's too late. Now get off your asses and do something, and let's fix the biggest crisis in the history of this country."[43] Federal authorities were not the only target of Nagin's ire. Louisiana Governor Kathleen Blanco was accused of delaying federal relief efforts: "I was ready to move today, but the Governor said she needed 24 hours to make a decision. It would have been great if we could have told the world that we had this all worked out. It didn't happen, and more people died."[44]
- *Louisiana Governor Kathleen Blanco*, believing the state had been unfairly criticized for its response to the storm, blamed the Federal Emergency Management Agency and President Bush for a slow initial response to the disaster and inability to effectively manage, care for and deliver promised resources to residents trying to evacuate from New Orleans.[45]
- *Government Agencies*, notably FEMA and the Department of Homeland Security, blamed local and state authorities for delays in engaging federal agencies for assistance, even after being approached by federal authorities. Police, fire and EMS organizations outside of the impacted region claimed to be hindered or slowed in their efforts to render assistance because of coordination problems between different levels of government.[46]

News media played a significant role in shaping public perception of response to Katrina during and after the storm. On the negative side were claims that media reporting on the disaster may have worsened its impact. Reporting was exaggerated, inaccurate and presented in an appalling manner. Coverage focused on government response rather than on preparedness and the plight of people and communities affected by the disaster. Worse yet, news organizations were criticized for reporting unsubstantiated accounts of widespread incidents of violence, rape and murder. In some cases, claims were repeated as facts without attribution. Elements of racial bias surfaced in media coverage as white flood victims were portrayed as "finding" supplies while a black flood victim was described as "looting" supplies. These images were widely used on the internet and criticized as an example of pervasive racism.

On the positive side were kudos given to the media for its extensive coverage of the disaster and the human condition in New Orleans. Media coverage helped raise awareness of the situation and mobilized resources to assist those in need by highlighting the need for emergency aid and supplies which led to an outpouring of support from people and organizations throughout the nation.

Behavior

Social scientists have long claimed that "natural" disasters are not natural in their social consequences. Instead, the distribution of damage exposes previously existing fissures in the fabric of society and communities. Katrina's greatest impact was on the social structure and political economy of New Orleans as evidenced in the behavior of its residents. New Orleans had one of the highest levels of income inequality in the country at the time Katrina made landfall. The actions of its residents during and after the storm followed the lines of social stratification.

Citizen Behavior. The actions of moneyed middle- and upper-class residents in response to the storm were predictable: make a hotel reservation or visit out-of-town friends, board the house windows, pack the car, get cash and get out of town. Most well-to-do residents had advance information about the storm's path through media and evacuated prior to Katrina's landfall. Yet, many who evacuated delayed leaving. Riding out a storm was an old New Orleans tradition with better-off New Orleanians staying in the city during hurricanes and evacuating "vertically" to the upper floors of hotels.[47]

Lower-income residents had few choices in preparation for Katrina. When the city began to flood, tens of thousands of poor black New Orleanians found themselves without food, water and shelter and were forced to rely on local and federal authorities to provide for their basic needs.[48] Many remained in their homes hoping for the best. Others headed toward the New Orleans Superdome and the Morial Convention Center on the belief that these shelters would provide sufficient protection until the storm passed. Significant numbers of elderly and disabled citizens perished in homes or public facilities of diseases that are easily managed under normal conditions but became lethal when access to medication and treatment was cut off by the storm.[49]

Social Disorder. Misinformation during Hurricane Katrina over how lawless New Orleans had become exacerbated an already dire situation. Media reports amplified stories of widespread looting and violence that could not be confirmed.[50] Television images captured people carrying electronics and valuable products out of retail stores but failed to present images of looters hunting for staples such as food, water, diapers and medicine. Looting was confused with people going into survival mode. Local officials added to the specter of disorder by warning residents of the presence of armed troops to prevent looting. Fear of looting led to the formation of quasi-militia groups, primarily made up of white residents and local police, who guarded areas in and around New Orleans, leading to racially motivated violence that would take years to prosecute.[51]

Putting the Pieces Together

Hurricane Katrina was a disaster within a disaster—a natural disaster transformed into a man-made disaster by human action. The human response to Katrina illustrates the social dynamics of risk—dynamics that can be modeled by structuring the variables underlying the relationship between risk and behavior. In the lexicon of social dynamics, behavior is a product of three interacting variables: *antecedent conditions* leading up to the onset of risk; *cognition and affect* igniting our response to risk; and *intervening factors*—social forces, group dynamics and institutional influence—which interact with cognition to mediate *behavior* in response to risk.

The most important element in this equation is ***cognition and affect***— the mental process and emotions underlying behavior in response to risk. The central nervous system is the hub that governs thought, movement and feeling. It controls muscles and coordinates movement enabling people to perform activities necessary for survival. Because of its centrality to thought and behavior, neuroscience and the biological processes that underlie cognition and affect are the focus of the next chapter.

Notes

1. Durlauf, S. and Young, P. *Social Dynamics*. Cambridge, MA: MIT Press, 2001.
2. Douglas, M. and Wildavsky, A. *An Essay on the Selection of Technical and Environmental Dangers*. Berkeley, CA: University of California Press, 1982.
3. Bye, R. and Lamvik, G. "Professional Culture and Risk Perception: Coping With Danger On Board Small Fishing Boats and Offshore Service Vessels." *Reliability Engineering System Safety*, 92(12) (2007), pp. 1756–1763.
4. Bye, R. and Lamvik, G. "Professional Culture and Risk Perception: Coping with Danger on Board Small Fishing Boats and Offshore Service Vessels." *Reliability Engineering System Safety*, 92(12) (2007), pp. 1756–1763.
5. Editor. "Fishing Revealed as World's Most Dangerous Industry." *The Fishing Daily,* October 21, 2121.
6. Bye, R. and Lamvik, G. "Professional Culture and Risk Perception: Coping with Danger on Board Small Fishing Boats and Offshore Service Vessels." *Reliability Engineering System Safety*, 92(12) (2007), pp. 1756–1763.
7. Editor. "Optimism for the Norwegian Seafood Industry." *High North News*, August 13, 2021.
8. Bye, R. and Lamvik, G. "Professional Culture and Risk Perception: Coping with Danger on Board Small Fishing Boats and Offshore Service Vessels." *Reliability Engineering System Safety*, 92(12) (2007), pp. 1756–1763.
9. Bye, R. and Lamvik, G. "Professional Culture and Risk Perception: Coping with Danger on Board Small Fishing Boats and Offshore Service Vessels." *Reliability Engineering System Safety*, 92(12) (2007), pp. 1756–1763.
10. Bye, R. and Lamvik, G. "Professional Culture and Risk Perception: Coping with Danger on Board Small Fishing Boats and Offshore Service Vessels." *Reliability Engineering System Safety*, 92(12) (2007), pp. 1756–1763.
11. Bye, R. and Lamvik, G. "Professional Culture and Risk Perception: Coping with Danger on Board Small Fishing Boats and Offshore Service Vessels." *Reliability Engineering System Safety*, 92(12) (2007), pp. 1756–1763.
12. Bye, R. and Lamvik, G. "Professional Culture and Risk Perception: Coping with Danger on Board Small Fishing Boats and Offshore Service Vessels." *Reliability Engineering System Safety*, 92(12) (2007), pp. 1756–1763.
13. Bye, R. and Lamvik, G. "Professional Culture and Risk Perception: Coping with Danger on Board Small Fishing Boats and Offshore Service Vessels." *Reliability Engineering System Safety*, 92(12) (2007), pp. 1756–1763.
14. Lewin, K. "Defining the Field at a Given Time." *Psychological Review*, 50(3) (May 1943), pp. 292–310.
15. Lewin, K. "Defining the Field at a Given Time." *Psychological Review*, 50(3) (May 1943), pp. 292–310.
16. Gastil, R. "The Determinants of Human Behavior." *American Anthropologist*, 63(6) (October 2009), pp. 1281–1291. Retrieved: September 30, 2022.
17. Gastil, R. "The Determinants of Human Behavior." *American Anthropologist*, 63(6) (October 2009), pp. 1281–1291. Retrieved: September 30, 2022.

18. Brittanica: The Editors of Encyclopaedia. "Hurricane Katrina." *Encyclopedia Brittanica*, 16 August 2022. https://www.brittanica.com/event/Hurricane-Katrina. Retrieved: November 25, 2022.
19. History.com Editors. "Hurricane Katrina." November 9, 2009.
20. Maldonado, C. "Katrina Fact-Check: Guesstimate of Katrina's Flooding in New Orleans Was Correct." *The Lens*, July 20, 2015.
21. Brittanica: The Editors of Encyclopaedia. "Hurricane Katrina." November 5, 2023.
22. Brittanica: The Editors of Encyclopaedia. "Hurricane Katrina." November 5, 2023.
23. Holthaus, E. "The Most Dire Weather Forecast Ever Issued." *Slate*, August 28, 2015.
24. Holthaus, E. "The Most Dire Weather Forecast Ever Issued." *Slate*, August 28, 2015.
25. Griffis, F. "Engineering Failures Exposed by Hurricane Katrina." *Elsevier*, 29(2) (April 2007), pp. 189–195.
26. Griffis, F. "Engineering Failures Exposed by Hurricane Katrina." *Elsevier*, 29(2) (April 2007), pp. 189–195.
27. Carey, P. "Floodwall's Collapse in New Orleans Linked to Soil Failure." *The Seattle Times*, October 8, 2005.
28. Wilson, D. and Kliger, E. "Flood or Hurricane Protection? The New Orleans Levee System and Hurricane Katrina." *IEEE Spectrum*, January 1, 2008.
29. Kay, J. "Cost-Cutting and Poor Planning Behind New Orleans Levee Failures." *Independent Panel Report on Hurricane Katrina*, May 23, 2006.
30. Johnson, S. "Hurricane Katrina: Challenges, Concerns, Policies and Needs." Environmental Public Health Impacts of natural Disasters: Hurricane Katrina: Workshop Summary (Chapter 2, pp. 12–15), *National* Academies Press, 2007.
31. Griffis, F. "Engineering Failures Exposed by Hurricane Katrina." *Elsevier*, 29(2) (April 2007), pp. 189–195.
32. Cole, T. and Fellows, K. "Risk Communication Failure: A Case Study of New Orleans and Hurricane Katrina." *Southern Communication Journal*, 73(3) (2008), pp. 211–228.
33. Vestal, C. "Katrina Brain: The Invisible Long-Term Toll of Megastorms." *Politico*, October 12, 2017.
34. Vestal, C. "Katrina Brain: The Invisible Long-Term Toll of Megastorms." *Politico*, October 12, 2017.
35. Wade, L. "Who Didn't Evacuate for Hurricane Katrina?" *Pacific Standard*, August 31, 2015.
36. Horney, J. "A Professor of Biostatistics Explains Why People Ignore Evacuation Orders." *The Conversation*, September 12, 2018.
37. Horney, J. "A Professor of Biostatistics Explains Why People Ignore Evacuation Orders." *The Conversation*, September 12, 2018.
38. Thomas, E. "The Government Response to Katrina: A Disaster Within a Disaster." *Newsweek*, September 18, 2005.

39. Weaver, R. *The Politics of Blame and Avoidance*. Journal of Public Policy. Cambridge, UK: Cambridge University Press, November 28, 2008.

40. "New Orleans Mayor, Louisiana Governor Hold Press Conference." (http://transcripts.cnn.com/TRANSCRIPTS/0508/28/bn.04.html) *CNN*, August 28, 2005.

41. "Who's to Blame for Delayed Response to Katrina?" *ABC News*, September 6, 2005.

42. Thomas, E. "The Government Response to Katrina: A Disaster Within a Disaster." *Newsweek*, September 18, 2005.

43. "Hurricane Katrina: Mayor Nagin's Emotional Interview." *BBC News Magazine*, August 20, 2015.

44. *American Morning*, CNN: Transcript (http://transcripts.cnn.com/TRANSCRIPTS/0509/05/ltm.01.html), September 5, 2005.

45. Pao, M. "Swept Up in the Storm: Hurricane Katrina's Key Players, Then and Now." *National Public Radio*, August 27, 2015.

46. .Bluesterin, G. "Firefighters Stuck in Ga Awaiting Orders. Greg Bluestein, Associated Press Writer." *USA Today*, September 7, 2005.

47. Fussell, E. "Leaving New Orleans: Social Stratification, Networks, and Hurricane Evacuation." *Social Science Research Council*, June 11, 2006.

48. Ibid.

49. Ibid.

50. Guarino, M. "Misleading Reports of Lawlessness After Katrina Worsened Crisis Officials Say." *The Guardian*. August 16, 2015.

51. Ibid.

SOCIAL DYNAMICS OF RISK

Part II

Chapter 4

Risk and Cognition

The human brain is the only object in the known universe that can predict its own future and tell its own fortune. The fact that we can make disastrous decisions even as we foresee their consequences is the great, unsolved mystery of human behavior. When you hold your fate in your hands, why would you ever make a fist?

Dan Gilbert, psychologist, Harvard University, 2018

There is much we don't know about how the human brain works. We do know, however, that one of its most important functions is to detect threats and protect us from harm. Our brain and nervous system are wired to sense peril and activate the body in response to threats. Given this fact, why is it that from the individual to the societal level, we are slow to react to threats and known forms of danger? Why do we avoid risk?

This chapter will dive into these questions from a neuroscience perspective. In today's world of ubiquitous risk, one cannot fully understand behavior in response to threats without considering inner workings of the brain and neurological influences that shape thought, emotion and behavior. Everything starts with the brain. It is the driving force behind what we think and do, the social dynamics we create and how we respond to threats.

DOI: 10.4324/9781003335658-6

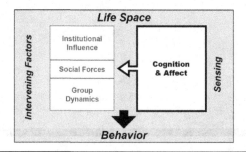

Cognition, Affect and Risk Behavior

Why the Brain Matters

Put yourself in a risk situation involving travel in inclement weather. You are scheduled to drive several hundred miles for a holiday visit with relatives. The weather forecast calls for high winds, heavy rain and dropping temperatures. Although most of the drive will be on an interstate highway, a back-road shortcut will shorten the drive and enable you to arrive on time for a family event. You depart on time and the first part of the trip goes according to plan. You take the shortcut, but shortly after leaving the interstate things change for the worse. A few miles down the road cars have skidded off icy pavement and trees have been uprooted by high winds. The car in front of you brakes suddenly to avoid a falling tree and you are close behind. You panic—your heart rate and breathing accelerate, your blood pressure elevates, your muscles tense and you break out in a sweat. This has all happened in seconds leaving little time to react. Your brain has taken over your body to protect you from harm.

Fight, Freeze or Flight?

Your response, also known as the acute stress response, is a physiological reaction that occurs in response to something that is terrifying either mentally or physically.[1] The state of panic you experienced on the road is part of a chain of rapidly occurring reactions inside your body to mobilize its resources in response to danger.[2] Your brain is hardwired for survival which prevails over everything. In response to acute stress, it signals the body to release hormones which activate the sympathetic nervous system. The sympathetic nervous system then stimulates the adrenal glands triggering the release of hormones that include adrenaline and noradrenaline.[3] Heart rate and respiration elevate, muscles tense and vision sharpens. Your brain has readied your body to respond to a harmful event.

You can probably think of numerous situations when you experienced a fight, freeze or flight response. Hearing footsteps behind you on a late-night walk, encountering a snarling dog, or experiencing anxiety prior to a presentation to executives at work. Although the brain's response to danger is designed to protect us from harm, it is not automatic nor is it entirely helpful or appropriate. Our brain is wired to respond to specific types of threats. Insidious threats like climate change are life-threatening, but invisible and beyond detection by the brain. Furthermore, our brain does not distinguish between appropriate and inappropriate responses to threats. Flight from an automobile accident in which you have been involved would be irresponsible. A fight response to a verbal exchange with a colleague at work would be ill-advised. A freeze response at the controls of an aircraft in distress could be disastrous. In a worst-case scenario, the brain's wiring to protect us from harm may actually impede our ability to respond meaningfully to threats.

Air France Flight 447

The tragic crash of Air France 447 (AF 447) in 2009 sent shock waves around the world. AF 447 was cruising at 35,000 feet over the Atlantic Ocean having departed Rio de Janeiro, Brazil, bound for Paris, France.[4] The Airbus A330 was carrying 216 passengers and 12 crew. Two hours into the flight, the captain left the flight deck and retired to the crew rest area leaving the first officer in charge of the aircraft. While passing through an intertropical convergence zone, AF 447 flew through powerful bands of convective thunderstorms within cumulonimbus clouds.[5] The aircraft experienced severe turbulence followed by icing conditions and hail. Its pitot tubes, which provide data including airspeed to the flight deck, became temporarily blocked due to ice crystal formation. The autopilot disconnected forcing the pilots to take manual control of the aircraft. A progression of errors occurred as the pilots, in a state of panic, failed to follow flight protocols[6]:

■ Rather than maintaining straight and level flight, the pilots made excessive control inputs, pulling back on the stick, making contradictory control inputs, raising the nose and exceeding the critical angle of attack, triggering a stall warning. During this time, vertical speed peaked at 7,000 feet per minute and the aircraft climbed to 38,000 feet.

■ Lacking experience on the characteristics of high-altitude manual flying, the pilots did not complete a procedure for verification of unreliable indicated airspeed—an oversight which led to disconnection of the automatic flight director—an instrument showing the attitude required to achieve a desired flight path.

■ Pilot error caused the critical angle of attack of the wing to be exceeded, thereby causing the aircraft to stall. Rather than reducing the angle of attack by lowering the nose and restoring lift, the pilots' reaction was the opposite—they pitched the nose up deepening the stall.

■ Not realizing the aircraft was in a stall, the pilots ignored the stall warning and, consequently, never applied the stall recovery maneuver.

Air France 447 remained in a stalled state for the entirety of its three minute and thirty second descent into the ocean. A post-mortem report based on data recovered from the aircraft's black box indicated that acute stress experienced by the pilots and their panic reaction may have caused them to ignore the stall warning.[7] The report also provided evidence of poor crew resource management on the flight deck. The crew became progressively disoriented as their awareness of the danger they were in mounted, and coordination fell apart to the point that situational awareness was lost.[8]

The panic reaction of AF 447's pilots is illustrative of the brain's response to immediate and present danger. It also illustrates the interplay between manufactured risk and human behavior. All of the elements of manufactured risk were present on AF 447: risk produced by advances in science and technology (an advanced jet aircraft with high-tech controls); a risk environment with limited historical reference (advanced jet technology is a relatively recent development); unpredictable technology (loss of human control is an unanticipated consequence of advanced technology); and transition in the source of risk (from nature to humans). The brain-body connection guiding behavior in response to danger was fully in play. The "fight response" of AF 447's pilots was instinctive as they struggled to gain control of the aircraft by making erroneous inputs to the flight controls. A challenging situation was transformed into a disaster through a combination of inexperience and decisions driven by instinct. Ironically, a simulation exercise after the accident demonstrated that with no pilot inputs to the flight controls, AF 447 would have remained at its cruise altitude following the autopilot disconnection.[9]

The Brain and Threat Response

Although our brain is at the center of everything we do, our survival is its primary function. The amygdala in the limbic system portion of the brain, located in the forebrain above the brainstem, is the brain's "threat detector and effector."[10] When our brain senses danger and prepares us to fight, the amygdala is at work. When we respond to danger by running away or freezing in fear, that's also the amygdala at work. This leaves unanswered, however, a question as to whether the brain's response to threats is indiscriminate or selective. Does the brain respond to all threats whether they are immediate or remote, tangible or intangible?

According to Harvard University psychologist Dan Gilbert, our brain is wired to respond to specific types of threats—those that are intentional, immoral, imminent and instantaneous.[11]

- **Intentional**: Our nervous system is constantly scanning for threats that intentionally want to hurt us. For example, our ancestors were sharply attuned to detecting a hungry bear in the brush that wanted them for its next meal. We take self-defense classes to prepare for the threat of being mugged late at night on the street. In the United States, we poured almost $35 billion dollars into the security alarm system industry from 2017 to 2022 to quell our fear of threats posed by robbers, burglars and abductors.[12]
- **Immoral**: As a species, we are concerned about right and wrong; who is good and who is evil. In reality, those categories are rarely clean-cut, but in audio, visual and printed media it is clear who poses a threat. Even as children, did we ever second guess whom to fear between the Big Bad Wolf or Little Red Riding Hood? Harry Potter or Voldemort? Through nature and nurture, our brains are conditioned to react positively to what is "good" and to fear and reject what is "bad."
- **Imminent**: "It's hard for the human brain to get excited about things that aren't happening now" (Gilbert, 2010).[13] Scientists, government officials and public health professionals issued warnings about the lack of preparation for a global pandemic decades, before COVID-19.[14] For example, a July 2019 risk assessment report from the Federal Emergency Management Agency predicted that, if a global pandemic happened, hospitals would become overcrowded, businesses would close and essential services would be disrupted on a large scale.[15] Because the idea of a global pandemic was tabled prior to 2020, it was viewed as something that *could* happen in the future and conceptualized as a distant, abstract threat. For this reason, the brain and nervous system did not activate in a way that prepared us for what was to come.
- **Instantaneous**: The human brain is not wired to discern gradual change and slow-moving threats. Instead, we are primed by the brain to respond quickly to abrupt change and instant threats. As soon as

it became clear that COVID-19 was *not* an abstract, distant threat, but rather a concrete threat with instant negative impact individually and collectively, the brain and nervous system went into alert mode. Researchers at the Harvard Medical School found that some individuals who did not contract COVID-19 experienced brain inflammation triggered by pandemic-induced disruption to their lives adversely affecting mental health.[16]

The intentional-immoral-imminent-instantaneous framework illustrates why our brains are not engineered to detect and respond to manufactured risk. Take, for example, global climate change. We are wired to respond to threats that are intentional, immediate and evil, but not wired to respond to threats that are unintentional or neutral. As Gilbert explains, "Global warming isn't trying to kill us, and that's a damn shame."[17] Further, as Marshall (2014) has written, "Climate change confounds a core moral formula: it is a perfect and undetectable crime everyone contributes to but for which no one has a motive."[18] If climate change was a force that was palpable, evil and intentionally trying to harm us, we would readily classify it as a threat and respond to it with urgency. Because there is no intent, however—neither good or bad—climate change falls into a gray area that makes it hard for the brain to assess and comprehend, let alone feel any urgency to respond.

In terms of imminence, clearly there are parts of the globe where the effects of climate change are being felt with intensity. Although circumstances are rapidly changing, a 2021 Yale University study indicated that among those who acknowledge the reality of global warming (65 percent of Americans), less than half (47 percent) believed global warming will harm them personally and just over half (55 percent) believed global warming should be a high priority for the government to tackle.[19] The general feeling was that climate change is something that will have a negative impact but at some point in the future.[20] It is not abrupt or instantaneous. It is an insidiously slow existential threat that doesn't trigger the amygdala to send alarm signals to the body in a way that would be characteristic of an immediate threat.

Kelley Fielding, a social and environmental psychologist at the University of Queensland, summed up the brain-threat connection in a sentence: "I think our brains haven't developed to deal with something as big and long-term as climate change."[21] Scientists working to convince individuals, organizations and societies that modern risk—like climate change—is a serious existential threat have a tough hill to climb. They must find a way to rewire the human brain—the oldest, strongest and most primal neurological wiring that exists.

The Brain-Behavior-Risk Connection

In 1944, American physicist Isidor Rabi discovered nuclear magnetic resonance—a discovery that revolutionized our understanding of the human brain and its connection to behavior.[22] No longer was our understanding of behavior limited to the effect of external stimuli. Behavior came to be understood as a product of neural activity integrating sensory information, perception and learning, and motor response.[23] When magnetic resonance imaging technology was first used on humans in 1977, the brain was revealed to be comprised of three main parts: the forebrain, midbrain and the hindbrain.[24] The hindbrain, located at the top of the spinal cord, controls involuntary bodily functions like breathing, heart pumping, sleeping and sneezing.[25] The midbrain connects the hindbrain and forebrain. It helps to regulate and coordinate body movement and is the area of the brain that helps to process auditory and visual signals. The forebrain, the largest portion of the brain, contains the cerebrum where most of our thinking occurs.[26] It fires up when we read, play, imagine, sense and access memory. Neurons which transmit information to nerve cells, muscles and other parts of the body are the building blocks of the brain.[27]

The brain is foremost among all parts of the body in shaping cognition, behavior and personality. Undergraduate students in Psychology 101 learn early on about the case of Phineas Gage, who when working on a railroad in 1848, suffered a terrible injury.[28] An explosion drove an iron rod through his left cheek and out the top of his head, destroying the left frontal lobe of his brain. Amazingly, Gage survived, but his personality changed. Previously known as a "quiet and respectable" 25-year-old man before the accident, Gage became "gross, profane, coarse, and vulgar," after the accident—as if he had no inhibitions at all.[23] Gage's brain injury changed his personality and behavior in radical, undeniable ways.

The brain, whether at a conscious or unconscious level, powers our response to threats. As information enters the brain through our sensory systems, it analyzes stimuli to identify threats and the potential for danger. If something is determined to be a threat, neural and hormonal processes kick in and a freeze, fight, or flight response is signaled to our autonomic nervous system (ANS) which regulates internal organs, including our eyes, salivary glands, blood vessels, sweat glands, heart rate and breathing—basically all of our vital functions.[24] The autonomic nervous system—comprised of two subsystems, one of which is the sympathetic nervous system (SNS)—jump-starts our body in response to threats.[25] It increases our heart rate which in turn increases the outflow of blood to our muscles. Our pupils constrict so we can focus on a specific threat and our digestive system slows to avoid pulling blood away from major muscles that require blood in order to fight or take flight. When blood flows to our muscles we are ready to act in response to danger.

The supercharging effect of the sympathetic nervous system does not continue unabated. Once a threat has passed, the parasympathetic nervous system (PNS) takes over and returns the body to a natural relaxed position.[26] The PNS reduces our heart rate and blood flow to the muscles and lowers blood pressure to a sustainable level. Our pupils dilate to open our field of vision and our digestive tract draws blood back to major organs to resume normal functioning. When everything returns to normal, our brain renews the search for threats.

Cognition and Affect

Beyond physically readying the body to act in response to danger, the brain plays a critical role in supporting cognitive functions which anticipate and detect threats. Imagine that you are a tourist returning from a two-week river cruise in Europe. You have risen at 5:00 in the morning in Frankfurt, Germany, to catch a 9:00 am flight to Boston with an eight-hour layover in JFK. Arrival in Boston is scheduled for early evening and your final destination is Portland Maine—a two-hour drive from Logan Airport. When you arrive in Boston, you will have gone 21 hours without sleep and face the prospect of a two-hour drive in total darkness. You will also be driving in inclement weather—the Boston-area weather forecast calls for heavy rain and limited visibility. Driving at night in foul weather following a long day of travel evokes past memories of travel in bad weather with little sleep. An earlier driving experience was marred by episodes of hydroplaning, double vision and near accidents caused by misjudgment. As you think about the danger that could lie ahead, intuition tells you to get in front of the situation and remove yourself from the possibility of harm. Upon arriving in Boston, you will need to make a decision: risk the two-hour drive or make a hotel reservation and drive the next day when you are rested and weather conditions are better.

Cognition. Your focus on danger that could be encountered on the return trip from Europe illustrates the pivotal role the brain plays in enhancing cognitive functions such as memory, comprehension, thinking and learning, and decision-making.[27] Not only does it prepare your body for response to an immediate threat, it anticipates danger and initiates danger control— a cognition-driven process that induces motivation to avoid threat events through change in behavior. The brain powers cognition by processing and storing sensory information which can be recovered for later use.[28] Parts of the brain involved in cognition include the prefrontal cortex, frontal and parietal lobes, temporal lobes and the occipital lobe.[29] The prefrontal cortex executes cognitive functions including planning, assessment of the outcomes of actions and the aptness of behavior in different social contexts.[30] The frontal lobes deal with language comprehension and memory, and the parietal lobes process sensory information by converting and consolidating sensory input into memory that is stored in the brain.[31] The temporal lobes process auditory sensory information for speech recognition and the occipital lobe processes visual information.[32]

Affect. Affect and the brain are intrinsically linked. Feelings shape who we are and how we behave. The amygdala, in the limbic system of the forebrain just above the brainstem, is critical to processing our emotions, including feelings of anger, joy and fear.[33] Within the prefrontal cortex is the anterior cingulate cortex, which connects the limbic system (known for emotional processing) and the prefrontal cortex (known for cognitive processing).[34] More specifically, the anterior cingulate cortex (ACC) is connected to the amygdala which is central to processing emotions. The ACC is also connected to the hippocampal region, which plays an important role in learning and memory, and the orbitofrontal cortex, which sits just above the eye sockets in the front of the brain and is believed to play a role in the decision-making and reward system of the brain[35] (see Figure 4.1).

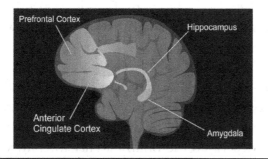

Figure 4.1   Brain Regions Involving Cognition and Affect

Cognition + Affect = Sensing

Cognition and affect comprise the *Sensing* dimension of the social dynamics model because they are neurobiologically connected. A simple example will illustrate their influence on behavior. Driving to an important meeting at work you have the misfortune of getting stuck behind a slow driver who would not let you pass. You arrive at the meeting 20 minutes late reeling with anger and ready to take on anyone who disagrees with you. The meeting is important and you know you should reel in your emotion, but you are unable to do so. Your behavior throughout the meeting is prickly, your interaction with colleagues is uncomfortable, and your ideas are not well received. Relationships have taken a hit all because something that happened earlier in the day put you in a foul mood.

Positive and negative emotions influence the way we interact with others, make sense of information and make decisions—basically, how our cognitive functions operate. Citing research by Garcia-Marques, Mackie and Claypool (2004), Stangor opined that "the influences of mood on our social cognition … extend to judgments about ideas, with positive mood linked to more positive appraisals than neutral mood."[36] Social science researchers Seth Duncan and Lisa Barrett argue that cognition and affect are so interconnected that there is no such thing as a "non-affective thought." Affect plays a role in perception and cognition, even when people cannot feel its influence.[37]

Social Neuroscience

The meeting example above illustrates how cognition and affect interact to influence behavior. The connection to behavior, however, is not direct. It is mediated by social forces primary among which are societal and group factors which shape behavior. The field of study focused on the relationship between social forces and biological systems is known as social neuroscience.[38]

Social Forces

Cognitive health—thinking, learning, remembering and interpreting is reinforced through participation in social networks. Our choices are made in the context of social forces and relationships. In *The Brain That Changes Itself* (2007), Doidge described the brain's ability to change itself in response to external stimuli and experience.[39] This is particularly true in totalitarian regimes which indoctrinate their citizens at a young age. Young brains are in a continuous state of development and therefore are more impression-able. Children in North Korea, for example, are placed in schools as young as two to four years of age, not just to learn numbers and academics but to assimilate into a "cult of adoration" for their leaders.[40] The outcome is deep changes in "perceptual emotional networks" throughout childhood that "do not merely lead to differences of opinion, but to plasticity-based anatomical differences which are difficult to bridge or overcome with ordinary per-suasion."[41] When the human mind is subject to forces of social control, the ability of individuals to think independently is reduced as well as their will-ingness to embrace new ideas and alter existing attitudes and beliefs.

Another example of the impact of social forces on cognition is the reduc-tion in cognitive capacity that occurred during the COVID-19 pandemic. In a study of 5000 volunteers from Spain, Italy and the United Kingdom—countries criticized for poor management of the pandemic—Bogliacino et al. determined that COVID lockdown and related restrictions on individual mobility affected cognitive functioning of many adults.[42] Results showed that those more vulnerable to the effects and consequences of lockdown experienced diminished cognitive capacity, made riskier decisions and suf-fered reduced civic-mindedness.[43] Decision-making abilities were impaired, and difficult choices were made without taking into account the social cost involved. Under the shock of the pandemic, people tended to want immedi-ate benefits and made on-the-spot decisions, some of them momentous.[44]

Group Dynamics

Group dynamics influence, and are influenced by, cognition and affect. Groups forge consistency in perception and behavior among members but also evoke a wide range of emotional reactions in their members. Research has shown that affect and emotional bonds fulfill key social functions in groups that maintain cohesion.[45] For instance, affect and emotion have been proposed to play a role in the allocation of roles and responsibilities among group members, the management of deviance and the coordination of col-lective efforts to attain shared goals. Research on group behavior has dem-onstrated that "emotional contagion"—the tendency to "catch" the emotions of others—via non-conscious processes and conscious, deliberate processes elicits a convergent emotional state facilitating bonding and coordinated action toward goals.[46]

Just as cognition and affect are influenced by group dynamics, these processes in turn shape group behavior. Field studies have shown that a positive affective tone within groups increases group harmony and coordination.[47] Expressions of anger on the part of group members can force deviant members into line as anger is interpreted as a signal of potential rejection by the group whereas expressions of happiness are interpreted as a sign of acceptance.[48] A similar effect has been observed in studies of leader emotional expressions on group performance.[49] Affect in the form of emotional signals from leaders has an influence on group dynamics. Expressions of anger on the part of a leader are interpreted by followers as an indication of dissatisfaction with performance whereas expressions of happiness are taken as an indication of acceptable performance.

Group Dynamics and Risk. Group dynamics play a powerful role in shaping perception and behavior in response to threats. Imagine you are part of a group of friends who have known each other for years, socialize together and share similar values and interests. Over the past several years, you have been following scientific reports and media accounts of climate change. You are keenly aware of aberrant weather cycles that have impacted different parts of the country—prolonged drought and non-stop rain in California, bomb cyclones in the Northeast, excessive snowfall in the Midwest, killer tornadoes in the Southeast and an Atlantic hurricane season that has gotten longer and more intense. Maine is your home state, and the Gulf of Maine is one of the fastest warming bodies of water on Earth. You can swim in the ocean in July—you don't have to wait until August. Winter temperatures are above freezing, nor'easters are getting more severe, and garden centers are stocking shrubs and plants native to Maryland and Virginia. You've seen enough—you are now a believer in climate change.

During a neighborhood gathering of friends, conversation shifts to climate change and whether it is real or part of a natural cycle. You voice an opinion—"given the mountain of scientific evidence, the sharp change in regional conditions and the rainfall and flooding in California—how can anyone deny the reality of climate change?" Hearing this, two of your friends react with shock and surprise. "Global warming is cyclical—everyone knows that." Others voice agreement and try to bring you into line with group opinion. You can't believe what you are hearing. Unquestionably climate change is real—just look at the evidence. Anxiety mounts as you experience the discomfort of rejection by friends. Will you stick to your guns and affirm your belief in climate change or waver and bend to group opinion?

Two processes are simultaneously at work: cognition and affect triggered by your brain and the influence of group dynamics on behavior. Contradictory information is being received by your brain and it needs to be reconciled. Which will prevail: *cognition* (thinking and knowing based on learning) or *affect* (feelings and emotion associated with group membership)?

Organizational and institutional Influence

One way of looking at organizations and institutions is that they are a common entity—cognitive systems occupied by people who gather and interact virtually or face-to-face with each another. As cognitive systems, what we know about institutions and organizations would not be complete without reference to neural substrates that underlie cognition. This has led to the integration of institutional behavior and neuroscience in a field of study known as *organizational neuroscience*—an important contributor to our understanding of the relationship between people and organizations because it incorporates a multilevel approach involving factors both internal and external to the individual.[50]

Neuroscientific methods and techniques have become increasingly important in the study of human behavior in organizations. In 2010, Beugre introduced the construct of neuro-organizational behavior, which he defined as the impact of the brain on behavior that occurs in organizations.[51] Lee and Chamberlain (2007) used the term organizational cognitive neuroscience to describe "processes within the brain that underlie or influence human decisions, behaviors, and interactions either within organizations or in response to organizational manifestations."[52] Neuro-organizational behavior includes three levels of analysis: neural, cognitive and behavioral.[53] The neural level focuses on identifying brain regions that are activated when organizational members display particular patterns of behavior. The cognitive level involves mental processes that rely on neural substrates such as memory and information processing—a linkage that helps us understand how organizational members acquire and organize information and make decisions. The behavioral level concerns observable actions displayed by organizational members.

Recent work in organizational neuroscience has bolstered our understanding of the importance of neuroscience for interpreting behavior in the context of organizations and institutions. A series of studies reported by Ward, Volk and Becker shed light on the neural basis of organizational dynamics[54]:

▪ Volk, Kohler and Pudelko (2014) demonstrated the utility of neuroscience in examining the effect of language-processing requirements in multinational corporations.[55] A model based on information about working memory and cognitive load was used to test the relationship between language, culture and cognition. Their work documented the utility of brain-level data in ascertaining why foreign language requirements can lead to lower performance and interpersonal issues among managers and workers.

■ Hannah et al. (2013) investigated leader self-complexity with the goal of improving our understanding of its effect on decision-making.[56] To measure self-complexity, they collected psychological data using a self-report survey and brain-level data using EEG to develop neural profiles of leader self-complexity. Their results showed that brain activity is related to important organizational outcomes such as adaptive decision-making.

■ In a series of four studies, Dietvorst et al. (2009) developed a scale to measure the relationship between salesperson theory-of-mind and performance.[57] Their goal was to understand the mechanisms that explain why some salespeople work smarter and perform better by correctly reading the mindsets of customers. They found that sales performance depends on what was happening inside salespeople's minds. Using neuroscience to interpret data, the researchers found that interpersonal-mentalizing skills—"mind reading" skills—of high-performing salespeople were consistently activated in the medial prefrontal cortex region of the mid-brain.

Neuroscience has a lot to say about the behavior of individuals and groups in organizations, including motivation and rewards, trust and cooperation, leadership and decision-making, and creativity and innovation. While neural activity alone does not provide a complete understanding of concepts like leadership and management, the neuro-organizational perspective is helpful in understanding behavior within organizations.

Mediating Forces

What is most interesting about the brain-behavior connection in response to danger is that not only is the brain wired to ensure our survival, it also has the potential to compound our exposure to risk. The panic reaction of the pilots on Air France 447 is a prime example of the brain-behavior connection and its effect on decision-making. It would be misleading, however, to attribute our response to danger principally to the brain. The brain-behavior connection is not direct. It is mediated by social dynamics which interact with cognition and affect to shape behavior:

■ *Social forces*—societally created patterns of behavior that influence how we think, act and relate to one another
■ *Group dynamics*—forces at play within groups that shape our attitudes, beliefs and behavior
■ *Organizational and institutional influence*—behavioral dynamics associated with organizational and institutional engagement that influence thought and behavior

These dynamics embody behavioral tendencies that shape our response to risk. Activism and polarization, for example, are contemporary forces in American society—one involving positive action toward social change and the other conflict as a result of division into groups holding different beliefs. Climate activists seek greater awareness of the effects of global warming by pushing change in support of climate goals. Naysayers circumvent the threat by quashing evidence of climate change. Both groups have the power to shape belief and behavior. The groups one belongs to—whether family, friends, work or social networks—have influence over thought and behavior. Opinions are formed and changed on the basis of group membership and norms. And then there are organizations and institutions. We work in them, acquire products and services from them and are subject to influence via information disseminated by them. They are an inexorable part of our lives. In tandem with social forces and group dynamics, they define who we are and how we think and act in response to risk.

Notes

1. Nunez, K. "Fight, Flight, Freeze: What This Response Means." *Healthline*. February 21, 2020.
2. Nunez, K. "Fight, Flight, Freeze: What This Response Means." *Healthline*. February 21, 2020.
3. Lanese, N. and Dutfield, S. "Fight or Flight: The Sympathetic Nervous System." *LiveScience*, February 9, 2022.
4. Wignall, A. "The Story of Air France Flight 447." *Aerotime Hub*, June 1, 2022.
5. Wignall, A. "The Story of Air France Flight 447." *Aerotime Hub*, June 1, 2022.
6. Wignall, A. "The Story of Air France Flight 447." *Aerotime Hub*, June 1, 2022.
7. Wignall, A. "The Story of Air France Flight 447." *Aerotime Hub*, June 1, 2022.

8. Wignall, A. "The Story of Air France Flight 447." *Aerotime Hub*, June 1, 2022.
9. Oliver, N., Calvard, T., and Potocnik, K. "The Tragic Crash of Flight AF447 Shows the Unlikely but Catastrophic Consequences of Automation." *Harvard Business Review*, September 15, 2017.
10. For more information, visit Brain Basics: Know Your Brain from the National Institutes of Health's National Institute of Neurological Disorders and Stroke website.
11. All Things Considered. "Why Climate Change Threats Don't Trigger an Immediate Response from Human Brains." *All Things Considered*, December 12, 2019.
12. IBIS World. *Security Alarm Services Industry in the US – Market Research*. IBIS World, January 29, 2022.
13. All Things Considered. "Why Climate Change Threats Don't Trigger an Immediate Response from Human Brains." *All Things Considered*, December 12, 2019.
14. Henig, R. "Experts Warned of a Pandemic Decades Ago. Why Weren't We Ready for This Virus?" *National Geographic*, April 8, 2020.
15. Frank, T. "FEMA Report Warned of Pandemic Vulnerability Months Before COVID-19." *Scientific American*, April 10, 2020.
16. Hampton, T. 2022, February 23. Pandemic Stress and the Brain. Referring to a study conducted by Ludovica Brusaferri et al. "The Pandemic Brain: Neuroinflammation in Non-infected Individuals During the COVID-19 Pandemic." *Brain, Behavior, and Immunity*, 102 (2022), pp. 89–97.
17. All Things Considered. "Why Climate Change Threats Don't Trigger an Immediate Response from Human Brains." *All Things Considered*, December 12, 2019.
18. Marshall, G. "Why Our Brains Are Wired to Ignore Climate Change and What to Do About It." *The Guardian*, September 23, 2014.
19. https://climatecommunication.yale.edu/visualizations-data/ycom-us/
20. https://www.indianaenvironmentalreporter.org/posts/the-psychology-of-climate-change-eminent-but-not-imminent.
21. Aron, A. and Fielding, K. The Climate Crisis: Interview with Social Psychologist Kelly Fielding." *Resilience.org*, July 14, 2021.
22. Questions and Answers in MRI. *The Discovery of NMR: Who Discovered NMR?* AD Elster, ELSTER LLC, Ballwin, Missouri, 2023.
23. Blue, C. "Predicting Behavior by Scanning the Brain: Does fMRI Really Resonate?" *Observer, Association for Psychological Science*, June 29, 2020.
24. National Institute of Health/ National Institute of Neurological Disorders and Stroke website. "Brain Basics: Know Your Brain."
25. Griffiths, B. "Understanding Your Sympathetic Nervous System's Fight or Flight Response." *Polar*, July 12, 2022.
26. Nall, R. "Your Parasympathetic Nervous System Explained." *Healthline*, April 23, 2020.
27. Tobin, J. "Cognitive Function of the Brain." *Brain Theory*, April 12. 2022.
28. Glees, P. *The Human Brain*. London: Cambridge University Press, 2005.

29. Roizman, T. "The Brain Functions Involved in Cognitive Functions." https://howtoadult.com/177861-the-brain-functions-involved-in-cognitive-functions.html.

30. Roizman, T. "The Brain Functions Involved in Cognitive Functions." https://howtoadult.com/177861-the-brain-functions-involved-in-cognitive-functions.html.

31. Roizman, T. "The Brain Functions Involved in Cognitive Functions." https://howtoadult.com/177861-the-brain-functions-involved-in-cognitive-functions.html.

32. Glees, P. *The Human Brain*. London: Cambridge University Press, 2005; Roizman, T. *The Brain Function Involved in Cognitive Functions*. London: Cambridge University Press, 2005

33. https://www.ncbi.nlm.nih.gov/pmc/articles/PMC8228195/pdf/biomolecules-11-00823.pdf

34. Stevens, F. L., Hurley, R. A., Taber, K. H., and Hayman, L. A. "Anterior Cingulate Cortex: Unique Role in Cognition and Emotion." *The Journal of Neuropsychiatry and Clinical Neurosciences*, 23(2) (2011), pp. 121–125.

35. Stevens, F. L., Hurley, R. A., Taber, K. H., and Hayman, L. A. "Anterior Cingulate Cortex: Unique Role in Cognition and Emotion." *The Journal of Neuropsychiatry and Clinical Neurosciences*, 23(2) (2011), pp. 121–125.

36. Principles of Social Psychology - 1st International Edition by Dr. Charles Stangor is licensed under a Creative Commons Attribution-NonCommercial-ShareAlike 4.0 International License, except where otherwise noted.

37. Duncan, S. and Barrett, L. "Affect Is a Form of Cognition: A Neurobiological Analysis." *Cognition and Emotion*, 21(6) (2007), pp. 1184–1211.

38. Cacioppo, J. "Social Neuroscience: Challenges and Opportunities in the Study of Complex Behavior." *Review*. National Library of Medicine/ PubMed.gov, April, 2011.

39. Doidge, N. *The Brain That Changes Itself*. London, UK: Penguin Books, 2008.

40. Norman Doidge as quoted by Kevin Weitz in https://library.psychology.edu/wp-files/uploads/2014/12/The_Neuroscience_of_Organizational_Culture_Ver3.pdf

41. Norman Doidge as quoted by Kevin Weitz in https://library.psychology.edu/wp-files/uploads/2014/12/The_Neuroscience_of_Organizational_Culture_Ver3.pdf.

42. Bogliacino, F. et al. "Negative Shocks Produce Change in Cognitive Function and Preferences: Assessing the Negative Affect and Stress Hypothesis." *Scientific Reports*, 2021. doi.org/10.1038/s41598-021-83089-0

43. Bogliacino, F. et al. "Negative Shocks Produce Change in Cognitive Function and Preferences: Assessing the Negative Affect and Stress Hypothesis." *Scientific Reports*, 2021. doi.org/10.1038/s41598-021-83089-0.

44. Bogliacino, F. et al. "Negative Shocks Produce Change in Cognitive Function and Preferences: Assessing the Negative Affect and Stress Hypothesis." *Scientific Reports*, 2021. doi.org/10.1038/s41598-021-83089-0.

45. van Kleef, G, Heerdink, M. and Homan, A. "Emotional Influence in Groups: The Dynamic Nexus of Affect, Cognition and Behavior." *National Library of Medicine/ PubMed.gov*, October 17, 2017.

46. van Kleef, G, Heerdink, M. and Homan, A. "Emotional Influence in Groups: The Dynamic Nexus of Affect, Cognition and Behavior." *National Library of Medicine/ PubMed.gov*, October 17, 2017.

47. Homan, A., van Kleef, G., and Sanchez-Burks. "Team Members' Emotional Displays as Indicators of Team Functioning." *National Library of Medicine/ PubMed.gov*, May 26, 2015.

48. van Kleef, G, Heerdink, M. and Homan, A. "Emotional Influence in Groups: The Dynamic Nexus of Affect, Cognition and Behavior." *National Library of Medicine/ PubMed.gov*, October 17, 2017.

49. van Kleef, G, Heerdink, M. and Homan, A. "Emotional Influence in Groups: The Dynamic Nexus of Affect, Cognition and Behavior." *National Library of Medicine/ PubMed.gov*, October 17, 2017.

50. Beugre, C. *The Neuroscience of Organizational Behavior.* Edward Elgar Publishing, Northampton, Mass., 2018.

51. Beugre, C. *The Neuroscience of Organizational Behavior.* Edward Elgar Publishing, 2018.

52. Lee, N. and Chamberlain, L. "Neuroimaging and Psychophysiological Measurement in Organizational Research." *Psychology, Biology Annals of the New York Academy of Sciences* (November 1, 2007).

53. Lee, N. and Chamberlain, L. "Neuroimaging and Psychophysiological Measurement in Organizational Research." *Psychology, Biology Annals of the New York Academy of Sciences* (November 1, 2007).

54. Ward, M., Volk, S., and Becker, W. *An Overview of Organizational Neuroscience. Organizational Neuroscience* (D. Waltman and P. Balthazard, eds.). Emerald Group Publishing, Somerville, Mass, 2015.

55. Volk, S., Kohler, T., and Pudelko, M. "Brain Drain: The Cognitive Neuroscience of Foreign Language Processing in Multinational Corporations." *Journal of International Business Studies*, 45 (2014), pp. 862–885.

56. Hannah, H., Balthazard, P., Waldman, D., Jennings, P., and Thatcher, R. "The Psychological and Neurological Bases of Leader Self-Complexity and Effects on Adaptive Decision-Making." *Applied Psychology*. National Center for Biotechnology Information. PubMed.gov. May 2013.

57. Dietvorst, R., Verbeke, W., Bagozzi, R., Yoon, C., Smits, M., and van der Lugt, A. "A Salesforce-Specific Theory of Mind Scale: Tests of Its Validity by Multitrait Multimethod Matrix, Confirmatory Factor Analysis, Structural Equation Models, and Functional Magnetic Resonance Imaging." *Semantic Scholar*, October 2009.

Chapter 5

Eclipse of Societal Guardrails

---

*In a liquid modern life there are no permanent bonds, and any that
we take up for a time must be tied loosely so that they can be untied
again, as quickly as possible, when circumstances change as they
surely will in our liquid modern society, over and over again.*

Zygmunt Bauman, Polish sociologist and philosopher, 2015

My workday in 1972 began with a cup of coffee, a quick check of headlines in the local newspaper and travel by car to a workplace detached from
home. As a senior administrator in a large college, I worked side-by-side with
administrators and support staff in a traditional hierarchy. My office routine
would begin with greeting colleagues and support staff in hallways and
offices, checking my schedule with a secretary, reviewing documents and
memos in the in-box on my desk and retrieving voice mail messages from my
desk phone. All communication was face-to-face, in writing and by phone.

I retired in 2012, but if I was working today everything would be different. The cup of coffee would be the same, but the newspaper would be
gone and communication would be digital—email, news and texts on my
cellphone; messages and images on Facebook, Twitter and Instagram; and
documents on my laptop. There would be more on my laptop than documents—information about sports teams I am following, tidbits of information
curated to attract my attention and ads featuring products and services that
could draw interest based on my online browsing history. Artificial intelligence would use algorithms constructed from my demographics, socioeconomics and life style to organize and deliver information matching my
needs, interests and preferences.

DOI: 10.4324/9781003335658-7

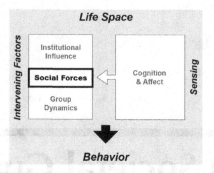

Social Forces and Risk Behavior

For boomers like me, communication has moved at a pace never before imagined and with greater urgency. I resisted the early wave of change brought on by social media. It was a clear departure from how I did things and it made me uneasy. Email was impersonal and technologically challenging. Writing articles and books using Microsoft Word was uncomfortable for one accustomed to thinking and writing long-hand. Online purchase of products and services was out of the question—buying something that could not be seen, touched or acquired through person-to-person contact was unthinkable. Eventually, however, I came to appreciate the advantages of the Internet and social media. Although the personal nature and reliability of communication had been lost in the avalanche of information delivered through media platforms, there was much to like about the speed and convenience of instantaneous communication. Faced with a choice of embracing or being bypassed by change, there really was no choice: embrace it—*but that is not everyone's choice*. Change is unstoppable in our fast-paced world. Some move with it because the risk of standing still is greater than that of moving in a new direction. Others stand still or push the pause button because it is an unwelcome departure from tradition.

Chapter Organization

One of three factors mediating cognition and behavior in response to risk, social forces are complex and have many moving parts. A brief description of chapter organization will help the reader understand these parts and their contribution to behavior.

- The chapter begins with a description of *cohesion and social change* as a framework for understanding the relationship between social forces and behavior. Cohesion is a state of common purpose uniting people in society. Working against it are change forces which break down norms and result in a state of disorder known as *anomie*.
- Forces contributing to anomie are described in terms of their impact on relationships and behavior. Two forms of relationship are presented: those based on community and altruism (*social capital*) and those predicated on self-interest and reciprocity (*social exchange*).
- In uncertain times, relationships shift from capital to exchange and the basis of interpersonal trust changes. Altruism gives way to self-interest and *cost* and *rewards* drive behavior.
- The chapter closes with an illustration of the impact of social forces on behavior in a risk circumstance. Relationships between people and institutions are put to the test when a choice must be made between altruism and self-interest in response to a crisis.

Social Cohesion and Change

Social cohesion is the "glue" that enables society to function with beliefs and values that enable people to trust one other.[1] It provides a sense of belonging and attachment to community while contributing in important ways to individual well-being. Despite its importance, however, a growing body of evidence suggests that cohesion has given way to collapsing levels of trust.[2] Norms lose their ability to guide the everyday behavior of people in periods of rapid social change. Connectedness gives way to transience and trust in the unknown becomes a precondition for safety.[3]

When boarding a commercial aircraft, your choice is either not to fly or to place your life in the hands of unknown people—the company that built the aircraft, the pilots at the controls of the aircraft, the mechanics who maintain the aircraft and air traffic controllers guiding the aircraft.

When buying produce at a grocery store, trust is placed in unknown growers and food handlers to deliver produce that is unspoiled and free of harmful bacteria. When ordering a meal at a busy restaurant, trust is placed in unknown personnel who prepare and handle food. When admitted to a hospital emergency room following an accident, trust is placed in the skill and training of unknown medical staff. Our safety is routinely placed in the hands of people we do not know. This is part of living with fast change and depersonalization in modern society. Trust in the unknown is a primary basis of cohesion in today's world.

Forces Precipitating Change

How could it be that we would consume a meal prepared by someone we do not know, travel on an aircraft with an unknown pilot at the controls or consent to a medical procedure under anesthesia rendered by someone we have just met? When one thinks about the extent of trust we place in unknown others, it can only be because that is what we have always known. We have grown up in a world of change in social institutions, in technology, in environment and in demographic makeup. More importantly, we have grown up in a world in which people and groups struggle for power and agency.[4] These forces contribute in important ways to our quality of life while simultaneously holding the potential for disruption. It is their potential for disruption that makes them important in the world of risk.

Technology

Advances in technology have impacted all aspects of our lives from the way we treat illness, to the way we grow food, and the way we educate children. The virtues of technology are obvious—improvement of just about everything from efficiency to quality of life to communication. Its drawbacks are just as obvious—job insecurity, misinformation and fake news and vulnerability created by technological dependence.[5] Consider the technology involved in keeping nuclear power plants running safely and securely. What happens if human error or faulty technology cause a power plant to malfunction, faulty systems cause a jet to crash, or a cyber-attack takes out critical infrastructure? What happens when millions of workers are displaced by automation and advanced technology? What happens when it becomes harder to determine what is true and what's not because of the spread of misinformation?

Population Growth and Composition

Declining numbers and changing composition of the U.S. population over the past two decades have altered economic growth and created enormous impact on social institutions.[6] Rapidly growing numbers of seniors are changing the way our social institutions are organized. Labor shortages coming out of the pandemic have put companies large and small out of business and resulted in wage and price inflation which has pushed families to the brink of financial collapse. Retiring boomers and skilled workers have created a knowledge gap that has strained the capacity of organizations and put the financial stability of the nation in peril as a result of lost tax revenue.[7] Automation and artificial intelligence have displaced millions of workers from jobs and had a profound effect on income inequality, not to mention mental health.[8] Colleges and universities are fighting for survival in an age of sharp decline in the number of high school graduates, rising tuition costs and questions about the value of higher education. Population dynamics have made the United States a nation of too few births, too many deaths and not enough skilled workers and migrants to grow the economy.

Social Institutions

Social institutions are undergoing dramatic change. Gallup Analytics have revealed diminishing confidence in organized religion, public schools, the news media, the Supreme Court, Congress and the presidency.[9] Americans continue to identify declining confidence in government as among the most important problems facing the nation.[10] The classic view of the American family as a support system of two married adults providing care and stability for their biological offspring has been altered by changing norms. Americans are increasingly likely to view previously stigmatized behavior as morally acceptable including having a baby outside of marriage, gay and lesbian relations, and sexual relations outside of marriage and divorce.[11] Yet in 2022, the Supreme Court reversed the constitutional right of women for access to abortion—a decision that altered the national understanding of freedom of choice in direct contradiction to opinion research regarding sexual behavior. The disjuncture between public opinion and judicial action is emblematic of the changing state of social institutions in America. Institutions that were once interdependent have become mutually exclusive—a circumstance that has contributed to declining confidence in institutions and a growing state of normlessness.

Environment

Extreme temperatures, rising sea levels, more frequent and intense weather events, flooding, prolonged drought, and food and water shortages—climate is now changing faster than at any point in recorded human history. Numerous studies conducted by researchers around the world have documented changes in atmospheric, ocean and surface temperatures; increasingly rapid glacial melting; rising sea levels and acidification which have affected marine life and coastal communities; and extreme weather which has destroyed communities and created climate refugees.[12] The impacts of changing climate on different sectors of society are interrelated. Drought has altered food production. Flooding has increased the spread of disease and damaged ecosystems and infrastructure. Rising temperatures have increased mortality and impacted food availability. Long-standing socioeconomic inequities have made underserved groups especially vulnerable to the effects of climate change.

Movements like 350.com have quantified the impact of climate change on vulnerable populations and ecosystems throughout the world. To preserve a livable planet, we must reduce the amount of CO_2 in the atmosphere from its current level of 400 parts per million(ppm) to below 350 ppm.[13] A report issued in 2023 by the University of Oxford's Smith School of Enterprise and the Environment found that on its current trajectory, the world will fall short of this target.[14] The frequency of deadly heat waves will triple by 2100, sea level will rise by 60 centimeters impacting 630 million people worldwide, and 90 percent of the world's population will live in nations with falling food production.[15]

Social Conflict

The struggle for power in the pursuit of self-interest is as old as society itself. When individuals and groups challenge boundaries, they bring about change in social policies and structures.[16] Consider, for example, the impact of the Me Too, Black Lives Matter, Pro Choice and Fridays for Future movements:

- *Me Too* initially appeared in 2006 and became a hashtag in 2017 as a way to call attention to the scope and magnitude of sexual abuse of women.[17] The hashtag has trended in 85 countries and made Me Too a worldwide movement.
- *Black Lives Matter*, a movement founded in 2013 to fight racism and anti-Black violence, especially in the form of police brutality, is international in scope.[18] Its name signals condemnation of the unjust killing of Black people and the imperative for society to value the lives and humanity of Black people as much as it values the lives and humanity of White people.
- *Pro Choice* supports the legal right to an elective abortion, meaning the right to terminate a pregnancy.[19] Emerging in 2022 in response to the restriction and criminalization of abortion in many states, the movement is comprised of a variety of organizations throughout the nation.
- *Fridays for Future* came into being in 2018 as a result of the efforts of one girl holding a protest sign outside of Sweden's parliament every Friday imploring politicians to act with immediacy on the climate

crisis.[20] In the short space of a year, the movement went worldwide and dominated headlines in 2019 when six million people attended climate protests.

Social movements are grassroots in origin and initiated by individuals and groups lacking conventional access to channels of social change. Influence is generated by peaceful means and subversive tactics to challenge authority and broadcast grievances from the margin of society. Protests, marches and boycotts are used to gain attention and to offset structural disadvantages. The Million-Man March in 1995, for instance, brought hundreds of thousands of demonstrators to Washington D.C. to promote unity and political participation among Black men.[21] Thousands of workers went on strike in 2021 to call attention to hardships of the pandemic and the sacrifices of workers in manual jobs deemed essential.[22] Workers at Frito-Lay, Nabisco, Kellogg's, John Deere, Volvo, Frontier Communications, New York University, Columbia University, Harvard, hospitals and airports walked away from their jobs in protest.[23] Workers at fast-food and retail chains including McDonalds, Walmart, Wendy's, Burger King, Bojangles, Jack-in-the-Box and Family Dollar held walkouts or short-term strikes to push labor law reforms in support of workers' rights.[24]

Constructive movements are emancipatory—they seek to pressure authorities into reducing systemic inequality, extending rights to previously excluded groups and alleviating material, social and political injustice.[25] Harmful movements tend to be reactionary and push polarizing aims and agendas. Constructive or harmful, a common goal of social movements is to disrupt and create disorder for the audience they are targeting. As movements grow in force and visibility, they challenge bonds that hold social structures together, leading to normative change and cultural shift.

Anomie

When societies undergo swift change, it can disrupt standing norms and values, leading to a loss of trust in institutions and a sense of normlessness among individuals—a condition of *anomie*. In American Requiem (2023), historians tendered an elegy of what America used to be and what it is becoming[26]:

> *Chris Rufo, Manhattan Institute Senior Fellow:* "With skyrocketing inflation, political division, social unrest, and a relentless effort

to wipe away the fundamental principles of the nation, America's future has come into question. The America of the 1980's has pretty much vanished."

Heather MacDonald, Manhattan Institute Senior Fellow: "We're now entering a period of unprecedented economic, social and cultural change. We are turning on our own legacy and declaring it evil, oppressive, and without any redeeming characteristics."

Steven Hayward, Resident Scholar at the University of California Berkeley: "There are some days I wake up and read the news and look around me and I don't recognize this country anymore."

Anomie in Theory

In *Suicide* (1897), French sociologist Emile Durkheim portrayed society as a combination of institutions functioning together to ensure stability and integration.[27] Norms, beliefs and values exert a powerful influence on thought and behavior. Working against norms, however, is progress. Rapid change weakens ties among people and withers away the collective consciousness of community. Forces of industrialization, urbanization and population growth fuel an inevitable progression toward modernity.[28] As population grows, interactions multiply and society becomes more complex. More and more people engage in economic activity and traditional bonds of family, religion and moral solidarity loosen ultimately leading to the disintegration of society.

In periods of rapid change, norms do not have the same regulating power as in periods of stability. People are left to their own devices regarding what to believe and value. This is known as *anomie*—a breakdown and blurring of norms that guide and regulate behavior.[29] Durkheim believed that all societies pass through three forms of anomie as they develop:[30]

■ *Mechanical Anomie*—a state of normlessness that occurs when rules and regulations that previously guided behavior fall by the wayside. New rules invariably replace traditions and norms established by long-held beliefs. When people resist change that is part of new rules, *social control* is weakened.
■ *Organic Anomie*—a breakdown in norms prohibiting aberrant behavior with little or no punishment. Organic solidarity holds people together and makes individuals feel attached to society. When people break free

of norms and established social patterns without sanction, the result is *social disorganization.*

■ *Cultural Anomie*—a condition that occurs when social goals, such as equal opportunity, are not achieved. When people follow institutionalized means for achieving social goals but are assigned marginal status, the result is *social disorder.* Feelings of meaninglessness and diss atis fac tion prevail, and acts against society become more common.

Anomie in Modernity

Partisan antipathy, disorder and incivility, and other forms of social disorder are manifestations of anomie in modern society. When standing norms give way to new ways of thinking and acting, people struggle to find footing with new norms. COVID-19 is a good example of the effect of changing norms on behavior. The virus changed nearly all forms of interaction. Little was known about how long it would last and social distancing, masking and quarantining dramatically altered connectivity with others. Connectivity is norm affirming. In the absence of affirmation, impulses become stronger and behavior more difficult to self-regulate. In a COVID-induced state of change, personal issues surfaced that had been repressed in better times. For some, relationships took a pathological turn—instead of stability there were problems with mental health, alcoholism, loneliness and isolation.

COVID-19 introduced behavioral changes that challenged people to adapt to a new normal.[31] In the transition to remote work, relationships between workers and employers became less interconnected and more siloed. In pre-pandemic society, employer-employee relationships were direct with a clear connection between workers and managers. Workers were removed from family for a significant portion of the day—a circumstance which fostered connectivity among employees. Enter the pandemic and workers were saddled with an overnight transition to remote work—a transition accomplished without time to balance conflicting interests of old and new ways of working. Social bonds frayed as workers were left adrift in the world of remote work—an anomic state that continues to evolve today.

COVID-19 is episodic—its contribution to anomie has a beginning and an end. Social inequality in American society and its contribution to anomie is perpetual—it is without end. In modernity we have been socialized to gauge success in terms of wealth and prosperity—the American dream. For those who buy into the dream but fail to achieve success, the outcome can be traumatic—financial loss, poverty, physical and mental illness, and worse. The disjuncture between goals and achievement can be resolved by a variety of means including invention, adaptation and marginalization.[32] Adapters align ends and means by accepting their position in life; inventors by pursuing alternatives in keeping with personal beliefs and values; and marginalists by rejecting socially approved goals and the means for achieving them. For inventors and marginalists, the experience of anomie can lead to a sense of disconnection from a community whose rules they can no longer respect. Connectedness is no longer to society as a whole but to others similar in outlook and interests.

Marginalization is pervasive in American society. Consider, for example, the mindset and behavior of people who engage in theft because they do not have legitimate means of accumulating wealth, people in cities feeling isolated due to a lack of connection to community, people from disadvantaged backgrounds losing hope because they are obstructed from achieving social goals, and extremists feeling ignored or neglected by government. The breakdown of social bonds between individual and community is a powerful force in thought and behavior. In extreme circumstances, it can render people incapable of navigating normative social situations such as forging a relationship or holding a job.[33]

Social Capital

In *Bowling Alone: America's Declining Social Capital* (1995) Robert Putnam profiled a decline of social capital in the United States over the course of the 20th century.[34] Using national data archives and state-level measures, Putnam examined seven dimensions of social capital: political participation, civic engagement, religious participation, workplace networks, informal networks, mutual trust and altruism.[35] He concluded that America had experienced a decline in the effective functioning of social groups and institutions manifested in waning civic and political participation, loss of membership in social organizations and estrangement from family and workplace networks.[36] Bowling was used to illustrate the decline. Although the number of people engaged in bowling increased during the 20th century, the number of people bowling in leagues decreased. People bowling alone do not participate in social interaction that would be part of bowling in leagues.

What is Social Capital?

In Putnam's view, social capital is the glue that holds American society together. It is best understood as "social networks and the norms of reciprocity associated with them." Networks involve a shared sense of identity, trust and reciprocity embedded in relationships among individuals in a group.[37] On a personal level, they create a sense of belonging and being connected to others. On a societal level, they establish norms for behavior that sustain strong social institutions and create ties that can be relied on in times of crisis. People come together in crisis, but only if strong institutions and relationships—*societal guardrails*—are in place.

Bonding and Bridging Capital. Social capital has different meanings depending on how it is applied. Capital is *bonding* when it describes ties among people of similar nature and interests and *bridging* when describing ties among people who are unlike one another in an important way.[38] The distinction between these forms of capital can most readily be understood in a comparative framework as illustrated in Table 5.1.

Bonding capital describes relationships among people who know each other, interact frequently and share similar characteristics and interests. The relationship among members is exclusive, inward-looking and promoting of homogeneity.[39] Examples include family members and neighbors, close friends, club members and employees who share a common outlook on life and work. Bonding capital fulfills a useful social function by providing emotional support to members and norms that facilitate trust and collective action. Among its negative effects is bias created by exclusivity which can foster ingroup-outgroup conflict.

Bridging capital can best be understood as the exchange that takes place between people with shared interests or goals but contrasting social identity.[40] Connections develop among people that "bridge" communities, groups and organizations normally divided in society. For example, lunch-and-learn

Table 5.1 Bonding and Bridging Social Capital

Bonding Capital		Bridging Capital
* Within	*Relationships*	* Between
* Exclusive	*Membership*	* Inclusive
* Closed	*Interaction*	* Open
* Inward-looking	*Mindset*	* Outward-looking
* Strong ties	*Association*	* Loose ties
* Like people	*Uniformity*	* Different people
* Unconditional	*Trust*	* Conditional

sessions where individuals from different interest groups learn from each other or workshops where employees from different organizations share best practices. Bridging capital traverses social boundaries by building consensus among groups representing diverse interests.[41] It is inclusive and transactional in nature. Its upside is the social function it fulfills by increasing tolerance and acceptance of different people, values and beliefs through contact with diverse others. It has few, if any, negative effects.

An understanding of social capital—what it is and how it works—is of obvious importance in societies besieged by forces which divide. At its most basic level, social capital conveys the importance of networks and relationships among people that enable institutions to function effectively through shared values, reciprocity and social support. With high social capital and strong networks, societies thrive. Without them, they falter—an argument central to Putnam's thesis that changing norms and behavior in America from 1950 on were eroding social bonds, damaging civic engagement and diminishing the power of institutions.

Trends in Social Capital

More than two decades have passed since Putnam's pioneering work sparked a vigorous debate about America's civic condition. Two decades into the new millennium, America finds itself in a period of transition. According to Isabel Sawhill, Senior Fellow of the Brookings Institution, current measures of social capital reveal a disturbing trend in the civic condition of the nation:[42]

- Data from the General Social Survey (National Opinion Research Council) indicate that trust has declined markedly since the early 1970s. In 1974, almost half of several thousand responding Americans indicated they could trust others. In 2020, the figure was less than a third.[43]
- Declining trust in others is paralleled by a trend of declining confidence in representative democracy.[44] In 1974, only 15 percent of General Social Survey respondents indicated a lack of confidence in fellow Americans "to make judgments under our democratic system about the issues facing our country." In 2020, four in ten had lost confidence in the ability of fellow Americans to make sound choices.
- Americans interact less with their neighbors and communities.[45] In 2008, seven in ten reported talking with neighbors a few times a month or more. The number had declined to half by 2017.

- Religious attendance declined from a level of 60 percent reporting service attendance at least once a month in 1972 to 40 percent in 2020.[46] The share of the public that never attended religious services increased from 10 percent in 1972 to 30 percent in 2018.
- Between 1974 and 2004, membership and participation in fraternal organizations decreased by 52 percent, in veterans' organizations by 42 percent, in labor unions by 41 percent, in school service organizations by 18 percent and in political organizations by 10 percent.[47]

A similar pattern of declining participation in institutions is evidenced in surveys conducted by Gilad Edelman, the Gallup Organization and the Pew Research Center. According to a 2019 survey conducted by Edelman, 49 percent of U.S. citizens distrust non-governmental organizations, businesses, government and media.[48] Gallup measures of "average confidence ratings for American social institutions" between 1993 and 2022 declined from a level of 38 percent of Americans expressing "a great deal" or "quite a lot" of confidence in 14 institutions in 1993 to 27 percent in 2022.[49] This was a historical low when compared to pre-2006 averages which consistently measured 40 percent. Americans' average confidence in major social institutions has steadily declined since Gallup started tracking 14 core institutions in 1993.[50] Of particular significance was the finding that a growing majority of Americans (five out of six) expressed lack of confidence in leaders of government and business.[51]

Respondents Indicating "A Great Deal" or "Quite a Lot" of Confidence

Congress	Business	Organized Religion	Police	Public Schools
2021 (12%)	2021 (18%)	2021 (37%)	2021 (51%)	2021 (32%)
2022 (7%)	2022 (14%)	2022 (31%)	2022 (45%)	2022 (28%)

Source: Gallup Poll of Americans' Confidence in Major U.S. Institutions/July 5, 2022

A 2021 survey of 1,015 American adults by the Advanced Studies in Culture Foundation (ASCF) and public opinion consultancy Heart+Mind Strategies found Americans' faith in themselves growing while their faith in institutions declined.[52] Although "rugged individualism" has been a trait historically ascribed to Americans, negative implications of this mindset have been held in check by social institutions. ASCF data reveal a trend away from reliance on social institutions toward self-reliance.[53] When asked to describe themselves, most ASCF survey respondents (58 percent) mentioned personal attributes of being "caring," "friendly" or "hardworking." Few mentioned group attributes like race (3 percent), gender (11 percent), age (12 percent) or sexual orientation. The focus on personal identity extended to where respondents placed their moral compass. Seven in ten said personal ethics and morals "came from within, not from something outside of or larger than themselves." Concurrent with the shift toward individualism was a concern voiced by some that "American society was decaying in a welter of self-interest."[54]

Declining confidence in social institutions and the pursuit of individual self-interest are classic symptoms of anomie. Decades earlier, the Great Recession, rising economic inequality and public- and private-sector corruption undercut confidence in institutions. More recently, Congressional gridlock and partisan politics, the pandemic, displacement of workers by automation and the transition to remote work have contributed to diminishing confidence in institutions. There is a growing sentiment that Americans on the whole have become more selfish, greedy and dishonest.[55] Some have gone as far as to make a connection between entitlement and declining effectiveness of social institutions.

Why Social Capital Matters

Social capital is central to strong institutions as evidenced in research linking social capital to higher levels of economic productivity, educational performance, personal happiness and the quality of democracy.[56] Without norms regulating appropriate and inappropriate behavior, without strong institutions that uphold unifying values and without a basis of trust, it is more difficult for people to come together to resolve problems. Decades of research have documented the relationship between declining social capital and alienation which can lead to dysfunctional behavior.[57] Social capital has been demonstrated to be an important contributor to the effective functioning of modern economies and a stable democracy,[58] as a basis for cooperation across sector and power gradients in society[59] and as a critical factor in community development.[60] Optimism, satisfaction with life, perception of government and political involvement—all have been shown to have a basis in strong measures of social capital.[61]

Social capital is associated with a wide range of beneficial economic effects including facilitation of growth in gross domestic product and more efficient functioning of labor markets (Aldridge et al., 2002; Halpern, 2004; Kawachi et al., 1997; Putnam et al., 1994).[62, 63, 64, 65] It is an important contributor to educational attainment,[66] public health[67, 68] and community governance.[69] Using Facebook proprietary data on 72.2 million young American adults and 21 billion friendships they had formed, Chetty et al. (2022) found that social capital in the form of cross-class connections at the community level elevated social mobility more than anything else including family structure and educational outcomes.[70]

Social capital is a double-edged sword, however, with an upside and a downside. It is an important contributor to societal well-being. Its binding nature, however, comes with a cost that may not be beneficial to community. Highly inclusive networks limit the freedom of individuals by channeling thought and behavior into patterns consistent with group norms.[71] They become a corridor of exclusion when outsiders perceived as representing different views and interests are marginalized, denied access to resources and excluded from full participation in social, economic and political life.[72]

Social Exchange

Dwindling social capital and the declining power of institutions are the most telling features of anomie in modern society. When institutions and norms lose their regulating power, altruism gives way to self-interest and relationships shift from collectivism to individualism. Individuals motivated by self-interest employ economic principles to calculate the value of relationships.[73] Relationships prosper when rewards are greater than costs and falter when costs exceed rewards. In periods of anomie, relationships forged on the basis of social capital give way to relationships in which the psychological, social and economic aspects of interaction are consciously or unconsciously weighed to determine rewards and costs.

Consider the following:

■ *In relationships*: We intuitively weigh the costs and benefits of friendship. We may value the caring attitude of a friend even if he/she belongs to a different social group or overlook aggressive behavior if a friend belongs to an esteemed group. In longitudinal research on college students, Rusbult (1983) found that in the early stages of a relationship, individuals tend to ignore the principle of exchange.[74] As the relationship progresses, satisfaction and cost come into the equation. Friends who felt that they were not benefitting from a relationship were more likely to terminate the relationship compared to friends who shared equal proportions of cost and benefit.[75]

■ *In the workplace*: Studies have shown that morale suffers when employees receive the same benefits irrespective of productivity and performance. Organizations use the principle of exchange to boost employee morale. Tags like "employee of the month," "best employee" and prizes are used to balance the relationship between rewards and costs. Employees leave jobs when costs exceed rewards for jobs where rewards and costs are equitable.

■ *In groups*: Emotional investment in group membership encourages individuals to think and act in ways they believe group members want them to act. For instance, if an individual is part of a close-knit group of friends, he/she will express opinions and beliefs consistent with group members even if, on occasion, group beliefs diverge from personal beliefs. The reward is good standing in the group; the cost is sublimation of personal belief to group belief.

In exchange, something of value (reward) is obtained in exchange for forfeiting something of value (cost). Relationships depend on the extent to which parity is achieved in the exchange. Six principles are integral to exchange:[76]

■ Economics is an important part of decision-making.
■ People are motivated by self-interest with maximum rewards and minimal costs sought in pursuit of the greatest profit.
■ Reward is a function of the amount of benefit received; it can be abstract or concrete, immediate or cumulative.
■ Cost is the value of what must be given up to receive a reward.
■ Cost subverts relationships when it rises to a level in excess of reward.
■ Exchange influences how people view social phenomena and engage with groups and organizations.

Recent findings from the Max Planck Institute for Human Development and the University of Konstanz suggest that perception of risk may be shaped and amplified in social exchange.[77] In our information-driven society, information about risk spreads rapidly. Dissemination occurs through multiple channels, but exchanges are often emotional—they carry subjective interpretations of risk. When risk information flows through exchange networks, it undergoes transformation and selective emphasis. This impacts how it is perceived with the result that risk behavior can take many forms.

Risk Behavior as Exchange

Risk behavior can be understood as the way in which we conduct ourselves in response to danger. It involves an intuitive process of exchange in which the costs and benefits of engagement determine how one responds to risk. When the "cost" of engagement (change in behavior to reduce exposure to risk) is perceived to be greater than the "reward" (avoidance of risk), one may forego engagement.

A climate change example will make the point. Imagine for a moment that you are a homeowner whose growing concern about climate change has reached a point where personal action is warranted. You have figured out what it will take to reduce your carbon footprint—get rid of your gas-powered car, use public transportation, install solar panels on the roof of your home, change to a plant-based diet and conserve electricity. The cost is clear: these actions will require behavioral change on your part and they will disrupt your life routine. The reward is less certain: you are only one person doing your part to address climate change and you wonder just how much impact your efforts will have. If you are one of many, your effort may be worthwhile. If you are going it alone, your effort may be fruitless. Considering the unknowns, you decide that the cost of your effort will exceed the reward. You defer action until you have more information and a better sense of return on investment.

Past experience and expectations play an important role in risk behavior. In the process of making a decision on climate change action, past experience weighed heavily on the homeowner. Favorable experience with a climate change advocacy group several years earlier elevated her expectation for success. Her next foray into climate activism, however, met with a different result. Neighbors and friends questioned her judgment and urged her to think twice before moving forward with the changes under consideration. In the interest of maintaining positive relationships, she scaled back her plans and put action on hold.

Risk behavior unfolds with growing awareness of the potential for harm. Attention initially focused on reward—minimizing exposure and avoiding the harmful effects of risk—morphs into consideration of cost. In the foregoing example, the homeowner initially focused on reduction of her carbon footprint (reward) in contrast to change in behavior to reduce carbon emissions (cost). As more was learned about the life style changes that would be necessary to achieve reward and negative reaction surfaced from neighbors and friends, attention turned to cost. When cost appeared to exceed reward, a tipping point was reached and a decision was made to defer action.

Paradise Lost

Following Robert Putnam's line of reasoning in *Bowling Alone,* one would think that social capital would be essential for building solidarity and trust in a risk environment. Quite to the contrary, a growing body of research has found lower levels of trust in societies functioning with high social capital.[78] Facing risk, people are more likely to establish trust through exchange with others. The reason is simple: the balance between rewards and costs in social exchange negates problems of inconsistency, impulsivity and unpredictability that are part of beneficent relationships in societies with high social capital. Think about it: Would you continue to lend money to a friend in the absence of reciprocity or payback of some sort? Would the relationship continue in its original form? If your answer to either question is "no," the relationship could be on unstable ground and its basis for continuation could shift to exchange.

In an environment of risk, exchange enhances one's ability to procure the resources necessary to reduce exposure to threats. Consider the circumstance of sea level rise on the Outer Banks of North Carolina and the crisis facing homeowners in the coastal community of Rodanthe:[79]

The Washington Post/March 13, 2023

Early in 2022, a house crumbled into the ocean in the small Outer Banks community of Rodanthe; home to some of the most rapid rates of erosion and sea level rise on the East Coast. Not long after, another house fell. And then another. Wave after wave, the ocean had clawed away at the beach until the stilted homes finally gave way. The collapses spread debris, and anxiety, for more than a dozen miles along the Cape Hatteras National Seashore....At least a dozen more houses in Rodanthe remain in serious danger of falling into the ocean. Faced with shrinking options, numerous homeowners are scrambling to move their homes—at a cost of hundreds of thousands of dollars—further from the tides that seem to creep ever closer. They have filed permits, lined up contractors, and teamed up with neighbors, all in a bid to buy more time from the encroaching sea.

In Rodanthe, there are ongoing tensions over what worsening erosion will mean for property values, tourism, and quality of life—and disagreement over exactly what should be done and who bears responsibility. Many homeowners argue the government should be doing more to help combat erosion, and that potential buyers should have more information about the growing risks. For their part, many government officials have expressed sympathy for homeowners, but they also say there is little they can do in the short term to help. No significant infusion of state or federal money seems likely in the short term.

Parties to Risk

Among the players involved in the effort to combat beach erosion at Rodanthe are homeowners, county executive officers, university professors with expertise in environmental planning, the Cape Hatteras National Seashore Association, the Division of Coastal Management in the North Carolina Department of Environmental Quality, the National Oceanic and Atmospheric Association (NOAA) and FEMA. Almost universally, homeowner requests for help have met with a blanket response: resources are not available to save homes and combat beach erosion. Dredging is estimated at a cost of $30 million and must be repeated every five years to be effective.[80] The tax base provided by Rodanthe homeowners, even if substantially increased, would be insufficient to offset the cost of dredging. Everything adds up to a negative bottom line: beach erosion will continue at a rate of 10–15 feet per year; abatement efforts are cost prohibitive; resources will not be forthcoming in the short-term to combat erosion; and long-term solutions are limited because sea level rise is projected to continue unabated to the close of the century.[81]

Social Exchange at Work

Homeowners and authorities have few options when it comes to beach erosion. Homeowners need help and they need it quickly. Authorities need committed resources and policy and processes that facilitate timely action. Standing in the way of a solution are obstacles that slow response and exacerbate risk:

- limited government resources
- gaps in federal and state laws and policies
- a lack of government plans and funding options to combat beach erosion
- delays and inaction caused by government bureaucracy
- public insensitivity and divisions among homeowners

Exchange by Default. Social capital is in short supply in Rodanthe. Bureaucracy and austere resources have made exchange the basis of strategy to combat beach erosion. For exchange to work:

Homeowners will *need to ask and answer important questions:* Will all homeowners participate in an organized effort to combat beach erosion? Will they come to consensus on a plan and contribute equally to its implementation? Will homeowners who moved homes inland at personal cost participate in the plan? Will homeowners unable to contribute full resources face repercussions of any kind?

Government agencies will need to remove bureaucratic obstacles that stand in the way of action. Efforts to combat the harmful effects of erosion have been repeatedly offset by federal policy, septic rules and private-versus-public property rights that limit options to address erosion. Flood insurance policies administered by FEMA, for example, force homeowners to wait until a house collapses into the ocean before paying out instead of buying and disposing of property ahead of disaster.[82]

Homeowners and government agencies will need to work together to identify and study innovative programs elsewhere to buy time or forge a solution to beach erosion.

Exchange, Risk and Paradox

Relationships among homeowners built on social exchange can be likened to a paradox involving simultaneously contradictory elements which shape behavior in response to risk. On the one hand, trust is more likely to develop among homeowners based on a balance between costs and rewards with all homeowners contributing equally to the resolution of beach erosion. Through exchange, problems of inconsistency and unpredictability that accompany altruism can be avoided and the door opened to collective action in response to risk. On the other hand, exchange can exacerbate social inequality when reciprocity cannot be negotiated among homeowners because some cannot contribute as much as others. Inequity among home-owners in exchange can lead to acrimony—a feeling of injustice in the exchange which could derail collective action in response to risk.

Given ongoing risk posed by beach erosion and people and organization issues standing in the way of resolution, can a path to resolution be forged through exchange? The answer is both "yes" and "no." For "*yes*," consider the example of a political initiative in California involving a novel approach to beach properties threatened by rising seas. California Senate Bill 83 would create a revolving fund for buying vulnerable homes.[83] Low-interest loans would be provided to beach cities which would then buy vulnerable homes from interested homeowners. Local governments would rent out the homes for enough money to partially or fully repay loans.

Tension among coastal homeowners in Honolulu, Hawaii, provides a good example of "*no*." For decades, coastal homeowners have used loop-holes to circumvent state laws prohibiting seawall construction.[84] Some have acquired permission from the state to build new seawalls or keep exist-ing walls through easements by leasing the public land under their homes. Others have acquired state approval to use sandbags and heavy tarps which create hazardous conditions during storms when the ocean is not able to naturally glide along the beach. Hostility resulting from a loophole in state laws regulating seawall construction and homeowner efforts to circumvent state laws has pitted residents against one another and effectively put a solu-tion out of reach.

Summing Up

Beach erosion in Rodanthe is manufactured risk caused by humanly induced climate change. It is exacerbated by social forces that contribute to instabil-ity. When bonds between individuals and community break down, social capital diminishes and exchange becomes the basis of relationships. Risk behavior assumes the form of an exchange process in which individuals weigh the benefits and costs of engagement. When costs outweigh rewards, engagement may diminish and individuals may forego response to risk.

Beyond social forces and their impact on behavior are group dynam-ics which predispose people to specific patterns of behavior in response to risk. In the context of groups, perception hinges, in large part, on subjective interpretations of risk by group members and compliance with group norms. If consensus emerges that a risk is significant or negligible, individuals are likely to adopt that view. In the next chapter, the focus shifts from social forces to group dynamics and their impact on individual behavior in response to risk.

Notes

1. Larsen, C. "Social Cohesion: Definition, Measurement and Developments." *United Nations.* https://www.un.org/esa/socdev/egms/docs/2014/LarsenDevelopmentinsocialcohesion.pdf
2. Brooks, D. "America is Having a Moral Convulsion." *The Atlantic*, October 5, 2020. Institute on Governance Canada. *Rebuilding Cohesion and Trust: Why Government Needs Civil Society.* Ottawa, Ontario: Canada, February 12, 2023.
3. Botsman, R. "We've Stopped Trusting Institutions and Started Trusting Strangers." *TED Talk*, November 7, 2016.
4. Schaeffer, K. "U.S. Has Changed in Key Ways in the Past Decade, from Tech Use to Demographics." *Pew Research Center*, December 20, 2019.
5. Andrea, H. "24 Pros and Cons of Technology in the 21st Century—What Are the Benefits and Drawbacks?" *Tech 21 Century*, February 21, 2023.
6. Frey, W. "What the 2020 Census Will Reveal About America: Stagnating Growth, an Aging Population, and Youthful Diversity." *Brookings*, January 11, 2021.
7. Gurchiek, K. "Employers Face Hiring Challenge as Baby Boomers Retire in Record Numbers." *Society for Human Resource Management*, June 28, 2021.
8. Holzer, H. "Understanding the Impact of Automation on Workers, Jobs and Wages." *Brookings*, January 19, 2022.
9. Brenan, M. "Americans' Confidence in major Social Institutions Drops." *Gallup News*, July 14, 2021.
10. Brenan, M. "Americans' Confidence in major Social Institutions Drops." *Gallup News*, July 14, 2021.
11. Newport, F. "Continuing Change in U.S. Views on Sex and Marriage." *Gallup News*, June 18, 2021.
12. Alfred, R. *CATASTROPHIC RISK: Business Strategy for Managing Turbulence in a World at Risk.* Oxfordshire, England, 2021.
13. Gooding-Call, A. "Inside 350.org and Why They Rise for Climate." *Resilience*, January 11, 2019.
14. Nakagawa, M. and Smith, B. "On the Road to 2030: Our 2022 Environmental Sustainability Report." *Smith School of Enterprise and the Environment*, University of Oxford, England, May 10, 2023.
15. Nakagawa, M. and Smith, B. "On the Road to 2030: Our 2022 Environmental Sustainability Report." *Smith School of Enterprise and the Environment*, University of Oxford, England, May 10, 2023.

16. Turner, R., Smelser, N., and Killian, L. "Social Movement." *Encyclopedia Britannica,* April 25, 2023. https://www.britannica.com/topic/social-movement. Retrieved: May 2, 2023.

17. Brittain, A. "Me Too Movement." *Encyclopedia Britannica*, May 15, 2023. https://www.britannica.com/topic/Me-Too-movement. Retrieved: May 26, 2023.

18. Brittanica, The Editors of Encyclopedia. "Black Lives Matter." May 19, 2023, https://www.britannica.com/ topic/Black-Lives-Matter. Retrieved: May 26, 2023.

19. Schultz, J. and Van Assendelft, L. "The American Political landscape." In *Encyclopedia of Women in American Politics* (1st ed.). Boston, MA: Greenwood Publishing Group, 1999.

20. Britannica, The Editors of Encyclopedia. "Greta Thuneberg." February 27, 2023. https://www.britannica.com/biography/Greta-Thuneberg. Retrieved: May 26, 2023.

21. King, B. "The Tactical Disruptiveness of Social Movements." *Social Problems*, 58(4) (2011).

22. Sainato, M. "They Are Fed Up: U.S. Labor on the March in 2021 After Years of Decline." *The Guardian*, December 21, 2021.

23. Sainato, M. "They Are Fed Up: U.S. Labor on the March in 2021 After Years of Decline." *The Guardian*, December 21, 2021.

24. Sainato, M. "They Are Fed Up: U.S. Labor on the March in 2021 After Years of Decline." *The Guardian*, December 21, 2021.

25. Turner, R., Smelser, N. and Killian, L. "Social Movement." *Encyclopedia Britannica,* April 25, 2023. https://www.britannica.com/topic/social-movement. Retrieved: May 2, 2023

26. Penley, T. "America 'Unrecognizable' and on the Brink of Collapse, Experts Warn: 'Turning on Our Own Legacy'." *Fox Nation Opinion*, February 7, 2023.

27. Durkheim, E. *Suicide*. London, England: Routledge & Kegan Paul, 1952.

28. Durkheim, E. *Suicide*. London, England: Routledge & Kegan Paul, 1952.

29. Durkheim, E. *Suicide*. London, England: Routledge & Kegan Paul, 1952.

30. Durkheim, E. *Suicide*. London, England: Routledge & Kegan Paul, 1952.

31. Yellowlees, P. "A Lot Has Changed During the Pandemic. How to Navigate Our New Normal." *UCDavis Health*, May 12, 2022.

32. Merton, R. (1938). "Social Structure and Anomie." *American Sociological Review*, 3(5). doi: 10.2307/2084686 JSTOR.

33. Merton, R. (1938). "Social Structure and Anomie." *American Sociological Review*, 3(5). doi: 10.2307/2084686 JSTOR.

34. Putnam, R. *Bowling Alone: America's Declining Social Capital*. New York: Simon & Schuster, 1995.

35. Putnam, R. *Bowling Alone: America's Declining Social Capital*. New York: Simon & Schuster, 1995.

36. Putnam, R. *Bowling Alone: America's Declining Social Capital*. New York: Simon & Schuster, 1995.

37. Putnam, R. *Bowling Alone: America's Declining Social Capital*. New York: Simon & Schuster, 1995.

38. Claridge, T. "Functions of Social Capital—Bonding, Bridging, Linking." *Social Capital Research*, January 20, 2018.
39. Claridge, T. "Functions of Social Capital—Bonding, Bridging, Linking." *Social Capital Research*, January 20, 2018.
40. Claridge, T. "Functions of Social Capital—Bonding, Bridging, Linking." *Social Capital Research*, January 20, 2018.
41. Claridge, T. "Functions of Social Capital—Bonding, Bridging, Linking." *Social Capital Research*, January 20, 2018.
42. Sawhill, I. "Social Capital: Why We Need It and How We Can Create More of It." *Brookings*, July 2020.
43. Ortiz-Ospina, E. and Roser, M. "Trust." *OurWorldinData.org.* https://ourworldindata.org/trust.
44. Newport, F. "Americans' Trust in Themselves." *Gallup News*, October 8, 2021.
45. Sawhill, I. "Social Capital: Why We Need It and How We Can Create More of It." *Brookings*, July 2020
46. Joint Economic Committee. "The Space Between: Renewing the American Tradition of Civil Society." *Social Capital Project* Report No. 8–19, 2019. Retrieved: March 11, 2023.
47. Joint Economic Committee. "The Space Between: Renewing the American Tradition of Civil Society." *Social Capital Project* Report No. 8–19, 2019. Retrieved: March 11, 2023.
48. Edelman. "2019 Edelman Trust Barometer." January 20, 2019.
49. Brenan, M. "Americans' Confidence in Major U.S. Institutions Dips." *Gallup News*, July 14, 2021
50. Jones, J. "Confidence in U.S. Institutions Down; Average New Low." *Gallup*, July 5, 2022.
51. Jones, J. "Confidence in U.S. Institutions Down; Average New Low." *Gallup*, July 5, 2022.
52. Advanced Studies in Culture Foundation. "Race, Ethics, and Culture: New National Survey of U.S. Adults." *HeartMind Strategies*, January 19, 2021.
53. Robinson, G. and Giles, M. "America Divided: Why It's Dangerous That Public Distrust in Civic Institutions Is Growing." *USA Today*, March 15, 2021.
54. Robinson, G. and Giles, M. "America Divided: Why It's Dangerous That Public Distrust in Civic Institutions Is Growing." *USA Today*, March 15, 2021.
55. Rainie, L., Keeter, S., and Perrin, A. "Trust and Distrust in America." *Pew Research Center*, July 22, 2019.
56. Duran, L. "Erosion of Social Capita, a Major Problem, Say Experts." *Politics*, May 17, 2017, Retrieved: March 17, 2023.
57. Sawhill, I. "Social Capital: Why We Need It and How We Can Create More of It." *Brookings*, July 2020.
58. Fukuyama, F. "Social Capital and Civil Society." *International Monetary Fund*, October 1, 1999.
59. Claridge, T. "Social Capital and Natural Resource Management: An Important Role for Social Capital." Unpublished Thesis, University of Queensland, Brisbane, Australia, 2004.

60. Claridge, T. "Social Capital and Natural Resource Management: An Important Role for Social Capital." Unpublished Thesis, University of Queensland, Brisbane, Australia, 2004.
61. Narayan, D. and Cassidy, M. "A Dimensional Approach to Measuring Social Capital: Development and Validation of a Social Capital Inventory." *Sage Journals*, 49(2) (March 2001).
62. Aldridge, S. and Halpern, D. "Social Capital: A Discussion Paper." *SCRIBD*, 2002.
63. Halpern, D. *Social Capital*. Hoboken, NJ: Wiley Publishing, 2004.
64. Kawachi, I., Kennedy, B., Lochner, K., and Prothrow-Stith, D. "Social Capital, Income Inequality, and Mortality." *American Journal of Public Health*, 87(9) (1997).
65. Putnam, R. et al. *Making Democracy Work: Civic Traditions in Modern Italy*. Princeton, NJ: Princeton University Press, 1994.
66. Israel, G. et. al. "The Influence of Family and Community Social Capital on Educational Achievement." *Rural Sociology*, 66(1) (2001), pp. 43–68.
67. Coulthard et. al. in Claridge, T. *Benefits and Importance of Social Capital*. Institute for Social Capital, University of Queensland, Australia, 2004.
68. Subramanian, S. et al. (eds.). "Social Capital and Health." *American Journal of Epidemiology*, 168(11) (December 2008), pp. 1340–1342.
69. Bowles, S. and Gintis, H. "Social Capital and Community Governance." *The Economic Journal*, 112(483) (November 2002), pp. F419–F436.
70. Chetty, R. et al. "Social Capital I: Measurement and Associations with Economic Mobility." *Nature*, August 1, 2022.
71. Wall, E. et al. "Getting the Goods on Social Capital." *Rural Sociology*, 63(2) (June 1998), pp. 1549–1831.
72. Westlund, H. and Frane, A. "Social Capital and Economic Performance: A Meta Analysis of 65 Studies." *European Planning Studies*, 18(6) (May 13, 2010), pp. 893–919.
73. Roeckelein, J. *Elsevier's Dictionary of Psychological Theories. Credo Reference*. Amsterdam: Elsevier, B.V., 2006. Retrieved March 2, 2023.
74. Rusbult, C. et al. "The Investment Model of Commitment Processes." *Purdue e-Pubs* (2011), 33p.
75. Clark, R. and Hatfield, E. "Gender Differences in Receptivity to Sexual Offers." *Journal of Psychology and Human Sexuality*, 2 (1989). Retrieved: March 15, 2023.
76. Redmond, M. "Social Exchange Theory." *English Technical Reports and White Papers*, 5 (2015). http://lib.dr.iastate.edu/engl_reports/5.
77. Moussaid, M. and Gaissmaier, W. "The Amplification of Risk in Experimental Diffusion Chains." *Max Planck Institute for Human Development*, 112 (April 21, 2015), pp. 5631–5636.
78. Yamagishi, T. et al. "Uncertainty, Trust and Commitment Formation in the United States and Japan." *American Journal of Sociology*, 104(1), (July 1998), pp. 165–194.

79. Dennis, B. "Another House Collapses into the Sea as This NC Town Erodes." *The Washington Post*, March 13, 2023.
80. Dennis, B. "Another House Collapses into the Sea as This NC Town Erodes." *The Washington Post*, March 13, 2023.
81. Dennis, B. "Another House Collapses into the Sea as This NC Town Erodes." *The Washington Post*, March 13, 2023.
82. Vargas, A. "Cleanup to Begin After Two Outer Banks Homes Collapse into the Ocean." *ABC News*, May 11, 2022.
83. Openstates. "SB 83 Sea Level Rise Revolving Loan Program." *Plural*, September 2, 2021.
84. Cocke, S. Hawaii Homeowners Face Stiff Fines for Illegal Seawalls." *Honolulu Star-Advertiser*, January 22, 2021.

Chapter 6

Group Dynamics and Risk Behavior

We are social creatures and it is the real or imagined pressure of others, when we act differently than if we were alone, that keeps things running smoothly.

Anonymous

I live in a coastal community in southeastern Maine with majestic trees and an abundance of flowering shrubs. Homeowners are drawn to this community because of its union of trees, shrubs and lawns which give it an aesthetic quite unlike that of other communities. Trees are the centerpiece. HOA approval is required to remove a tree, and removal is a rare occurrence.

Several years ago, a new group of homeowners moved into the community and rattled our collective sense around tree conservation. Oak trees drop an abundance of acorns in the Fall, and shade created by them suppresses lawn growth. After a year of coping with acorn litter and patchy lawns, a small group of new homeowners challenged HOA policy on tree removal. Their appeal was denied, but persistence paid off and eventually the HOA board of directors gave in and approved the removal of 12 trees. The sight of 100-ft. heirloom oaks stacked on the street created a furor in the community. Policy and aesthetics had been violated and a long-standing norm of conservation had been broken. Homeowners who removed trees were shunned and subjected to derisive comments. The Board was criticized for its failure to uphold policy, and a petition was circulated among

DOI: 10.4324/9781003335658-8

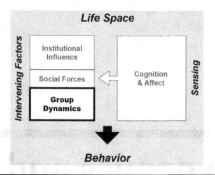

Group Dynamics and Risk Behavior

homeowners requesting a moratorium on tree removal. Group dynamics were at work. Homeowners on both sides of the issue engaged in behavior collectively that they would not have engaged in individually.

The Power of Groups

The seeds of group behavior are sown early in life. Group affiliation begins at an early age through family and socialization experience with friends. As we move from adolescence to adulthood, affiliation broadens to include groups of all kinds—classmates, sports teams, clubs, work groups, political parties, community service groups, neighborhood friends and more. Groups influence much of what we do, even in the most fleeting of circumstances. Social science experiments have shown that individuals randomly brought together can be made to perceive a stationary object as moving under group influence.[1] Decades of research have shown that psychological pressure in a group situation can prompt individuals to move their perception and judgments in the direction of group consensus. And recent research has shown that brain activity changes when people are in the presence of others.[2] Standing out inappropriately in a social situation is an experience to be avoided. It can cause stress and, in extreme circumstances, affect emotional and physical health.

Group Dynamics

Many, if not most, of the activities we engage in are performed within the context of a group. Whether it is part of a team at work, participating in a social club or political organization, or volunteering for a service project, groups are a fundamental part of our social experience. They touch everything we do, particularly the way in which we interact with others. Research has shown that *group dynamics*—the behavioral and psychological processes that occur in a group—shape behavior by rewarding adherence to group norms.[3] Norms remove the doubt and stress that come from uncertainty and help individuals feel socially connected and in tune with their environment. As groups become more cohesive, a shared identity emerges leading to trust and rising levels of member satisfaction. With group membership comes a sense of belonging and identity that makes people feel good about themselves.

Group dynamics contribute in important ways to our understanding of behavior but defy easy understanding because of attributes that complicate analysis. On the one hand, group dynamics help us understand how people interact in groups, how interaction influences behavior and how behavior is managed and channeled toward socially desirable goals.[4] On the other hand, group dynamics are complicated by patterns of human interaction which can be simple or complex depending on the situation and people involved. Some aspects are simple, such as how we communicate with one another and how we make decisions. Other aspects are complex, such as how relationships form within a group and how group norms influence behavior. The sheer number and layers of relationships among people in a group make it hard to separate the individual from the group and determine the cause of behavior.[5]

Perspectives from Theory

How important are group dynamics in understanding behavior in social situations? Consider the extent to which you would be influenced by group sentiment in the following example:

> *Put yourself in a social situation—say a happy hour with colleagues after work at a local restaurant. After a couple of drinks, conversation turns to climate change and whether it is natural or humanly created. Group consensus seems to be that it is natural and cyclical—not something to worry about. You strongly disagree with this opinion. What would you do:*

> ■ *voice your objection*
> ■ *say nothing, keep your opinion to yourself*
> ■ *verbally agree with group opinion*

Many would choose a path of diplomacy and refrain from saying anything. We value harmony and want to remain on good terms with a group so we remain silent but hold fast to our opinion—a course of action known as "optimal distinctiveness."[6]

Here is what theory and research have to say about group dynamics:

- *Conditioning*. Early in life we learn to associate positive outcomes with group membership. Through repeated interaction with family and friends, we develop attitudes toward others which become a basis for behavior throughout life. We learn that compromise, for example, is more likely to lead to a positive outcome with others than intransigence.
- *Social Exchange*. We are motivated by self-interest in interactions with others. Group membership is a means to gain resources that might otherwise be unavailable—a process of negotiated exchange between parties based on an expectation of mutually beneficial rewards.[7] Joining a professional organization, for example, could provide one with access to job opportunities, networking events and other resources that could advance a career. Joining a group with similar interests—a group with a specific medical condition, for instance—could provide emotional support and practical advice that could help one weather health challenges.
- *Social Cohesion*. We are drawn to groups on the basis of shared values and a sense of belonging. A psychological bond develops when we believe we are working with others toward a common goal. "Liking" is an important factor in cohesion with solidarity rising or falling on the strength of reciprocal positive attitudes among group members. For example, emergency responders, firefighters and successful sports teams are known to have high levels of cohesion which are important to their success.
- *Social Identity*. Social groups contribute to identity through processes of categorization and comparison with individuals defined by the group to which they belong.[8] Groups are differentiated through a process of comparison resulting in favorable feelings toward the group to which one belongs and less than favorable feelings toward other groups. Classic rivalries such as Michigan versus Ohio State in football and Duke versus North Carolina in basketball confer strong identification to individuals based on group membership.
- *Social Comparison*. Our drive to be part of a group stems, in part, from a need to enhance self-esteem by comparing ourselves to others.[9] We interpret information gained through comparison to see ourselves more positively because holding a favorable opinion of oneself is gratifying.

Further, we make upward or downward comparisons to others depending on which strategy will enhance self-esteem. When we identify with an upward target—say to someone who has achieved a goal we aspire to—self-image is enhanced evoking feelings of motivation and inspiration. Conversely, identifying with a downward target can have the opposite effect. It may decrease self-image and motivate one to change the cognitive representation of the target.[10] An example of upward comparison would be a friend going on a diet and meeting her target weight: "If she can do it, so can I." Downward comparison would enhance self esteem through elevation of position in relationship to a comparison target. "At least I don't weigh as much as other people I know."

■ *Self-categorization.* Groups give us an idea of who we are, how we see the world, what we should believe and how we should behave. They affirm identity through a process of accentuation, where behavior and beliefs are grounded in the norms and values of a salient category.[11] If an individual's salient category is that of "physician," he/she will act in terms of the norms associated with "physician" (exercise careful control over emotions and adhere to medical protocol) and less so in the norms and values of other social categories.

■ *Optimal distinctiveness.* We have a desire to be similar but also to differentiate ourselves from others to balance needs for belonging and autonomy. Research has shown that individuals become uncomfortable and cognitively disadvantaged in situations in which they feel dissimilar from others, or too much like outsiders.[12] Excessive similarity, however, does not provide a basis for self-definition—a circumstance which could cause discomfort in social situations in which distinctiveness is valued. Social identity is aimed toward achieving a balance between inclusion and differentiation in social situations.[13] Optimal distinctiveness can readily be observed in the clothing choices and hairstyles of: teens—anxious to be as much like others of their age group as possible, while also seeking to differentiate themselves by calling attention to a look that sets them apart.

Social Conformity

Theories of group dynamics reduce to a common denominator: groups have a powerful influence on individual behavior in social situations. Behavior is driven in large part by pressure to conform to norms in social situations, and nowhere is the pressure to conform greater than in groups. The conforming power of groups is particularly evident in risk situations when uncertain conditions impel people to align their behavior with the behavior of others. Consider what research has disclosed about the mask-wearing behavior of Americans during COVID-19:[14]

> Over the course of the COVID-19 pandemic, health authorities strongly advocated the wearing of face masks as a crucial measure in combating the virus. The recommendation or legal requirement to wear a face mask, however, was no guarantee of adherence to the rules. For many, mask wearing came down to a personal decision based on observation of public behavior and a desire to protect oneself and others. It was also a function of group membership. People followed mask-wearing tendencies of the groups of which they were a part. Mask-wearers were more likely to be part of groups with a higher mask-wearing rate whereas non-maskers affiliated with groups with a lower mask-wearing rate.

These findings parallel those of early research on the causal influence of social norms on behavior. From classic to contemporary research on conformity, behavioral research has shown that individuals align their behavior with the observed behavior of people around them.[15] In risk situations, we mimic the behavior of others acting in a common way in response to threats. Standing alone is not an option as people behaving differently from us make us aware of being different. We conform because we want to remain on good standing in a group and because we believe that our potential for avoiding harm is greater with a group than going it alone.[16]

Dimensions of Conformity

Conformity is two-dimensional. On the one hand, it is *internal and individual* because of our need to internalize the values of a group and achieve a sense of belongingness. It is *external and collective* when social pressure induces us to "fit in" and look to groups for guidance in ambiguous situations. In "Facing Ambiguous Threats," Roberto, Bohmer and Edmondson (2006) described the influence of conformity on group dynamics following the Challenger space shuttle disaster:[17]

> *NASA's hurriedly assembled postlaunch Debris Assessment Team—*
> *the group responsible for evaluating the foam strike—was poorly*

structured and had limited data with which to work. Its members had no experience working together on critical, time-sensitive problems. The group lacked a well-defined charter, budget, reporting structure, and formal standing within NASA. It tried to operate with an awkward leadership structure which left some members wondering who was in charge.

A team's atmosphere is just as important as its design. Many groups lack a climate of psychological safety; thus, members do not feel comfortable raising tough questions, expressing dissenting views, or speaking candidly about ambiguous threats. Team members who call attention to such threats find themselves marginalized or ostracized, perhaps even derided as Chicken Littles. Group dynamics at NASA did not encourage a candid discussion of threats. Meeting transcripts revealed that managers did not actively seek dissenting views. Packed agendas inhibited thoughtful discussion of potential threats. Hierarchy and status differences made it difficult for lower-level engineers to express their concerns.

Group dynamics during the Challenger post-disaster analysis offer an excellent illustration of the influence of conformity on behavior in a crisis situation. Within NASA, a culture of closed communication existed which precluded free-flowing exchange of information between departments and people at different levels.[18] During post-disaster evaluation, NASA managers did not listen to engineers who had technical knowledge of the rocket booster. Much of the evidence pertaining to the disaster was dismissed and input was not sought from technical experts. Shut out of communication and devoid of evidence, engineers and technical staff deferred to pressure from managers for consensus. The outcome was an illusion of unanimity based on groupthink—a psychological phenomenon of self-deception and conformity to group belief that occurs when a group in pursuit of harmony reaches consensus without reasoning or evaluation.[19]

Groupthink

Groupthink was at the heart of the process that culminated in the *Challenger* space shuttle disaster. National, group and political pressure on NASA and Morton Thiokol to launch on schedule fueled events leading up to the disaster. NASA had averaged five missions a year after a projected space shuttle frequency of 50 flights a year.[20] Against the backdrop of a gap between expectancy and reality and a cut in its federal budget, NASA was working feverishly to maintain national interest in its shuttle program. *Challenger* had to fly and it had to launch on schedule.

The day before the launch, Thiokol engineers warned that the launch might be risky.[21] They worried about the below-freezing temperature forecast for the morning of the launch and its impact on the O-ring rocket booster seals—a critical component of the rocket motor that had never been tested below 53 degrees Fahrenheit.[22] When Thiokol engineers raised the safety issue in a teleconference, NASA personnel discounted their concerns and urged them to reconsider their recommendation. After an off-line caucus with company executives, Thiokol engineers reversed their "no-go" launch position and announced that their rocket boosters were ready for flight.[23] When NASA executives later certified that *Challenger* was flight ready, they never mentioned a concern about the O-rings. The rest was history: 73 seconds into flight, *Challenger* disintegrated in a fiery explosion killing all seven crew members.

Psychology of Groupthink

The *Challenger* disaster drew the attention of Yale social psychologist Irving Janis who was fascinated with the question of how an acknowledged group of experts could make a terrible decision. He was convinced that their error wasn't an isolated instance limited to NASA decision-making, corporate boardrooms or matters of a technical nature. The same dynamics were believed to be at work in other tragic decisions: Roosevelt's complacency before Pearl Harbor, Truman's invasion of North Korea, Kennedy's Bay of Pigs fiasco, Johnson's escalation of the Vietnam War, Nixon's Watergate break-in and Reagan's Iran-Contra scandal coverup.

Janis used the Bay of Pigs disaster in 1961, the Japanese attack on Pearl Harbor in 1941 and the 1986 *Challenger* space shuttle disaster as case studies to examine the effect of group dynamics on decision-making in social situations.[24] His research uncovered a tendency for individuals to avoid raising controversial issues or alternative solutions in social situations with a resulting loss of creativity and independent thinking. Group dynamics produced an "illusion of invulnerability"—a sense of certainty that the right decision had been made.[25] Groups overrated their own abilities in decision-making and underestimated those of other groups. Furthermore, they pressured members to "go along with the crowd" and act in ways that will be favorably perceived by the group. He labeled the phenomenon "groupthink" with ear-marks that include:[26]

Belief in the power of the group

- *Illusion of invulnerability.* A feeling of optimism or cognitive bias that makes group members feel safe and secure when they are in dangerous situations.
- *Belief in the inherent morality of the group.* A tendency among group members to overlook the consequences of what they decide. Whatever the group does, it will be all right because members know the difference between right and wrong.

Close mindedness

- *Collective rationalization.* A group tendency to obscure potential problems and opportunities through reinforcement of shared beliefs and exclusion of contrary evidence and viewpoints.
- *Out-group Bias.* The tendency to dislike or disavow members of groups who are different from an in-group. Negative feelings mark the interchange between in-group and out-group members even if nothing is known about individuals in the out-group.

Pressures toward uniformity

- *Self-censorship.* The act of censoring or classifying one's own discourse out of fear, or deference to, the preferences of others and without pressure from others.
- *Illusion of unanimity.* An unquestioned belief which leads group members to ignore possible moral problems and not consider the consequences of individual and group actions. In situations involving risk, group members find comfort in believing that everyone is in agreement and feels the same way—a feeling that makes it difficult to speak out when group members are on the same page.
- *Direct pressure to conform.* When no one speaks out or voices an alternative opinion, consensus prevails and group opinion holds sway. Members breaking from consensus are subjected to direct pressure to fall into line or face the prospect of being branded as disloyal.

■ *Self-appointed mindguards.* The tendency of group members to protect leaders from information that is problematic or contradictory to the
group's cohesiveness, beliefs and decisions. Mindguards filter information to control dissent and direct decision-making toward a specific,
limited range of possibilities. The techniques employed by mindguards
consciously or subconsciously include time pressure in regard to decision-making, bandwagon effect, information cascades and reframing
situations to increase pressure toward or away from a specific outcome.

Cohesiveness is a major contributor to groupthink, but it is not sufficient
in and of itself to produce unity of thought and action. The likelihood of
groupthink increases when there are structural faults within an organization
and a decision must be made during a period of high stress.[27] When a group
is confronted by a challenge, concurrence-seeking is a rapidly unfolding
process which can lead to an inferior solution. There are occasions in organizational life, however, when groupthink is helpful because it raises issues
that must be addressed for a successful resolution to occur. Groupthink
was clearly at work in the college strategic planning example presented in
Chapter 2.

Southeastern College

*The Context. In 1994, Southeastern College (SC) was in the enviable position
of serving a city undergoing dynamic growth. The city was among the fastest-
growing metropolitan areas in the country and was on the cusp of becoming
a regional center for business, finance and transportation. Antithetical to its
growth was Southeastern College—a single-campus institution located near
city center. Rich in tradition, SC was served by a veteran faculty committed to
in-person learning, student success and academic excellence. Faculty maintained a strong sense of purpose. Their collective mindset was clear: "We're
good—our reputation is earned and it speaks for itself."*

The Onset. SC's strategic planning process began in Fall 1994 under the
leadership of a new president and national recognition as one of the top
two-year colleges in the nation. College faculty enthusiastically bought into
the recognition—it was an affirmation of deeply held values and beliefs.
The new president did not buy into the acclaim. Systems and processes
were dated, faculty and staff were seen as living on past laurels, and their
focus was inside rather than outside on the external community. The president was working against the tide of belief, sentiment and three decades of

history. An unvarnished look was necessary—a process that could best be accomplished through external consultants brought in to assist the college in planning for the future. The table was set: the planning process launched in a college divided along lines of old versus new, outsiders versus insiders and inside-out versus outside-in thinking.

The Process. After months of meetings with a wide array of campus and community constituencies, a review of economic and demographic projections, and analysis of public policy and competitor behavior, rudiments of a draft strategic plan were unveiled. The plan called for transformation of SC from a single-campus institution into a multi-campus system serving a growing metropolitan region. It was met with skepticism by faculty leaders. The move would fracture the college. The central campus would be fragmented into satellite campuses, faculty and staff would be parceled out among the campuses, and a holistic culture would be broken into cultural enclaves with no center.

The draft plan split SC into two factions—the president and senior administrators in full support and faculty leaders opposed. Faculty leaders took every opportunity to vocalize their opposition to the plan. Indicative of their displeasure was an all-campus holiday luncheon which left the consulting team sitting alone at a table on the periphery of the room. The team had disrupted the culture. It was the "enemy," and anyone choosing to sit with the team would do so at their own risk. Groupthink was in full bloom. As the Christmas holiday approached, a move was underway to suspend work on the plan. The consultants met with the executive team to chart next steps. After much soul-searching, the president indicated that faculty sentiment could not be ignored. The college would put the planning process on hold until things settled down. His words disclosed the power of groupthink: "If they don't like you, you aren't going to get where you want to go." The consultants returned to homebase with an appreciation of groupthink and the reinforcing power of culture. In the words of Peter Drucker, "Culture eats strategy for breakfast." Even if your cause is moral and right, a cohesive group working in opposition will derail your cause.

The Outcome. After a two-month hiatus, the consultants returned to campus with a revised plan. Originally presented as a single document issuing thirty recommendations with supporting information, the plan ballooned into a two-volume report consisting of an executive summary and a lengthy companion document providing detailed data backing all recommendations. Upon receiving the revised plan, faculty leaders asked:

> *Why is it necessary to include so much information in a plan that has laid out a direction we cannot support?*

A good question. Groupthink was a large part of the answer.

Analysis. The faculty culture at SC was a prime example of a cohesive in-group with a clubby atmosphere. Many instructors had a long record of service and were deeply rooted in college history and tradition. Elite national organizations of which the college was a part had a cozy reinforcing feel. SC administrators and faculty leaders interacted with peers in these organizations and, in doing so, were, essentially talking to themselves. SC's culture was strong, it was continually reinforced, and it was compelling. It took outsiders—a newly appointed president and external consultants asking a lot of questions—to rain on the parade.

In the language of groupthink, years of working together had given the faculty a sense of connectivity that made them feel invulnerable. Their work was important, their cause was just, and their accomplishments were many. Ties among colleagues were such that they would overcome any threat—an illusion of inviolability. As the consulting team pushed deeper into the inner workings of the college, out-group bias surfaced in the form of vitriol directed toward the president and the consulting team. Faculty leaders were particularly troubled by findings pointing to a gap between community needs and college programs and services. Their inward focus had obscured awareness of community needs even in the face of compelling evidence. Objective characteristics of the situation (community needs for programs and services) were subordinated to subjective interpretation through groupthink driven by prevailing norms and values.

Figure 6.1 diagrams groupthink at SC in terms of Janis's theory. The boxes on the left present preconditions for groupthink and the boxes on the right the behavior and consequences of groupthink. Long-serving faculty at SC were the embodiment of a cohesive group with norms that insulated them from the external community and from being receptive to new information. The likelihood of groupthink increased because of structural faults in the college and decision-making pressure in a time of high stress. The hire of a new president and entry of a consulting team challenged long-standing values and beliefs and created a moral dilemma for faculty leaders: coming up with a rationale for rejecting the plan other than violation of group norms.

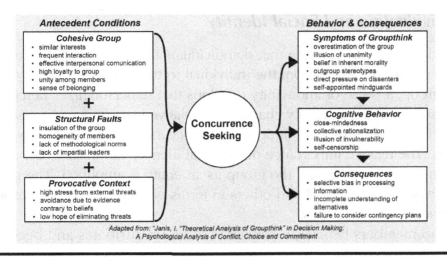

Figure 6.1 Attributes and Processes of Groupthink

Conclusion. On the surface, one would think that groupthink contributed to low probability of a successful planning outcome at Southeastern College. Exactly the opposite happened. Faculty criticism forced an intensive, multi-source approach to documentation of planning findings. Information supporting planning recommendations was double- and triple-checked to ensure accuracy. Recommendations formulated on the basis of contradictory evidence were eliminated as were recommendations that could not be verified through multiple-source data. The end product was a vastly improved plan that could stand the test of scrutiny from multiple audiences.

Deindividuation

Taken to the extreme, group dynamics can morph into deindividuation—a loss of one's sense of self occurring as a result of group immersion.[28] There are many theories of deindividuation beginning with the notion of crowd mentality advanced by French psychologist Gustave Le Bon in *The Crowd: A Study of the Popular Mind* (1895) and furthered by collective psychology theories promoted by Freud, McDougall, Blumer and Allport.[29] Festinger (1952) put Le Bon's theory of the crowd into scientific terms, describing deindividuation as a state of being wherein individuals put more emphasis on the group than on themselves.[30] Concerns individuals have for their own thoughts and feelings are marginalized through group involvement—a process leading to loss of internal standards and over-reliance on external cues.[31]

Deindividuation and Social Identity

Social identity theorists argue that deindividuation does not cause a loss of self but a shift in identity from the individual to the group. As identity shifts to the group, a sense of anonymity develops that depersonalizes perception of self and others. Anonymity changes the relative importance of personal vs. social identity. A process of detachment occurs that obscures individual features. The relative importance of personal identity diminishes, depersonalization is accentuated, and the group as an entity is amplified. The result is a tendency to perceive self and others in terms of group features in contrast to individual characteristics.

Group members behave in ways that fit group attributes and become interchangeable through stereotyping. For instance, if an individual defines herself as an environmentalist, she may conserve water, recycle whenever possible and march in rallies for climate change awareness. Members of sports teams who personally take the blame for a team loss, participants who remain with an unsuccessful group when they have the opportunity to leave, and activists who jeopardize their personal well-being for causes or principles that are unlikely to yield immediate personal benefit—all are examples of the impact of group identity on perception and behavior. People will go to great lengths to maintain group affiliation—to render "personal self" subservient to the "collective self"— as these examples suggest.

The ramp-up to launch of the *Challenger* space shuttle is a good example of the process by which individual identity is subordinated to group identity. The group identity for flight engineers was "aeronautical engineer" and Thiokol's engineers acted in accord with the norms of this profession in contrast to the norms of other groups (e.g., NASA administrators). In doing so, the engineers accentuated similarities among themselves and other members of the "aeronautical engineers" profession and distinguished themselves from NASA administrators and Thiokol managers working with a different set of norms. Facing pressure to launch from NASA administrators and Thiokol managers, Thiokol's engineers opposed the launch arguing that freezing overnight temperatures meant that the O-rings at the booster rocket joints could stiffen and fail to contain the explosive fuel burning inside the rocket booster. Allan McDonald, director of the booster rocket program at Thiokol, agreed with this assessment and refused to sign off on the launch.[32] Despite his refusal, his superiors at Thiokol ignored his warnings, overruled their engineers and proceeded with the launch.

Reflecting on contrasting group norms for engineers and administrators, one must ask whether Thiokol senior executives who approved the launch had a dual normative orientation—that of administrator and engineer. Did they experience a state of deindividuation in which an unstructured situation and sensory overload affected judgment? Did these factors combine to minimize self-evaluation and weaken controls based on group norms? Were thresholds for behavior lowered thereby silencing valuable input from engineers?

Depersonalization

Depersonalization is similar to but distinct from deindividuation in that it is an experience of detachment from oneself and others because of group immersion.[33] The self and others are seen in terms of group identity. In extreme circumstances, depersonalization can be a coping mechanism in response to stress—a mechanism unconsciously used to reduce the intensity of a disturbing event.[34] This was undoubtedly the experience of Thiokol engineers and NASA administrators during the *Challenger* space shuttle disaster. Executives in charge of Thiokol's engineering division had an engineering background sufficient to assign credence to safety warnings from engineers. They may have been caught between two value systems leading up to the disaster—one administrative and the other of the engineering profession.[35] Under pressure from NASA, administrative values prevailed and Thiokol executives approved the launch despite warnings from engineers. Interpreted in terms of the psychological phenomenon of depersonalization, Thiokol executives may have alleviated stress associated with dual identities by detaching themselves from the norms and experience of one identity (engineer) and adhering to norms of the other (administrator). Accompanying this action may have been emotional numbing, a loss of feeling and a lapse in emotional reactivity associated with group identity.

Executives in charge of Thiokol's engineering division undoubtedly had sufficient background in engineering to assign credence to safety warnings from their engineers. Under pressure from NASA to launch and caught between two value systems—one administrative and the other of the engineering profession—a choice had to be made. and administrative values prevailed. Executives may have alleviated stress associated with dual identities through depersonalization in which the values of one identity were surrendered to the other. Emotional numbing—a loss of feeling and lapse in emotional reactivity—eased the process by detaching executives from the value system of engineers and reinforcing the binding power of administrative norms.

Group Dynamics and Risk

Group immersion may increase the likelihood of flawed decision-making in relationship to risk by reducing mental acuity and moral acumen.[36] Group members may prioritize consensus over critical thinking and independent decision-making—an occurrence that can lead to faulty judgment as evidenced in the *Challenger* disaster. As a group, Thiokol executives refrained from voicing opinions contrary to those of NASA administrators when it became clear that NASA was not going to accept anything other than a "go" decision for launch.

The effect of group dynamics on risk behavior is manifested in research showing that:[37]

■ the risk behavior of individuals is shaped to a considerable extent by the behavior of others in the immediate social environment
■ group identity and immersion have a powerful impact on individual decision-making in situations involving risk
■ decision-making is more complex in risk situations when groups are involved--multiple influences at play within groups are exacerbated when the focus of group activity is uncertain and important
■ group dynamics amplify the power of the group in decision-making and decrease the randomness of member behavior in response to risk
■ groups are more susceptible to decision-making pitfalls when facing risk because of a need to balance the demands of time and urgency with group cohesion

Groupthink is at the heart of the relationship between group dynamics and risk. Flawed policy decisions such as the Bay of Pigs invasion and Enron corporate strategy disaster serve as prime examples of groupthink in high-risk situations. A consistent strand of behavior in risk situations is a tendency of individuals to value the group and being part of it more highly than anything else, causing them to buy into an illusion of unanimity. In the Bay of Pigs invasion, presidential advisors had good reason to think the mission would fail but never voiced their concerns out of fear of being labeled "soft" or "undaring" in the eyes of colleagues. The problem at Enron was one of a cohesive board of directors comprised of members sharing similar backgrounds and interests which made it difficult to challenge each other's ideas. Staying together as a group and loyalty to the company and its executives were priorities. Questioning corporate decisions was tantamount to an act of disloyalty.

Group Dynamics and Risk Behavior

Group dynamics have a significant impact on risk perception and behavior, but its impact is variable depending on group properties. Smaller groups composed of members with tightly held beliefs may filter input and narrow behavior in response to risk.[38] As groups become larger, interaction among members may diminish thereby enabling other factors to weigh more heavily in behavior. Among them are *individual* factors such as personal beliefs, values and needs and *contextual* factors such as the environment, social influences and type of risk. These factors, in combination with *group dynamics*, comprise a three spheres framework of risk behavior as illustrated in Figure 6.2).

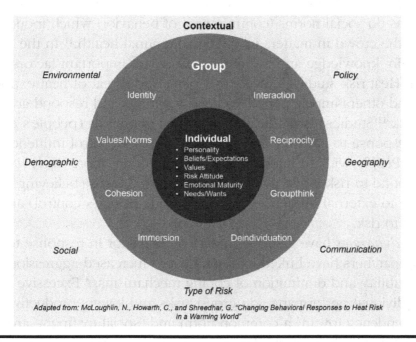

Adapted from: McLoughlin, N., Howarth, C., and Shreedhar, G. "Changing Behavioral Responses to Heat Risk in a Warming World"

Figure 6.2   Three Spheres Framework of Group Dynamics and Risk

Three Spheres Framework

Heat risk in a warming world provides a timely illustration of the effect of individual, group and contextual factors on risk behavior. In 2022, the Intergovernmental Panel on Climate Change (IPCC) warned that the percentage of the global population exposed to heat stress will increase from one in three today to three-quarters of the population by the end of the century.[39] Furthermore, much of the world's population lives in cities that amplify risk due to "heat island" effects that intensify air pollution and trap heat. Extreme heat events created by climate change have resulted in human mortality on every continent and led to thousands of deaths. The 2003 heatwave in Europe, for example, is estimated to have led to more than 70,000 deaths, and a 2019 University of Washington study examining death records in nine countries determined that at least 356,000 deaths were caused by extreme heat.[40] Consequences of heat exposure include heat stress, heat stroke, dehydration, accelerated morbidity from chronic illnesses, mental health disorders and increased risk of collective violence.

In the three spheres framework, individual, group and contextual factors combine to shape heat risk behavior. *Contextual* factors include demographics, social influences and characteristics of risk. Demographic characteristics (age, ethnicity, income and educational level) account for differences in behavior as do social norms (commonness of behavior) which induce people to follow the crowd in matters involving communal health.[41] In the *individual* domain, knowledge and awareness of risk are important factors in risk behavior. Heat risk studies indicate that perceived threat of heat exposure to oneself and others impels people to heed warnings and respond adaptively to heat risk.[42] Studies also indicate that coping appraisals (people's evaluations of response to hazards) and personal sense of control influence risk behavior. People with an internal locus of control are more likely to proactively respond to risk while those with an external locus (believing events occur due to external influences and are outside of one's control) are likely to give in to risk.

Group dynamics have a strong impact on behavior in response to heat stress. Researchers have linked extreme heat to increased aggression, lower cognitive ability and diminution of coping mechanisms.[43] Excessive heat affects individual performance on group tasks and lowers productivity as a result of tendency toward a common norm and "social loafing"—an inclination to put forth less effort when part of a group.[44] When group dynamics take hold in risk situations, three things happen: (1) individuals tend to respond in terms of patterns of behavior shared by group members, (2) psychological pressure causes individuals to move their perceptions and judgments about risk in the direction of group consensus and (3) group norms become personal norms. When group norms become personal norms, risk behavior may deviate from personal preference to group preference. Individuals may exert less effort than they would alone due to reduced accountability, blurring of personal contributuion, and diffusion of responsibility. And they may feel less responsible for taking action because there are other people who could take action.

From Groups to Institutions

Next up in the behavioral world of risk are institutions—specifically organizations and the media. Organizations shape how we perceive and respond to risk through collective values and norms which comprise a "risk culture"—the way people think about and act on risk within an organization. Media influence on risk attitudes and behavior happens through its portrayal of behavior as acceptable or unacceptable—a process that can help or hinder organizational efforts in building a risk culture.

Risk culture is the very heart of an organization's capacity to manage risk. For some organizations, it is a liability; for others, a source of stability and competitive advantage. Ultimately it comes down to leaders and employees and the extent to which they are part of a culture attuned to risk and its consequences—the subject of the next chapter.

Notes

1. Sherif, M. *The Psychology of Social Norms*. New York: Harper & Bros, 1936.
2. Hirsch, J. "Zoom Conversations vs. In-Person: Brain Activity Tells a Different Tale." *Neuroscience News*, October 26, 2023.
3. Tasca, G. *Group Dynamics: Theory, Research and Practice*, July 12, 2023.
4. Nowak, A. "Social Influence and Group Dynamics." *Wiley Online Library*, April 15, 2023.
5. Cherry, K. "How Does Group Size Influence Problem-Solving?" *VeryWellMind*, February 6, 2021.
6. Ma, A. and Rast, D. "Optimal Distinctiveness Theory." *Encyclopedia of Personality and Individual Differences*, June 5, 2017.

7. Cook, K and Rice, E. "Social Exchange Theory." In *The Handbook of Social Psychology,* ed. J. DeLamater, New York; John Wiley & Sons, 2013, pp. 53–76.

8. Mcleod, S. "Social Identity Theory: Definition, History, Examples and Facts." *Simply Psychology,* April 14, 2023.

9. Festinger, L. "A Theory of Social Comparison Processes." *Human Relations,* 7(2) (1954), pp. 117–140.

10. Festinger, L. "A Theory of Social Comparison Processes." *Human Relations,* 7(2) (1954), pp. 117–140.

11. Haslam, A.A. "Stereotyping and Social Influence: Foundations of Stereotype Consensus." In *The Social Psychology of Stereotyping and Group Life,* eds. R. Spears, P. Oakes, N. Ellemers, et al. Oxford: Blackwell, 1997, pp. 119–143.

12. Brewer, M. "Optimal Distinctiveness, Social Identity and the Self." In *Handbook of Self and Identity*, eds. M. Leary and J. Tangney. Guilford Press, 2003, pp. 480–491.

13. .Brewer, M. "Optimal Distinctiveness, Social Identity and the Self." In *Handbook of Self and Identity*, eds. M. Leary and J. Tangney. Guilford Press, New York, NY, 2003, pp. 480–491.

14. Mladenovic, D., Jirasek, M., Ondracek, T., Opatrna, Z., and Stangova, R. "The Influence of Social Conformity on Mask-Wearing Behavior During the COVID-19 Pandemic." *Heliyon*, 9(3), National Library of Medicine (March 2023).

15. Crossman, A. "How Our Aligning Behavior Shapes Everyday Life." *ThoughtCo,* November 6, 2020.

16. Cherry, K. "What Is Conformity." *VeryWellMind*, November 14, 2022.

17. Roberto, M., Bohmer, R., and Edmondson, A. "Facing Ambiguous Threats." *Harvard Business Review,* November, 2006.

18. Roberto, M., Bohmer, R., and Edmondson, A. "Facing Ambiguous Threats." *Harvard Business Review,* November, 2006.

19. Cherry, K. "How Groupthink Impacts Our Behavior." *VeryWellMind*, November 12, 2022.

20. Penn State University. "How Groupthink Played a Role in the Challenger Disaster." sites.psu.edu/aspsy/2020/10/07/how-groupthink-played-a-role-in-the -challenger-disaster/#:text.

21. Grinstein, J. "What the Challenger Disaster Teaches Us About Speaking Up in a New Era of Spaceflight." *NeuroLeadership Institute*, February 27, 2020.

22. Grinstein, J. "What the Challenger Disaster Teaches Us About Speaking Up in a New Era of Spaceflight." *NeuroLeadership Institute*, February 27, 2020.

23. Siddharth, R. "Challenger: A Management Failure." *Space Safety Magazine*, September 8, 2014.

24. Janis, I. *Groupthink*. New York, NY: Houghton Mifflin, 1982.

25. Janis, I. *Groupthink*. New York, NY: Houghton Mifflin, 1982.

26. Janis, I. *Groupthink*. New York, NY: Houghton Mifflin, 1982.

27. Janis, I. *Groupthink*. New York, NY: Houghton Mifflin, 1982.

28. Hopper, E. "What Is Deindividuation in Psychology? Definition and Examples." *ThoughtCo*, February 29, 2020.

29. Reicher, S., Spears, R., and Postmes, T. "A Social Identity Model of Deindividuation Phenomena." *European Review of Social Psychology*, 6, 1995, pp. 161–198.
30. Nickerson, C. "Deindividuation in Psychology: Definition and Examples." *Simply Psychology*, April 14, 2023.
31. Zimbardo, P. *The Cognitive Control of Motivation: The Consequences of Choice and Dissonance*. Glenview, IL: Scott, Foresman & Co.,1969.
32. Berkes, H. "Remembering Allan McDonald: He Refused to Approve Challenger Launch, Exposed Cover-Up." *Houston Public Media*, March 7, 2021.
33. Sierra, M. and Berrios, G. "The Phenomenological Stability of Depersonalization: Comparing the Old with the New." *The Journal of Mental and Nervous Disease*, 189(9) (2021), pp. 629–636.
34. Mayo Clinic Press Editors. "How to Cope with Depersonalization and Derealization." *Mayo Clinic Press*, April 18, 2023.
35. Berkes, H. "Remembering Allan McDonald: He Refused to Approve Challenger Launch, Exposed Cover-Up." *Houston Public Media*, March 7, 2021
36. Schaedig, D. "Groupthink: Definition, Signs, Examples and How to Avoid It." *Simply Psychology*, July 31, 2023.
37. Hillson, D. "How Groups Make Risky Decisions." Paper presented at PMI Global Congress 2009—EMEA, Amsterdam, North Holland, The Netherlands. Newton Square, PA: Project Management Institute, 2009.
38. Gu, Q. and Mendonca, D. "Group Information-Seeking Behavior in Emergency Response." In *Real-Time and Deliberative Decision Making. NATO Science of Peace and Security Series C: Environmental Security*, eds. I. Linkov, E. Ferguson, and V. Magar. Springer Science, New York, NY, 2008.
39. International Panel on Climate Change. "Climate Change 2022: Impacts, Adaptation and Vulnerability." *IPCC Sixth Assessment Report*, February 28, 2022.
40. Christensen, J. "Study Finds 'Very Concerning' 74% Increase in Deaths Associated with Extreme Heat Brought on by the Climate Crisis." *CNN Health*, August 19, 2021.
41. Rudert, S. and Janke, S. "Following the Crowd in Times of Crisis: Descriptive Norms Predict Physical Distancing, Stockpiling, and Prosocial Behavior During the COVID-19 Pandemic." *Sage Journals*, July 23, 2021.
42. Toloo, G., Fitzgerald, G., Aitken, P., Verrall, K., and Tong, S. "Are Heat Warning Systems Effective." *Environmental Health*, April 5, 2013.
43. Gupta, S. "How Extreme Heat from Climate Change Distorts Human Behavior." *Science News*, April 18, 2021.
44. Hoffman, R. "Social Loafing in Psychology: Definition, Examples & Theory." *Simply Psychology*, September 7, 2023.

Chapter 7

The Shaping Power
of Institutions

More essential than working on attitudes and behavior is examining the paradigms out of which attitudes and behavior flow.

Stephen Covey, American Educator and Author

Institutions shape and are shaped by human behavior. Their power lies in the structure they provide for interaction and norms which guide behavior in a given situation. In times of crisis, they are a source of stability, which is essential for maintaining social order. Among the most potent of institutions are organizations and the media because of their capacity to control information and the environment in which people interact. Organizations use structure and authority to influence behavior and resources to shape consumer preferences. The media exert power through selective reporting of information and framing issues in ways that shape belief and opinion.

Organizations and Affect

Organizations are complex systems with a significant impact on their members and those who interact with them. Their very complexity, however, complicates our understanding of them. Among the myriad of factors contributing to their effect are *rules* that set standards for conduct, *informal norms* that influence how members interact with one another and *systems* that shape relationships with the organization.[1] The importance of formal

DOI: 10.4324/9781003335658-9

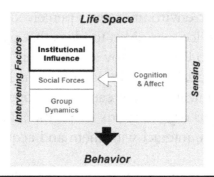

Institutions and Risk Behavior

controls is indisputable: they provide a framework for behavior that delivers a predictable outcome. In and of themselves, however, they do not make organizations work. Parallel to them is an informal network that does the heavy lifting. Its influence on behavior is inestimable. In fact, it has been argued that the informal organization is a far more powerful influence on behavior than organizational rules and regulations.[2]

The Power of Culture

As a consultant to scores of organizations during a 50-year career in academe, the most oft-repeated term I heard was "culture." Leaders were fervent in their belief that culture is a powerful driver of organizational success, yet many on the front lines saw it in a different way. Culture was a root cause of things that were going wrong. Typical of their comments were references to culture as a toxic entity permeating the organization: "the culture here sucks," "motivation and morale are low," "communication is top-down and one-way," "the budget is more important than people," "the executive team is out of touch with the people who do the work," "people don't listen— they talk past each other," "what people say doesn't match what they do," "this is not what I signed up for."

Employee silence—withholding information by failing to speak up—was especially troubling. I repeatedly observed instances where staff members went silent in group settings when their ideas and opinions were sought. Privately, however, they had much to say and did not hesitate to voice their opinion. For some, silence was a function of personality and background. They lacked the disposition to speak up because of introversion or fear of being shunned for using their voice. For others, silence was driven by fear: speaking up could jeopardize their job. For most, however, silence was situational: the work environment was perceived as unwelcoming of employee input. Lip service was given to ideas that ultimately went nowhere, and there was nothing to be gained by speaking up.

The "social cost" of speaking up in organizations intrigued me. What is it? What is it about organizations that causes employees to think and act in a particular way? How do organizations shape the attitudes and behavior of those who work in them, interact with them and acquire products and services from them?

The Underside of the Iceberg. Organizational culture can be likened to an iceberg with the bulk of the iceberg, which is submerged, comprised of shared beliefs and assumptions with the power to derail a corporate initiative. *It* sets *industries* apart due to variation in values and goals in different types of enterprises. *It* sets *organizations* apart—performing a job for Walmart is different than performing the same job for Kohl's, as is performing a job at General Electric compared to the same job at Boeing and performing a job at Accenture compared to the same job at McKinsey. Culture sets *people* apart—involvement in a culture of engagement is an entirely different experience than involvement in a top-down authoritarian culture.

Culture limits what organizations and leaders can do. If an organization has a tradition of shared governance and inclusive decision-making, a shift in style to top-down decision-making would invariably meet resistance and hamper a leader's ability to enact change. I experienced this first-hand as part of a consulting project with a college in California in 2008. The college was in the middle of an enormous wave of economic and technological development in the Tri-Valley region of California. New program development was essential to keep pace with rapidly developing occupational and job opportunities in the region. The college's program mix did not match up with the emerging economy—a matter of concern to a newly arrived president from a midwestern city flush with economic development. The president felt compelled to push a program development agenda—a decision that ran head-on into an academic culture which valued dialogue and consultation over change. Matters came to a head in an on-campus retreat involving senior administrators and faculty leaders to discuss workforce development for new industries moving into the region. The president and executive team were committed to a fast change agenda and faculty leaders were having none of it. Discussion was lengthy and fraught with difficulty. With time running out and the meeting soon to end, the consultants posed a question to the participants:

If a major employer moved into the college service region and indicated that programs would be needed to train 2,000 workers in three job categories in the next 12–18 months, would you mobilize and create the programs?

For the executive team, this was a no-brainer—the response was an enthusiastic *"yes."* The answer from faculty leaders was *"no."* Union policies and an entrenched culture of shared governance in which faculty, professional staff, administrators and the governing board participated jointly in policy development and decision-making would prevent timely action in response to the employer. Discussion was over—culture prevailed and the president's initiative was dead.

Culture in 3-D Perspective

Lochner (2020) argues that organizational culture can be understood through three lenses: what is *seen*, what is *said* and what is *believed*.[3] We can observe behavior in people that indicates their feelings about an organization: how they interact and communicate with one another, how they participate in meetings and contribute ideas and how leaders and managers treat personnel. People talk about work and their feelings toward fellow employees. Positive remarks may suggest a culture that values well-being and engagement. Silence and withdrawal may indicate a toxic culture where people are hesitant to speak out because of distrust, fear of backlash or norms which encourage competition.

People bring values to work they believe in. Consider the project experience of strategy consulting network PwC using culture as a vehicle for managing change:[4]

Even though our practice of using culture to manage change had proven effective with hundreds of clients, our methods were about to be chewed up and spit out by executives of a highly analytical financial services firm. Why? This client's business was centered on finding information others missed using an analytically thorough methodology and critical thinking. The company had a strong culture of skepticism, necessary for its business, but incompatible with our usual efforts. Phrases we usually used such as "sources of pride" and "emotional energy" were "too squishy" and abstract to be successful here....

After our first meeting at the financial services company, we set out to unearth the true nature of the organization's wariness around cultural initiatives. We observed how employees at all levels interacted with one another and found that, in this organization, success was built on relentless challenging. Employees took great pride in asking thought-provoking questions, diving into data to understand and analyze it, and pushing past conventional wisdom to get to the right answer. Understanding how things really worked at this company and the culture of steadfast skepticism helped us use these sources of pride to draw in the organization....

In highly analytical cultures, change efforts should appeal to emotions through logic and reasoning. Start with facts and figures. Use data to explain why the change is important and why it has to happen now. For example, show how competitors are gaining market share or illustrate the effects of low growth on the stock price. Demonstrate the expected benefits and costs of the change. Analytical minds will internalize the data and build their own personal case for transformation. With our financial services client, we unlocked powerful emotions by showing how key changes would allow analysis to reconnect with and do more of the parts of their job they liked. We made this case through facts and figures, but it resonated emotionally with analysts who had been bogged down for years by workarounds and inefficient processes....

With our financial services client, we established a communications schedule early and made sure to hit every deadline, building credibility along the way. Our messaging led with the facts and explained how transformation would benefit employees' day-to-day work, which we learned about by engaging with and listening to authentic informal leaders or employees who may not hold formal authority, but possess and exhibit leadership strengths and an in-depth knowledge of how the organization operates.

Cultural Congruence

Companies with a strong culture have a discernible impact on employees who, in turn, reinforce the power of company culture. *Pixar*'s trademark is originality.[5] It promotes psychological safety among its employees to nurture and encourage originality. Employees provide feedback to each other to improve ideas. Workers are expected to get accustomed to feeling embarrassed in public by sharing works in progress with colleagues. Radical candor is used to promote transparent conversations. Colleagues respect one other—no one pulls punches to be polite.

- *Zappos* is known for its family spirit and fun workplace culture. It has a customer-centric culture based on the idea that customers should be treated like family and happy employees make for happy customers.[6] Zappos places high importance on doing whatever it takes to deliver an optimal experience to customers. Its culture is built on core values: deliver WOW through service, embrace and drive change, create fun and a little weirdness, be adventurous and creative, pursue growth and learning, build a positive team and family spirit and be humble.
- *Patagonia* is renowned for its commitment to environmental sustainability and social responsibility.[7] Its culture aligns with its core values which include enjoining employees to live purposeful lives. The company encourages employees to participate in environmental activism and supports their involvement through paid environmental internships.
- *Walt Disney* prioritizes customer satisfaction in its theme parks to provide a memorable experience for its guests.[8] Every decision is centered around the guest experience. Employees are valued for their unique stories and their contribution to the customer experience through actions and words.
- *Meta Platforms* has a culture characterized by continuous learning, risk-taking and innovation.[9] Known for its mantra "Move Fast and Break Things," Meta maintains an environment where rapid innovation is the norm and employees are expected to push boundaries in order to keep the company at the forefront of social media.

Cultural congruence—alignment between an organization's culture and the values of its employees—is reinforced through self-selection and attrition. People are drawn to organizations where they feel they will fit in. Organizations, in turn, reinforce alignment by seeking candidates who will work seamlessly into their culture. Some organizations prioritize cultural fit over specific job-related skills in the hiring process. Southwest Airlines, for example, focuses on hiring employees based on personality and attitude rather than just technical skills. When employees feel that their cultural identities are valued, they buy into a culture and reinforce it with their values and beliefs. Culture is further reinforced through attrition—a process of separation when employee values, work style or behavior clash with the organization and lead to departure. The process of attraction-selection-attrition in which organizations bridge the gap between individual and organizational values is the cradle of organizational culture.

Unfortunately, cultural congruence is not a common experience among organizations. While Pixar, Patagonia and Zappos have been successful at creating a culture of alignment between personal and organizational values, others have struggled to do so. Research has shown that highly rated organizational values often do not overlap with top-rated values of employees.[10] It has further shown that employees' personal values are not systematically championed by organizations. In cultures marked by congruence between individual and organizational values, engagement is a positive experience. In hostile cultures, low morale can lead to disengagement and high rates of turnover.

The Behavioral Influence of Culture

Every member of an organization experiences and absorbs the effects of its culture. While some organizations choose members on the basis of fit, others choose them on the basis of acculturation—a belief that over time personal values will overlap with those of the organization.[11] Assessment of cultural fit can be so complex, that many organizations avoid it altogether opting instead to let cultural norms align organizational and employee values. As norms take hold, members begin to live the organization's values and become "carriers" of its culture.

In the early part of my career, I served as a senior administrator in colleges in Kansas City and New York. In both institutions, administrators dressed formally and senior-level officers were addressed by title—president, vice president or dean. Relationships among administrative peers were boundaried, communication was filtered, and power struggles were part of the turf. A busy schedule of meetings and appointments was a workday reality—not only to conduct the business of administration but to limit access of subordinates and, at times, colleagues. Limited availability was a sign of importance. Support staff were trained to control traffic and to maintain decorum appropriate for the office of a senior administrator.

Power, competition for resources and pursuit of advantage were the normative basis of administration in these institutions. Understanding and navigating organizational politics was essential not only for personal success but also for survival. I learned power dynamics by focusing on the behavior and mindsets of administrative peers—their goals, their body language, their modus operandi and preferred outcomes in decision-making. I never went into a meeting or a decision process without an outcome in mind and a strategy to achieve it. Wins and losses coming out of decision processes were calculated and remembered. Accumulated losses were a liability and information was priceless. Even more important than information itself, however, was a realization that acquisition of sensitive information without having to fish for it was integral to success. Competition was intense, and information was the key to advantage. The more one had that others didn't have, the greater the advantage.

Familiarity breeds comfort. When one is exposed to norms repeatedly, one becomes comfortable with them. I bought into the administrative norms I had come to know, I became adept at them, and I was good enough to move up the ranks of administration to vice president. My next stop would likely have been a college presidency, but fate intervened and took me in different direction. Thinking that I would enter the ranks of university teaching later in career, I developed name recognition through publications and presentations while serving as an administrator. My writing and speaking were well-received and drew the attention of university programs leading to an invitation to join a university graduate faculty in 1980.

I carried values of political awareness, power dynamics and competitiveness from administration to academe. My arrival as a newly minted professor at a midwestern research university in 1981 was met with a complete absence of fanfare. It was early January and I came in ready to roll, but no one was around. When colleagues, staff and students showed up a few days later, the professional decorum I was accustomed to in administration was nowhere to be seen. All were on a first name basis, casually dressed and observed few boundaries in conversation. When colleagues learned where I had chosen to reside, I was asked "Why did you move way out there?" I quickly learned that one has no "boss" in a university academic department. You are your own boss, and how you manage your time is key to your success. Other than classroom teaching, there were no hours for work and no deadline for results. One's body of work happened over years, not weeks or months. Merit was the sole basis of reward—articles and books, published research, grants and national recognition. Step increases for years in position did not exist. Professional visibility was synonymous with university visibility. One was expected to be among the top five academics nationally in one's field—anything less was not acceptable.

These contrasting environments illustrate the power of culture and its effect on behavior. Cultural norms dictate what is acceptable and "right." To gain acceptance, one aligns values and behavior with prevailing norms. As an administrator, I dressed for the role, engaged in power dynamics and sought leverage over others to achieve advantage. As an academic, I dressed casually, followed loosely structured norms for the conduct of work and fell into line with the academic reward system. Different cultures, different norms and different behavior. I internalized the norms of each culture and became a culture carrier.

The Media and Affect

As a purveyor of information that can reach audiences anywhere in real time, the media has become personal space for people to relate to others. We are inundated by non-stop information telling us what to believe, what others think, and what we need. Influence comes through the valence media brings to thought. Positive in ways such as increasing our knowledge of current events or promoting social change. Negative in ways, such as spreading misinformation and bias which fuels intolerance of others. The media is our window to the world beyond immediate experience. It influences our perception of reality, our sense of self, and our relationships with others.

Media Power

Traditional technologies including screen media, print, audio and multimedia have historically had a wide reach. Their influence has been augmented by the Internet and social media which are now an integral part of life. Seven in ten adults in the United States now use social media sites.[12] Information about anything can be acquired, and anyone can be a source of information. Unlike traditional media where the source is often authoritative after screening and verification, a social media post on anything can be published at any time, usually neither screened nor verified. The Internet and social media have created a virtual reality that we cannot live without, leading to a fragmented version of one's self pulled in many directions.

Media influence travels through four mediums: (1) a *direct effect* involving information about evolving norms and persuasion to accept them, (2) a *conditional effect* varying from person to person involving psychological and personality factors, (3) a *cumulative effect* involving repetition and exposure to information across multiple channels which changes or reinforces existing thought and (4) an *indirect effect* on individuals who are not directly exposed to media content.[13] Psychological and neurological research reveals a media impact on brain functioning that affects *attentional capacities, memory processes* and *social cognition.*[14]

Attentional Capacities. The widespread use of social media has divided our attention across multiple media sources at the expense of sustained concentration.[15] The ability of the Internet to capture and hold attention is not solely due to online content. An "attraction mechanism" is at work whereby aspects of the Internet which fail to gain attention are absorbed by incoming information some of which captures our attention. Cognitive capacity declines when people are unable to filter or ignore incoming distractions. Smart phone technologies further the process of distraction through email and social media prompts that compete for attention.

Memory Processes. Online information and social media have shifted the way we gather, store and use knowledge.[16] Among the advantages of volumes of information at our fingertips is reduction of dependence on memory, particularly memory of facts. Online access to information leads us to remember where facts can be retrieved rather than the facts themselves. This can result in "cognitive offloading" where we make less effort to remember information since we know it will be available for future reference through the Internet and social media.[17] As we become more dependent on technology, personal capability may diminish thereby creating an illusion of "greater than actual knowledge" retained in memory.[18]

Social Cognition. Online media settings resemble and evoke real-world social processes which has created a new interplay between technology and our social lives. We are drawn to online sociality to exchange information and ideas and to gain support just as we would in real-world interaction. Research indicates that neurocognitive responses to online social occurrences are similar to those of real-life interactions.[19] However, online sociality bends rules of the game. For example, whereas real-world acceptance or rejection is often ambiguous and subject to interpretation (who initiated the rejection), social media platforms directly quantify social success or failure, by providing labels in the form of "friends," "followers," and "likes."[20]

Internet of Behaviors

As digital technologies become more integrated with everyday life, they exert greater influence over cognitive processes and, ultimately behavior and attitudes. The Internet of Behaviors (IoB) describes the process through which behavior is shaped through continuous release of information compatible with individual behavior.[21] Data and information are collected from the interconnected devices of users, studied to discern trends in user behavior and interests and analyzed through behavioral science to understand how it affects individual behavior and attitudes. The Internet is tuned into the political persuasion of users, their favorite sports teams, their shopping preferences, topics that draw are likely to draw their interest and positions on issues that correspond to personal beliefs and preferences. The result is reinforcement of existing attitudes, interests and beliefs.

Not only does the IoB reinforce existing attitudes and beliefs, it forges new beliefs through individual and social channels. Individual channels provide new information to individuals and persuade them to accept it. Social channels inform users about what others learn, thereby facilitating coordination.[22] Media channels are frequently used by anti-stigma groups to share their work and to influence public attitudes. For example, New Zealand's "Like Minds, Like Mine" Facebook page entitled "Stigma Watch" encourages members to post and discuss media articles of concern because of their stigmatizing content, thereby facilitating conversation.[23] Diverse representation is another tactic used by social media to promote behavioral change. By showcasing a variety of perspectives and experiences, media break from traditional stereotypes and encourage a fresh outlook on issues.

There is obviously a downside to social media. It spreads false information which can alter our sense of reality. In the early months of the pandemic, posts and videos promoting natural remedies for the virus—everything from steam inhalation to ginger—proliferated online. While some scholars posited that people share falsehoods out of bias or flawed thought, research turned up evidence of a relationship between social media platform design and user spread of misinformation.[24] By constantly posting "likes" and "comments," media platforms create habitual users who are largely unconcerned with the accuracy and partisan slant of the content they post. They post simply because the platform rewards posting in the form of likes, comments and re-shares. Platforms aim for profit and engagement—more users spending more hours using them. By rewarding and amplifying engagement of any type regardless of its quality or accuracy, platforms create users who share indiscriminately.[25]

Risk Behavior

Risk behavior, like behavior in general, is a social process in which learning occurs through exposure to norms and interaction with others. Norms help individuals understand behavior that is expected in a risk situation while interaction helps them understand behavior that is common in the situation. When employees observe colleagues and superiors behaving in a particular way, they often mirror their behavior. When information is accessed through media, socially common behaviors are learned which, in turn, may affect individual behavior. Risk behavior is a product of social learning through interaction in organizations and media exposure—observing others and behaving in the same way, learning about evolving norms, and altering behavior to fit new norms.

Organizations and Risk Behavior

Risk behavior in organizations varies as a function of culture and the way in which risk is managed. Organizations with a strong risk culture have a well-defined understanding of risk and an enterprise-wide approach to managing it. They have a robust infrastructure supported by standards and controls that help units meet their risk management responsibilities with full accountability. Employees understand risk and they act on it in the course of their work.

Organizations vulnerable to risk are reflexive rather than proactive. They underestimate its impact and fail to recognize potential vulnerabilities. Short-term gains are prioritized over long-term mitigation. Departments operate independently leading to fragmented decision-making. Employees do not tend to risk—it is not part of their work and will be handled elsewhere in the organization. Flaws in systems, controls and infrastructure heighten vulnerability to risk.[26] Organizations with a weak risk culture are characterized by:

- *Lack of engagement.* Employees perceive risk as outside of their responsibility—a circumstance which can lead to complacency and a lack of accountability. The causes of complacency are many: excessive workload, leader and managerial neglect, lack of support and recognition, low autonomy and intolerance for rules which are seen as getting in the way of job performance.[27]
- *Inadequate internal controls.* Limited emphasis on risk in policy and protocols. In the absence of protocols, employees may lack information about how to handle risk and be at a loss for making decisions which can alleviate its threat and consequences.
- *Risk creep.* Growing tolerance of risk when the nature, immediacy and severity of risks are not defined—a circumstance which can lead to increasingly precarious behavior without regard for consequences.[28]
- *Narrow focus.* A focus on managing risk through controls and compliance tools which ignore the big picture of risk. A narrow focus limits employee perception to a small universe of risk and reduces their ability to detect and address emerging forms of risk.
- *Mismanagement of risk behavior.* A failure to understand causative factors underlying risk behavior. Leaders mismanage risk by failing to understand the influence of the informal organization on employee behavior, failing to evaluate critical input from employees and failing to learn from past mistakes.

Behavior in strong and weak cultures diverges in important ways that impact an organization's ability to manage risk. The dichotomy between strong and weak is simple: In strong cultures, a feeling of psychological safety among employees who understand risk and are committed to acting on it in strong cultures. In weak cultures, a feeling of inculpability among employees who do not fully understand the consequences of risk and avoid taking responsibility for it.

Media and Risk Behavior

The influence of media on risk behavior runs through multiple channels. Risk is learned *directly* through personal experience or *indirectly* through people and the media. A 2017 working paper by Hye-Jin Paek and Thomas Hove at Hanyang University provides a comprehensive analysis of media factors that shape risk perception and behavior:[29]

Media coverage. Media coverage heightens public attention to risk and magnifies or trivializes its effect leading people to elevate or minimize the potential for harm.[30] People evaluate risk on the basis of limited information and inferences made from media coverage. This is known as "availability heuristic"—a mental shortcut that relies on information that immediately comes to mind when evaluating an issue.[31] Heightened coverage of dramatic events leaves a lasting impression. The longer an event occupies one's attention, the more available it will be for reference in a future risk event, and the more likely one will buy into the possibility that the event could occur.

Media framing of risk issues. Compared to the amount of coverage that the media devote to a risk issue, what is often more important is the way the issue is presented.[32] *Framing* is a process of "selecting and highlighting particular facets of an event or issue, and making connections among them so as to promote a particular interpretation."[33] Information about a risk issue is presented in "frames" using words, images, phrases and presentation styles that serve as the cognitive framework in which people interpret the issue. Frames emphasize the issue's dramatic characteristics; for instance, news accounts that emphasize who or what is responsible for causing a risk issue and actions that need to be taken to neutralize its potential for harm.

Valence and tone of media coverage. News media tend to pay attention to the emotional aspects of risk issues and select issues for coverage that generate strong feelings.[34] Emotional content is a powerful force shaping risk perception as evidenced in feelings such as worry, anger, distrust and distress felt by the public in response to an event.[35] News media draw interest by focusing on human interest topics, worst-case scenarios, and emotionally charged language in contrast to presenting emotionally neutral information about risk.

Risk information sources. The sources used in media coverage of risk issues have a strong influence on perception.[36] Journalists tend to favor sources with opinions capable of generating strong debate or those with controversial views on an issue. Risk perception may also be affected by conceptions of a source's trustworthiness. In risk communication literature, trust has been found to play a significant role in predicting risk perception and risk- preventative behavior.[33] For abrupt and unexpected natural or humanly-created risks, people instinctively turn to scientists, experts or government officials in media coverage. The higher their trust in information from a knowledgable source, the more likely they will accept the risk. Conversely, If they distrust an information source or find the valence to be objectionable, they may reject the information. People assign more credibility to negative news—a tendency that colors their perception of risk[37]

Risk presentation formats. The manner in which media present information can affect the way people respond to risk.[38] Verbal and numeric estimates are commonly used for presenting risk information.[39] Verbal estimates present information using words that can be vague or misleading. Numeric estimates present information with numbers that stand alone or in ranges, sometimes accompanied by verbal qualifiers. Research findings have shown that: 1) numeric presentation generally yields a higher level of risk perception than verbal presentation and 2) a combination of quantitative and qualitative information formats may yield a higher level of risk understanding than a single format.[40]

Research has revealed a bimodal impact of media on risk behavior. *Impersonal impact* makes a distinction between personal-level and societal-level judgments about risk.[41] Personal-level judgments refer to individual beliefs about the personal harm that can be caused by risk, while societal-level judgments refer to beliefs about the extent to which risk threatens collectives such as a city, nation or the world population.[42] Personal-level judgments have been found to be more likely to lead to preventative behavior while societal-level risk judgments are less likely to have a direct impact on behavior. The reason is simple: media coverage presenting risk as a threat to generalized others is likely to be perceived as a problem specific to a group but not to the individual.[43]

The *differential impact mode* predicts that entertainment media are more likely to influence personal-level risk judgment while news media are more likely to influence societal-level risk judgment.[44] Entertainment media present risk in dramatic and emotional ways that tone threats in a way that makes them personally relevant to people. By comparison, the effect of news media is cognitive in nature thereby rendering perception less subject to emotion and error.

Risk Culture

Organizations cannot rely on instinct and reflex to predict and control risk in a widening risk universe. An obvious need is to strengthen their *risk culture*—the awareness, attitudes and behavior of leaders and employees toward risk and how it is managed in the organization.[45] Despite its importance, however, risk culture is imprecisely defined. It is often spoken of narrowly, usually in the context of organizational controls, while its psychological and behavioral attributes are left undetermined. Instead of an organization-wide priority and a cultural imperative, the behavioral side of risk is neglected in favor of controls and oversight by risk professionals. And when management goes awry, the consequences can be devastating, even fatal. Failures such as the Challenger Space Shuttle disaster in 1986 had their origin in management flaws that allowed risk to take root and grow.

Every organization has a culture that determines how it identifies, analyzes and acts on risk. Organizations with a poor risk culture set themselves up for failure through neglect or improvident actions that damage reputation and performance. Organizations with a strong risk culture cultivate a shared understanding of risk that results in consistent risk-based decisions across the organization.[46] In a risk intelligent organization, employees are aware of the effects and consequences of risk and make informed decisions. Risk is everyone's business.

Elements contributing to the risk culture of an organization are:[47]

- *Risk tolerance*—the degree of risk or uncertainty that is acceptable to an organization.
- *Risk appetite*—the amount of risk an organization is willing to accept to achieve its goals.
- *Checks and balances*—the balance between risk-taking functions and control functions.
- *Risk awareness*—the degree to which employees are aware of risks that are relevant to their job and to the organization as a whole.
- *Risk values*—the values of an organization that are relevant to risk such as prioritizing safety, health, environment and sustainability.
- *Due diligence*—the expectation that employees will exercise responsibility for managing risk.
- *Tone at the top*—the values and diligence required to manage risk at the top of an organization.
- *Authority*—the distribution of authority to manage risk.

■ *Resilience*—the ability of an organization to withstand stress.

Risk culture has a powerful influence on employees. Consider the following corporate examples of poor and strong risk cultures and their effect on employee attitudes and behavior:

Poor Risk Culture

Wells Fargo. In 2016, Wells Fargo was fined $185 million for opening millions of unauthorized accounts and credit cards for its customers.[48] A culture of intense competition had been instilled among employees to improve sales performance, including preparation of daily score cards and hourly monitoring.[49] Employees were under extreme pressure to meet sales targets with incentives tied to meeting minimum goals; a move which led to unethical practices such as "pinning"—assigning PIN numbers to fake accounts opened without customer knowledge or consent. Deficient controls were maintained to prevent and detect misconduct leaving employees no choice but to follow management directives. Wells Fargo's culture of high-pressure sales was part of a business strategy prioritizing growth over risk—a formula for neglect of warning signals and eventual disaster.

Uber. The world first became aware of Uber's toxic culture in 2017 when Susan Fowler, a former employee, wrote a public post about sexual harassment and discrimination she experienced during her employ at Uber.[50] The company prized "meritocracy" and "hustlin" over teamwork and caring for each other. Results were valued above everything else. Uber drivers cited physical and mental health concerns—eating unhealthy food, lack of exercise, being distracted by customer demands, dealing with potentially dangerous situations and negative ratings from passengers which could lead to being removed from the ride share platform. Job and income security were driven by a need to remain in good standing in work designed around passenger ratings which took precedence over health and safety concerns.[51]

Strong Risk Culture

JPMorgan Chase. JPM has long prided itself as having the best risk management practices in the financial industry.[52] Risk management is overseen and managed on an enterprise-wide basis. Risk teams throughout the organization research and measure risk with a goal not to eliminate it, but to understand, anticipate and mitigate it.[53] JPM's commitment to risk management is reflected in its Risk Management and Compliance Program—a training program for employees designed to develop insight and expertise in risk assessment and compliance.[54] The program provides hands-on experience in evaluating and assessing credit risk, conducting risk reviews, developing end-to-end risk models, forecasting risk and evaluating the firm's risk readiness and controls.

Goldman Sachs. Goldman Sachs has an enterprise-wide risk management framework that includes a standardized risk assessment process to identify, quantify and prioritize expected and unexpected events that may have an adverse impact on the firm.[55] Risk management is keyed to a culture of continuous improvement and structured oversight. Risk teams drive how the firm analyzes and manages risk in coordination with risk professionals who execute day-to-day risk management activities. The company's partners and managing directors participate in a Chairman's Forum, a mandatory in-person training program focused on reputational risk management and the responsibility of every employee to strengthen the firm's culture and protect its reputation.[56] The firm also has a comprehensive Reputational Risk Framework to manage reputational harm to the firm, its employees and its clients. The framework includes training, regional vetting groups, a heightened whistleblower program, sophisticated search tools, electronic surveillance and tone at the top.[57]

Clearly, these corporate examples of poor and strong risk cultures are extreme. What they reveal, however, is that risk tracks back to a cultural root cause, leading to actions that can plunge an organization into crisis. Risk is exacerbated when leaders neglect the *people side* of risk—the mindsets and behaviors of individuals and groups that determine an organization's ability to act on risk.[58] Employees are at a disadvantage in managing risk without established protocols. They may be uncertain about their roles and responsibilities and, ultimately, their accountability for identifying and acting on risk.

Managing the People Side of Risk

On the heels of the pandemic, most organizations put robust processes and oversight structures in place to detect and manage risks before they become full-blown crises. These structures have helped, but they alone do not suffice. The difference maker in a widening risk universe is *people*. Crises emerge or are exacerbated when people are not tuned in to risk. Employees, not controls, are an organization's first line of defense against risk. Managing the people side of risk is as important, if not more important, than risk controls. It is integral to organizational and leader success and requires an understanding and appreciation of individual differences in dispositon toward risk.

Controls Versus People

Controls that treat people *en masse* reduce the role of individuals to compliance and do not cover the full spectrum of risk. Nor does leaving the risk management function in the hands of specialists. Reliance on specialists, while essential, can have the effect of devaluating individual judgment. Kaplan and Mikes (2012) put the issue of people vs. controls into perspective with a description of the Deepwater Horizon oil rig disaster in 2010:[59]

> *When Tony Hayward became CEO of BP, in 2007, he vowed to make safety his top priority. Among the new rules he instituted were the requirements that all employees use lids on coffee cups while walking and refrain from texting while driving. Three years later, on Hayward's watch, the Deepwater Horizon oil rig exploded in the Gulf of Mexico, causing one of the worst man-made disasters in history. A U.S. investigation commission attributed the disaster to management failures that crippled "the ability of individuals involved to identify the risks they faced and to properly evaluate, communicate, and address them."*

BP's experience illustrates that despite the resources invested in systems and controls, risk management is more than a control and compliance process that can be executed by instituting systems that people are expected to follow. It is a people process requiring an understanding of *risk attitude*—the disposition of individuals toward risk driven by perception and evidenced in their behavior.[60]

Risk Attitude

Because organizations are constantly facing risk and manned by individuals with a wide range of attitudes, there is a varied potential for risk at any time. Ingram and Thompson (2012) have created a framework that depicts risk in two contexts: (1) as an attitude or opinion held by individuals and (2) as an event or circumstance.[61] In times of peril, prevailing opinion is never unanimous. COVID-19, for example, elicited an array of opinions about risk of which four rose to prominence: *optimists*, who were positive in outlook and looked toward a favorable outcome; *fatalists*, who were consumed by the epidemic and a future that was uncertain; *equilibrists*, who viewed the epidemic as cyclical and self-correcting; and *managers*, who viewed the epidemic as ominous but capable of being mitigated if managed properly.

Over time, risk attitudes such as the above are tested through circumstances that pose a mismatch between what individuals think will happen and what actually happens.[62] With the pandemic, for example, individuals might anticipate a resilient world with a positive outcome; a volatile world engulfed in danger; a world in transition, but ultimately in equilibrium; or a world in chaos, but capable of being righted if capably managed. This means that when a risk event of the pandemic's magnitude happens, it could be met in 12 different ways as shown in the matrix in Figure 7.1.[63]

Risk Attitude	Actual World of the Pandemic			
	Propitious	Resignation	Stasis	Tractable
Propitious (Optimist)	No surprise	Unexpected, look for silver lining	Predictable, change is cyclical	Predictable, people overcome adversity
Resignation (Fatalist)	Danger is ongoing	No surprise	Outcome is predetermined	Holding fast to belief in fate
Stasis (Equilibrist)	World is in balance	World is out of balance	No surprise	Predictable, COVID curbed by science
Tractable (Manager)	Effective management gets results	Unexpected, sells management short	Predictable, management creates stability	No surprise

Figure 7.1 Typology of risk attitudes. Adapted from Ingram, D. and Thompson, M. "What's Your Risk Attitude? (And How Does It Affect Your Company)" Harvard Business Review. June, 2012.

Along the diagonal of the matrix the world is the way it is expected to be—there are no surprises. In the remaining 12 boxes, there is the element of surprise—a difference between what individuals think would happen in relationship to the pandemic and what would actually happen.[64]

■ In a ***Propitious*** world, the pandemic is brought under control by science, and there are varied opinions ranging from cynicism (danger is ongoing) to predictability (science and management get results). *Fatalists* are surprised by the turn of events with a contagion brought under control. *Equilibrists* and *Managers* who believe in long-term stability are surprised at how quickly stability is achieved following mass vaccination.

■ In a world of ***Resignation***, the effects of COVID-19 linger and social and economic recovery is slow. *Optimists* are disappointed by the slow pace of recovery and look for light at the end of the tunnel. For *Equilibrists* and *Managers*, stability is the expected long-term outcome, but recovery has fallen short in spite of the best efforts of science, business and government.

■ In a world of ***Stasis***, balance between losses and gains has been achieved in the war against COVID. Optimists and Fatalists are surprised—*Optimists* because progress is slower than expected and *Fatalists* because COVID is in situ when they thought it would be raging toward a bleak outcome. *Managers* see stability as a predictable outcome resulting from effective management.

■ In a ***Tractable*** world, the effects and consequences of COVID have been neutralized by effective health policy and economic controls. *Optimists* see this outcome as predictable because adversity can be overcome through scientific and technological advances. *Fatalists* are puzzled and see neutralization as implausible over the short term; they hold fast to their belief in fate. *Equilibrists* see neutralization as predictable given the discovery of a vaccine and the cyclical nature of an epidemic.

The process of changing risk attitudes can run two routes. First, individuals can change their attitude if their experience with risk is sufficient to wear away their convictions. If they are adaptable, their attitude could shift to a perspective on risk that aligns with the current environment. If they are intransigent, they may maintain or adopt a risk attitude that does not align with the environment at significant cost to an organization.[65] The second route poses a challenge to leaders requiring resolution. Persuasion, rules, reorganizations, resignations, promotions, retirements and layoffs are some of the tools leaders can use to balance employee attitudes toward risk with environmental conditions.[66]

The scond route of change is through tone at the top by changing leaders. Leaders coming into an organization face the challenge of adapting to or shifting the prevailing risk attitudes of individuals and he organization as a whole. Through persuasion, rules, reorganizations, resignations, promotions, retirements and layoffs, new leaders will eventually obtain the balance in risk atitudes needed for the organization to prosper.

A Perfect Storm

From its roots in human cognition, its grounding in social forces and group dynamics and its basis in institutions, we have come full circle with the social dynamics of risk. We know that group and organizational factors have a profound influence on risk behavior. We also know that there is a strong correlation between risk perception and behavior in a variety of social settings. Much less is known, however, about how group and setting factors interact to affect the way organizations see and respond to risk. And even less is known about their influence on decision-making and engagement with risk. This brings into focus the role of leaders. Risk management does not function in a vacuum and rarely does it survive leadership failure. Leaders shape the collective mindset and behavioral norms that determine how an organization identifies and manages risk—its risk culture. Organizations with a strong risk culture are not predisposed to self-inflicted wounds while those with a weak culture are more vulnerable to risks.

In a growing universe of risk, culture and the capability of leaders are critical elements that distinguish high- from low-performing organizations and effective from ineffective leaders. In the next chapter, social dynamics are considered in the context of a perfect storm that will challenge the capacity of organizations and leaders in managing risk. The perfect storm will need to be navigated by risk intelligent organizations and leaders who understand the importance of asymmetry and paradox in tomorrow's world of risk. The focus of closing chapters in the book.

Notes

1. Jindal, S. "Formal Vs. Informal Culture." *All Things Talent*, March 2018.
2. Kazuhito, I. "The Theory of the Informal Organization." *Springer Briefs in Business*, October 27, 2020.
3. Galli, M. "Organizational Culture and Its Importance." *ResearchGate*, March 2022.
4. PwC. Business Consulting Case Studies. https://www.pwc.com/us/en/library/case-stu.
5. Shah, R. "Pixar Culture: 5 Principles That Rescued Disney." *Shortform*, December 30, 2020.
6. Aaron Hall. "Zappos: Revolutionizing Culture and Customer Service." August 14, 2023. aaronhall.com/insights/zappos-revolutionizing-culture-and-customer-service/
7. Lebovitz, S. "Patagonia's HR Chief Says He Reads Resumes 'From the Bottom Up' to Avoid the Culture-Fit-Trap." *Business Insider,* October 18, 2019.
8. Williams, A. "Disney's Organizational Culture: An Analysis of Cultural Traits." *Panmore Institute*, September 20, 2023.
9. Lombardo, J. "Facebook's (Meta's) Organizational Culture & Its Traits (An Analysis)." *Panmore Institute*, August 30, 2023.
10. Workstars. "Reconciling Organizational and Personal Values: Dissecting the ILM's Latest Research." Retrieved: November 22, 2023.
11. Sackman, S. *Culture in Organizations*. Contributions to Management Science, https://doi.org/10.1007/978-3-030-86080-6_4. Retrieved: November 26, 2023.
12. Auxier, B. and Anderson, M. "Social Media Use in 2021." *Pew Research Center,* April 7, 2021.
13. Arias, E. "How Does Media Influence Social Norms: Experimental Evidence on the Role of Common Knowledge." *Cambridge University Press*, February 20, 2018.
14. Firth, J., Torous, J., Stubbs, B., Firth, J., Sreiner, G., Smith, L., Alvarez-Jimenez., Gleeson, J., Vancampfort, D., Armitage, C., and Sarris, J. "The 'Online Brain': How the Internet May Be Changing Our Cognition." *Journal of World Psychiatry*, 18 (2) (June 2019), pp. 119–129.
15. Firth, J., Torous, J., Stubbs, B., Firth, J., Sreiner, G., Smith, L., Alvarez-Jimenez., Gleeson, J., Vancampfort, D., Armitage, C., and Sarris, J. "The 'Online Brain': How the Internet May Be Changing Our Cognition." *Journal of World Psychiatry*, 18(2) (June 2019), pp. 119–129.
16. Firth, J., Torous, J., Stubbs, B., Firth, J., Sreiner, G., Smith, L., Alvarez-Jimenez., Gleeson, J., Vancampfort, D., Armitage, C., and Sarris, J. "The 'Online Brain': How the Internet May Be Changing Our Cognition." *Journal of World Psychiatry*, 18(2) (June 2019), pp. 119–129.
17. Firth, J., Torous, J., Stubbs, B., Firth, J., Sreiner, G., Smith, L., Alvarez-Jimenez., Gleeson, J., Vancampfort, D., Armitage, C., and Sarris, J. "The 'Online Brain': How the Internet May Be Changing Our Cognition." *Journal of World Psychiatry*, 18(2) (June 2019), pp. 119–129.

18. Firth, J., Torous, J., Stubbs, B., Firth, J., Sreiner, G., Smith, L., Alvarez-Jimenez., Gleeson, J., Vancampfort, D., Armitage, C., and Sarris, J. "The 'Online Brain': How the Internet May Be Changing Our Cognition." *Journal of World Psychiatry*, 18(2) (June 2019), pp. 119–129.
19. Firth, J., Torous, J., Stubbs, B., Firth, J., Sreiner, G., Smith, L., Alvarez-Jimenez., Gleeson, J., Vancampfort, D., Armitage, C., and Sarris, J. "The 'Online Brain': How the Internet May Be Changing Our Cognition." *Journal of World Psychiatry*, 18(2) (June 2019), pp. 119–129.
20. Firth, J., Torous, J., Stubbs, B., Firth, J., Sreiner, G., Smith, L., Alvarez-Jimenez., Gleeson, J., Vancampfort, D., Armitage, C., and Sarris, J. "The 'Online Brain': How the Internet May Be Changing Our Cognition." *Journal of World Psychiatry*, 18(2) (June 2019), pp. 119–129.
21. Thomas, L. "The Internet of Behaviors—A Paradigm Shift." *TC Global*, June 21, 2022.
22. Bump, P. "The 5 Types of Social Media & Pros and Cons of Each (Research)." *Hubspot,* May 16, 2023.
23. Thornicroft, C., Wyllie, A., and Mehta, N. "Impact of the Like Minds, Like Mine Anti-stigma and Discrimination Campaign in New Zealand on Anticipated and Experienced Discrimination." *Australian & New Zealand Journal of Psychiatry*, 48(4) (November 2013), pp. 360–370.
24. Allen, S. "How Social Media Rewards Misinformation." *Yale Insights,* March 31, 2023.
25. Allen, S. "How Social Media Rewards Misinformation." *Yale Insights,* March 31, 2023.
26. Posey, C. and Shoss, C. "Research: Why Employees Violate Cybersecurity Policies." *Harvard Business Review*, January 2022.
27. Posey, C. and Shoss, C. "Research: Why Employees Violate Cybersecurity Policies." *Harvard Business Review*, January 2022.
28. Logg, J., Tinsley, C., and Leitao, M. "Risk Creep: A COVID-19 Longitudinal Field Study." Georgetown McDonough School of Business Research Paper No. 4219931, September 19, 2021.
29. Paek, H-J. and Hove, T. "Risk Perceptions and Risk Characteristics." In *Oxford Research Encyclopedia of Communication*, ed Eric Kramer. Oxford: Oxford University Press, March 2017.
    This online paper presents an excellent synthesis of literature and research on media factors that shape risk perception and behavior. Theoretical perspectives on risk perception presented by Paek and Hove are extensively used in this chapter to describe the way in which media condition perception and behavior.
30. Paek, H-J. and Hove, T. "Risk Perceptions and Risk Characteristics." In *Oxford Research Encyclopedia of Communication*. Oxford: Oxford University Press, March 2017.
31. Gleason, C. "Availability Heuristic and Decision Making." *Simply Psychology*, July 10, 2023.

32. Paek, H-J. and Hove, T. "Risk Perceptions and Risk Characteristics." In *Oxford Research Encyclopedia of Communication*. Oxford: Oxford University Press, March 2017.

33. Entman, R. *Projections of Power: Framing News, Public Opinion, and U.S. Foreign Policy*. Chicago: University of Chicago Press, 2004.

34. Paek, H-J. and Hove, T. "Risk Perceptions and Risk Characteristics." In *Oxford Research Encyclopedia of Communication*. Oxford: Oxford University Press, March 2017.

35. Paek, H-J. and Hove, T. "Risk Perceptions and Risk Characteristics." In *Oxford Research Encyclopedia of Communication*. Oxford: Oxford University Press, March 2017.

36. Paek, H-J. and Hove, T. "Risk Perceptions and Risk Characteristics." In *Oxford Research Encyclopedia of Communication*. Oxford: Oxford University Press, March 2017.

37. Paek, H-J. and Hove, T. "Risk Perceptions and Risk Characteristics." In *Oxford Research Encyclopedia of Communication*. Oxford: Oxford University Press, March 2017.

38. Paek, H-J. and Hove, T. "Risk Perceptions and Risk Characteristics." In *Oxford Research Encyclopedia of Communication*. Oxford: Oxford University Press, March 2017.

39. Paek, H-J. and Hove, T. "Risk Perceptions and Risk Characteristics." In *Oxford Research Encyclopedia of Communication*. Oxford: Oxford University Press, March 2017.

40. Paek, H-J. and Hove, T. "Risk Perceptions and Risk Characteristics." In *Oxford Research Encyclopedia of Communication*. Oxford: Oxford University Press, March 2017.

41. Tyler, T. and Cook, F. "The Mass Media and Judgments of Risk: Distinguishing Impact on Personal and Societal Level Judgments." *Journal of Personality and Social Psychology*, 47, 1984, pp. 693–708.

42. Tyler, T. and Cook, F. "The Mass Media and Judgments of Risk: Distinguishing Impact on Personal and Societal Level Judgments." *Journal of Personality and Social Psychology*, 47, pp. 693–708.

43. Tyler, T. and Cook, F. "The Mass Media and Judgments of Risk: Distinguishing Impact on Personal and Societal Level Judgments." *Journal of Personality and Social Psychology*, 47, pp. 693–708.

44. Paek, H-J. and Hove, T. "Risk Perception and Risk Characteristics." In *Oxford Research Encyclopedia of Communication*. Oxford: Oxford University Press, March 2017.

45. Deloitte. *Cultivating a Risk Intelligent Culture: Understand, Measure, Strengthen and Report*. Deloitte LLP, London, England, UK, 2012.

46. Higgins, R., Liou, G., Maurenbrecher, S., Poppensieker, T., and White, O. "Strengthening Institutional Risk and Integrity Culture." *McKinsey & Company*, November 2020.

47. Spacey, J. "11 Examples of Risk Culture." *Simplicable*, November 2023.

48. Veetikazhi, R. and Krishnan, G. "Wells Fargo: Fall from Great to Miserable: A Case Study on Corporate Governance Failures." *Sage Journals*, 8(1) (November 2018), p. 227797791880347.

49. Veetikazhi, R. and Krishnan, G. "Wells Fargo: Fall from Great to Miserable: A Case Study on Corporate Governance Failures." *Sage Journals*, 8(1) (November 2018), p. 227797791880347.

50. Bartel, E., MacEachen, E., Reid-Musson, E., Meyer, S., Saunders, R., Bigelow, P. Kosny, A., and Varatharajan, S. "Stressful by Design: Exploring Health Risks of Ride-Share Work." *Journal of Transport and Health*, 13 (March 2020), pp. 115–127.

51. Bartel, E., MacEachen, E., Reid-Musson, E., Meyer, S., Saunders, R., Bigelow, P. Kosny, A., and Varatharajan, S. "Stressful by Design: Exploring Health Risks of Ride-Share Work." *Journal of Transport and Health*, 13 (March 2020), pp. 115–127.

52. Zeissler, A. and Metrick, A. "JPMorgan Chase Whale D Risk-Management Practices." *Journal of Financial Crises,* 1(2) (2019),pp. 92–102.

53. Zeissler, A. and Metrick, A. "JPMorgan Chase Whale D Risk-Management Practices." *Journal of Financial Crises,* 1(2) (2019).

54. JPMorgan Chase & Co. "Risk Management and Compliance." https://careers.jpmorgan.com/global/en/our-businesses/riskp-compliance.

55. Goldman Sachs. "Risk Management—Goldman Sachs." https://www.goldmansachs.com/.../risk-management.pdf.

56. Goldman Sachs. "Risk Management—Goldman Sachs." https://www.goldmansachs.com/.../risk-management.pdf.

57. Goldman Sachs. "Risk Management—Goldman Sachs." https://www.goldmansachs.com/.../risk-management.pdf.

58. Kaplan, R. and Mikes, A. "Managing Risks: A New Framework." *Harvard Business Review*, June 2012.

59. Kaplan, R. and Mikes, A. "Managing Risks: A New Framework." *Harvard Business Review*, June 2012.

60. Kaplan, R. and Mikes, A. "Managing Risks: A New Framework." *Harvard Business Review*, June 2012.

61. Ingram, D. and Thompson, M. "What's Your Risk Attitude? (And How Does It Affect Your Company?)" *Harvard Business Review*, June 2012.

62. Ingram, D. and Thompson, M. "What's Your Risk Attitude? (And How Does It Affect Your Company?)" *Harvard Business Review*, June 2012.
The concept and design for the risk framework presented in Table 7.1 were adapted directly from Ingram and Thompson's framework depicting risk as operating in two contexts (*attitude* held by individuals and *event or circumstance*) in "What's Your Risk Attitude" (*Harvard Business* Review, 2012). In contrast to the risk attitudes profiled by Ingram and Thompson in the financial industry, differential attitudes toward risk in this chapter are described in the context of the COVID-19 pandemic for four categories of people: Optimists, Fatalists, Equilibrists and Managers.

63. Ingram, D. and Thompson, M. "What's Your Risk Attitude? (And How Does It Affect Your Company?)" *Harvard Business Review*, June 2012.

64. Ingram, D. and Thompson, M. "What's Your Risk Attitude? (And How Does It Affect Your Company?)" *Harvard Business Review*, June 2012.

65. Ingram, D. and Thompson, M. "What's Your Risk Attitude? (And How Does It Affect Your Company?)" *Harvard Business Review*, June 2012.

66. Ingram, D. and Thompson, M. "What's Your Risk Attitude? (And How Does It Affect Your Company?)" *Harvard Business Review*, June 2012.

Chapter 8

A Perfect Storm

There are some things you can only learn in a storm.

Anonymous Quote

On October 20, 1991, the captain and crew of the Andrea Gail, a 70-foot fishing vessel working out of Gloucester, Massachusetts, left port for the Grand Banks of Newfoundland in a quest for commercially profitable swordfish. Having no luck in the Grand Banks, the Andrea Gail turned east toward the Flemish Cap, filled its hold and began the 900-mile return journey. Flush with excitement at the prospect of returning home with a big catch, the captain and crew paid little attention to the storm brewing off the coast. A cold front from the east coast of the United States carrying a wave of low pressure and a high-pressure ridge from Canada were coming together to create a massive Nor'easter. When the fronts met over the Atlantic, air moving between high and low pressure created 70 mph wind gusts and 30-foot waves. Further out to sea, warm air remnants of Hurricane Grace compressed into a cyclone creating the final element of what was to become a "perfect storm"—a rare combination of circumstances which made the storm unusually powerful. Exacerbating its effect was inattention of the captain and crew to weather reports and their almost singular focus on returning to home port with a profitable catch. The rest is history—the Andrea Gail and its captain and crew were lost to the fury of the storm on October 30, 1991.[1]

Storm and Stress

"Perfect storm" is an idiom oft used to describe a situation where multiple factors come together to create a catastrophic event.[2] It can be a combination of events in multiple contexts. In a meteorological context, it is a confluence of forces so powerful that the resulting storm can only be described as "perfect." In politics it could be a situation in which a number of factors come together to create a worst-case scenario. In a social context, it could be a convergence of economic, political and social factors that create a crisis.

■ The *Great Recession* of 2008 was caused by a combination of factors including the collapse of the housing market, the credit crunch and decline in bank lending, the erosion of consumer confidence and the naivete of lawmakers who did not understand the financial crisis.[3] Excessive borrowing by consumers and corporations created asset bubbles which when devalued wiped out net worth of investors and caused businesses to fail.

■ In the aftermath of *Hurricane Katrina*, flaws in levee construction, government bureaucracy and long-standing racism were found to have contributed to the storm's damage.[4] Katrina exposed a harsh reality facing low-income populations—social and economic challenges exacerbate risk in catastrophic events. Forced onto rooftops to escape flooding, sheltering in squalid conditions in the Louisiana Superdome and encountering bureaucratic hurdles, impoverished residents were caught in a perfect storm of inequality, poor planning and government ineptitude. They were doomed before Katrina's landfall.

■ A highly infectious virus, a worldwide economic depression, the collapse of global governance and the absence of a coordinated international response vaulted *COVID-19* from an outbreak to a pandemic of historic proportion.[5] From a public health standpoint, the contagion spread because of its unique molecular structure, high risk of human transmission, long incubation period, presence in asymptomatic or mildly symptomatic carriers and viral shedding after symptom relief.[6] From a social standpoint, its spread was influenced by human factors including a lack of compliance with distancing guidelines, misunderstanding of the threat posed by the virus, mistrust of leaders and misguided expectations as to the long-term impact of the virus.[7]

Common to all of these events is the principle of **asymmetry**—augmentation of the effects and consequences of risk due to a lack of symmetry in social dynamics. When cognition, social norms, group dynamics and institutional behavior do not align, processes that make social life fluid can break down exposing people to conflict of their own making. Returning to the examples above, asymmetry would play out as follows:

- In the **Great Recession**, the disjuncture between *social norms* (standing consumer expectations about borrowing, spending and retirement) and the behavior of *institutions* (banks issuing faulty loans and government officials failing to understand the financial system) contributed to a crisis that caused significant financial hardship.
- In the specter of **Hurricane Katrina**, the disconnect between *social norms* (behavior and attitudes perpetuating inequality), *group dynamics* (communication and coordination among officials within and between government agencies) and the behavior of *institutions* (lack of government oversight in levee construction and bureaucratic obstruction) led to unspeakable suffering for low-income New Orleans residents.
- In the grasp of **COVID-19**, rapid evolution of the virus from an outbreak to a pandemic resulted, in part, from asymmetry of cognition, social norms, group dynamics and institutional behavior. *Norms* around social distancing and mask-wearing designed to prevent spread of the virus were subverted by *group dynamics* which encouraged resisters to perceive COVID-19 as a low-level threat. Slow-moving government agencies (*institutions*) accelerated spread of the virus by failing to impose social restrictions early on in response to the virus.

Flow

In a perfect world, alignment would exist among social dynamics factors. One's cognitive state would match prevailing social norms, the norms of one's in-group and the influence of institutions with which one is engaged. By way of example, let's say you are a climate change naysayer. Your gut instinct tells you that warming and cooling are cyclical and climate conditions balance out over time. Important others share this view—friends, members of social groups to which you belong and coworkers all feel the same way. Your view is further reinforced by an absence of policy related to sustainability in your workplace and negative information about climate change you have curated from social media. All of the dynamics line up. Affirmed by group norms and social media and in the absence of workplace policy on sustainability, your view on climate change is rock hard.

When social dynamics align, a condition of *flow* is realized. Not in a business sense as value or efficiency or in positive psychology as an optimal state of consciousness.[8] In the context of social dynamics, flow refers to patterns of change and stability in behavior over time. When individual, group and setting factors align, as shown in Figure 8.1, flow is achieved. The whitespace in the graphic signifies a melding together of cognition, social norms, group dynamics and institutional influence leading to consistency in behavior and attitudes.

Flow is an individual experience encompassing five factors:

■ commitment to a central attitude or belief
■ a union of attitude and behavior
■ attenuation of reflective capability
■ an ability to control perception and subjective experience
■ an ability to interpret information, situations and events in ways consistent with personal beliefs

People in flow, look at things in a singular way without consideration of alternatives. In the world of organizations, an example would be employees holding a singular attitude toward risk in a weak or strong risk culture. In a *weak risk culture*, flow could take the form of aversion to risk reinforced by similarly inclined coworkers in an organization with a narrow structural approach to risk.[9] In a *strong risk culture*, flow could be realized as an

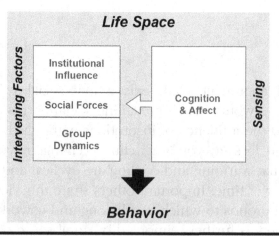

Figure 8.1 Social Dynamics as Flow

individual and collective attitude toward risk consistent with an organization-wide risk strategy supported by robust standards and controls.[10]

Flow is situational. A shift in group sentiment, a change in organizational risk strategy, a change in social norms about risk—all are factors which could alter alignment and interrupt flow.

Asymmetry

When social dynamics do not align, it is for lack of symmetry. This is ***asymmetry*** as illustrated in Figure 8.2—an absence of flow in social dynamics. Using the example above, consider a situation in which your view of climate change is challenged by friends claiming that it is a scientifically proven reality. Further complicating the situation is the commitment of your company to sustainability and a risk intelligent culture. You are expected to embrace this culture and sharpen your understanding of climate change and other forms of risk. Company and friends are important, but they are not paramount. Reinforcing your view are naysaying members of a social group to which you belong and media posts quashing evidence of climate change. You are caught in a web of competing perspectives. Which will prevail?

Unlike the psychological flexibility that is part of flow, asymmetry can cause stress when people encounter evidence and beliefs contrary to their own. Flow eases adjustment to situations that diverge from expectation. When evidence and belief clash, people will do everything in their power to restore flow. They may seek information that reinforces existing belief,

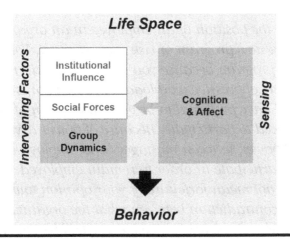

Figure 8.2   Social Dynamics as Asymmetry

alter belief to match evidence, adopt a new belief or remove themselves from the situation altogether.[11] We are capable of remarkable cognitive leaps to achieve the psychological comfort of flow even to the point of self-deception—denying or rationalizing away evidence or belief contrary to expectation. Flow is the converse of asymmetry—a state that when achieved channels discomfiting conditions into a positive emotional state.

Paradox

When contradictory forces in social dynamics persist over time and cause discord, paradox is realized.[12] Flow is difficult to achieve when groups promote norms and values that contradict individual beliefs and organizations push agendas that put people in a place they do not want to be. With discord comes the reality of choice—achieve flow by resolving the contradiction or embrace the contradiction. If the choice is "embrace," asymmetry will prevail which, if not resolved, can morph into paradox.

Integral to flow is the notion that discord caused by contradiction in social dynamics can be resolved by finding common ground among countervailing forces. Paradox, however, disrupts flow through the persistent interplay of contradictory forces that cannot be united. For instance, stability versus change or efficiency versus flexibility. In the world of social dynamics, paradox involves a tension between individual, group and setting factors that cannot be resolved. For example, a tension between power asymmetry and voluntary engagement in an organization when employees and managers are on different sides of a management issue.[13]

> *Put yourself in the position of an employee in an organization that has instituted a new program of risk management. You are strongly opposed to the program because you think it will add responsibility to an already oppressive workload. Participation is mandatory, but you would have preferred to be given the option of choice rather than being forced to participate. Because of power asymmetry—the imbalance of power between managers and employees—you feel compelled to participate in order to remain employed. Participation, however, does not mean forfeiture of your opinion toward the program. The contradiction between what the organization is mandating and your view of participation will be ongoing without resolution.*

Similarly, consider a counterintuitive situation in which an orga-
nization invests significant resources in improvement of its safety
practices only to have employees walk out in protest against prac-
tices they believe will get in the way of performing their jobs. The
contradiction between management intention to protect employees
from harm and employee perception that harm will be caused by
the actions of management will evolve into paradox if allowed to
persist without resolution.

In both situations, social dynamics of *cognition, group dynamics* and *orga-*
nizational behavior are out of alignment and will evolve into paradox if the
contradiction cannot be resolved. Paradoxes involve hardcore contradictions
in organizational life that must be resolved, or at least balanced, if organizations and leaders are to perform optimally. For this reason, paradox is the
third factor in a three-factor framework—flow, asymmetry and paradox—
that will test the proficiency of organizations and leaders in a widening risk
universe.

Risk Attitude

Among the more prominent risks facing organizations are external factors
which can wreak havoc on best-laid plans. Events such as a climate disaster, global pandemic or a cyberattack test the risk mettle of organizations
and people in them with a *risk attitude*—a disposition toward risk driven
by perception and a tendency to evaluate risk in a particular way.[14] Risk
attitudes vary among people. There are people who embrace risk, people who avoid risk and risk neutral people who gauge a situation before
responding. For some, risk attitude is a personal matter forged on the basis
of deeply held values and beliefs. For others, it is malleable—opinions
or beliefs, for example, that change with variation in situation or circumstance. For this reason, multiple risk attitudes are possible at any one time
in an organization with a given situation eliciting different attitudes from
personnel.

Risk attitudes play out in different ways depending on context and mental
state. Individuals in a state of *flow* could see risk in an exclusively positive
or negative way with cognition, group dynamics and institutional influence
in alignment creating consistency in thought and behavior. Individuals in a
state of *asymmetry* created by non-alignment could vacillate in their attitude

toward risk depending on situation and circumstance. Individuals in a state of *paradox* could embrace contradictory forces shaping their attitude toward risk and forego pursuit of flow through compartmentalization—a defense mechanism in which they mentally separate countervailing forces to avoid the discomfort of contradiction. In this state, simultaneously contradictory forces in social dynamics would persist over time and color risk attitude.

These contextual states contribute to an environment in which attitudes toward risk find expression in different ways as shown in Figure 8.3. To understand how flow, asymmetry and paradox in social dynamics influence risk attitude, the mental state specific to each is described for seven categories of people: *Embracers, Avoiders, Joiners, Conformists, Followers, Nonconformists and Compartmentalists*. Climate change is the medium for description of risk attitude.

Risk Attitude	Social Dynamics			
	Cognition	Social Forces	Group Dynamics	Inst. Influence
Flow	Aligned			
Embracer	Optimism—risk is manageable and must be addressed	Social norms endorse action in response to risk	Group values promote engagement with risk	Organizational culture fosters risk accountability
Avoider	Pessimism—risk is a threat and must be avoided	Social Norms are meaningless in relation to risk	Group values encourage avoidance of risk	Organizational risk culture is weak
Asymmetry	Non-aligned / Flexible			
Joiner	Group membership is a basis for self-identity and risk perception	Social norms promote action in response to risk	**Group values deter engagement with risk**	Organizational culture promotes risk engagement
Conformist	Social norms are a primary basis of risk perception	Norms relevant to risk are accepted and followed	Group values and norms promote engagement with risk	**Organizational risk culture is weak**
Follower	Organizational citizenship is important--org values drive risk perception	**Social norms are perceived as meaningless in relation to risk**	**Group values do not support engagement with risk**	Organizational risk culture is strong--requires accountability
Nonconformist	Risk perception driven by intuition differs from the majority of people	Social norms lack relevance to risk	Group values reflect ambivalence in relationship to risk	**Strong org risk culture-compliance is expected**
Paradox	Non-aligned / Inflexible			
Compartmentalist	**Risk perception driven by intuition**	Social norms are seen as irrelevant to risk	**Group norms drive perception of risk**	Organizational risk culture is weak

Figure 8.3 Typology of Risk Attitudes

Flow

- **Embracers** are optimistic about risk. Their natural reaction when faced with a threat is to act. They believe climate change is capable of being managed through collective effort. They seek affiliation with climate change advocacy groups and organizations with a strong risk culture. Knowing what an organization stands for and its position on climate change are important factors in affiliation.
- **Avoiders** are risk averse. Their tendency when facing a threat is to avoid the problem altogether. Social norms encouraging engagement with risk are meaningless. Avoiders identify with climate deniers, and affiliation is sought with groups that are skeptical about climate change. Organizational culture is not a driving force in risk attitude for Avoiders. They resist participation in organizational efforts to mitigate risk because they perceive such efforts as getting in the way of their job or as a challenge to their autonomy.

Asymmetry

- **Joiners** take meaning through group affiliation. Group norms influence risk perception and behavior. When social norms and organizational policy for climate action come into conflict with group norms, a condition of non-alignment is realized. The resulting tension may cause feelings of anxiety which, if not resolved, could become harmful. Joiners achieve a sense of belonging through conformity to group norms about climate change but face the possibility of rejection from people outside the group subscribing to different beliefs.
- **Conformists** see social norms as a binding force in risk perception. Social policy and the behavior of others exert a strong influence on their feelings about climate change. They seek affiliation with like-minded people in climate action groups and are shocked and disappointed by the lack of a climate action policy in the organization of their employ. They are not willing to sit quietly while their organization considers the merits of a climate action strategy. They want action in the form of an ESG framework that aligns their organization with social policy.
- **Followers** take much of their orientation toward risk from organizations—particularly those in which they work and look to for value.

Followers prefer to work in organizations with a culture that matches their values and beliefs whether they be pro- or anti-climate action. Loyalty is an important part of the Follower-organization relationship when personal and organizational values match. The fly in the ointment for a Follower in an organization with a strong commitment to climate action would be workgroup resistance to company policy and a negative reaction among friends to the organization's position on climate action.

■ ***Nonconformists*** define risk through the lens of intuition. They think for themselves and do not choose to conform to social or cultural norms which they view as constrictive and limiting. Nonconformists are more likely to think outside of the box and come up with new ideas— a tendency which could be of great value to an organization but also a source of consternation. In the arena of climate change, Nonconformists are a wild card—capable of forging a viewpoint that may or may not be consistent with norms at the societal, group or organizational level. These norms are largely irrelevant. What matters most is personal belief.

Paradox

■ ***Compartmentalists*** view risk in mutually exclusive ways depending on circumstance and situation. In interaction with members of a social group holding a negative view of climate change, they may express support for group sentiment. In the employ of an organization with a strong risk culture and climate action commitment, they may suppress personal values and beliefs and support company policy. Compartmentalists are masters of paradox. They put risk in compartments and move between compartments as situations and circumstances dictate.

The distinguishing feature of risk attitudes is disposition toward change. The risk attitudes of individuals in a state of *Flow* and *Asymmetry* are subject to change. Access to new information, a shift in group membership, changing patterns of organizational behavior, or the emergence of new social norms— all can trigger a shift in risk attitude. The risk attitude of *Compartmentalists*, however, is different. Essentially, it is an amalgam of multiple risk attitudes that are simultaneously contradictory and impervious to change.

Navigating the Storm

Varying attitudes toward risk pose a significant challenge to organizations and leaders. The enormity of this challenge can be understood in the spectrum of risk attitudes shown in Figure 8.4.[15] The same situation will elicit different attitudes from different people depending on how they perceive risk. And because attitude drives behavior, different people will exhibit different responses to the same situation as a result of their differing risk attitudes. What one person may see as a threat another will see as an opportunity. What one person may hold as a fixed attitude toward risk, another may hold as fluid depending on the situation. What for one person may be an attitude shaped by group membership, for another would be an attitude shaped by intuition.

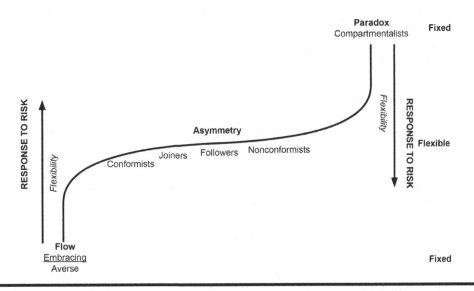

Figure 8.4 Risk Attitude Spectrum. Adapted from Hillson, D. and Murray-Webster, R. Understanding and Managing Risk Attitude (2nd Edition). Routledge: Oxfordshire, UK, 2007.

Differing risk attitudes among employees can derail an organization's risk strategy if not effectively managed. Mismanaged risk attitudes can lead to misunderstanding and confusion among employees who interpret risk differently. It can impede decision-making as employees with different attitudes struggle to understand each other. And it can squander overall risk strategy if leaders and employees are not on the same page. Balancing diverse attitudes into a unified risk strategy can be tricky for leaders. How this can be accomplished in a risk intelligent organization is the focus of the next chapter.

Notes

1. Redd, W. "The Wreck of the Andrea Gail and the 'Perfect Storm' That Caused It." July 5, 2018. https://allthatsinteresting.com/andrea-gail.
2. Osmond, C. "Perfect Storm—Idiom, Origin & Meaning." *Grammarist*, January 12, 2024.
3. Field, A. "What Caused the Great Recession? Understanding the Key Factors That Led to One of the Worst Economic Downturns in US History." *Business Insider*, August 8, 2022.
4. Britannica. "Hurricane Katrina/ Deaths, Damage & Facts." https://www.britannica.com/event/Hurricane-Katrina.
5. Singh, S., McNab, C., Olson, R., Bristol, N., Nolan, C., Bergstrom, E. et al. "How an Outbreak Became a Pandemic: A Chronological Analysis of Crucial Junctures and International Obligations in the Early Months of the COVID-19 Pandemic." *The Lancet*, December 4, 2021.
6. Lippi, G., Sanchis-Gomar, F., and Henry, B. "Coronavirus Disease 2019 (COVID-19): The Portrait of a Perfect Storm." *NIH*, April 8, 2020.
7. Jetten, J., Bentley, S., Crimston, C., and Haslam, S. "COVID-19 and Social Psychological Research: A Silver Lining." *Asian Journal of Social Psychology*, McKinsey (March 24, 2021).
8. Congdon, M. "Finding Flow: The Point Where Process Meets Performance." *Forbes*, February 5, 2024.
9. Higgins, R., Liou, G., Maurenbrecher, S., Poppensieker, T., and White, O. "Strengthening Institutional Risk and Integrity Culture." *McKinsey & Company*, November 2, 2020.
10. Higgins, R., Liou, G., Maurenbrecher, S., Poppensieker, T., and White, O. "Strengthening Institutional Risk and Integrity Culture." *McKinsey & Company*, November 2, 2020.
11. Mcleod, S. "What Is Cognitive Dissonance Theory?" *Simply Psychology*, October 24, 2023.
12. Smith, W. and Lewis, M. "Toward a Theory of Paradox: A Dynamic Equilibrium Theory of Organizing." *Academy of Management Review*, 36 (2), (2011), pp. 381–403.
13. Cao, N. and Cheung, S. "The Paradox of Power Asymmetry and Voluntary Participation in Construction Dispute Mediation." Chapter in *Construction Dispute Research Expanded*, January 25, 2024.
14. Hillson, D. and Murray-Webster, R. *Understanding and Managing Risk Attitude*, 2nd ed. Oxford: Routledge, 2007.
15. Figure 8.4 is adapted from a graphic representing the concept of *risk attitude spectrum* created by David Hillson and Ruth Murray-Webster and published in *Understanding and Managing Risk Attitude,* 2nd ed. Oxford: Routledge, 2007.

LEADING AND MANAGING RISK

Part III

Chapter 9

Building a Risk Intelligent Organization

Gauging risk and building a risk intelligent organization is not rocket science. It is deceptively simple—a matter of common sense, logic and, most of all, commitment.

Richard Alfred, Author and Professor,
University of Michigan

In the wake of the pandemic, organizations invested heavily in controls to manage risk. While essential for avoiding damaging oversights and maintaining organizational effectiveness, internal controls are not sufficient to shield organizations from harm. Most risk incidents can be traced back to a cultural root cause embedded in the attitudes and behavior of people. Crises emerge and deepen when organizations neglect to manage their first line of defense against risk—employees with insights into operations and systems that put them in a position to identify vulnerabilities.

What Is Risk Culture?

Risk culture encompasses the collective knowledge, attitudes and understanding about risk shared by people with common purpose in an organization.[1] It is a key indicator of how widely an organization's risk management policies and practices have been adopted. Unlike traditional risk management which focuses on structure and processes, risk culture emphasizes

DOI: 10.4324/9781003335658-12

the human decisions that drive operations. It is not the province of leaderrs and risk managers, but of people in every part of the organization. In a *risk intelligent culture*, everyone understands the organization's approach to risk, takes personal responsibility in managing it, and encourages others to follow their example.[2] Key elements of a robust risk culture are a clear risk strategy, commitment to information sharing across the organization, rapid response to threats, role-modeling of desired behavior, and incentives to think about risk in terms of overall organizational health.[3]

Research has shown that leaders play a critical role in developing and managing risk culture in industry-leading firms.[4] Leaders who view risk more broadly than compliance anticipate challenges better, seize opportunities faster and emerge from setbacks stronger. They ask tough questions about their organizations' approach to risk management and do not accept soft answers. What drives how we manage risk? Who is responsible for risk? Is risk information widely shared with our employees? What is more important—keeping our operations moving or protecting the organization from risk? Do we devote more resources to internal controls or to building a human-centered risk culture?

Questions of this type need to be asked and answered by leaders in every organization. Get a pencil and rate your organization.

Who is *most important* in shaping the risk strategy of your organization?

Board of directors ** Risk professionals ** Executive officers ** Employees

Does your organization have a clear and coherent strategy for managing risk?

No   *   *   Strategy in place, but unclear   *   *   Yes

Are warning signs of risk broadly shared within your organization?

No   *   *   Don't know   *   *   To some extent   *   *   Broadly shared

Do employees have a clear and broadly shared understanding of risks facing your organization?

No   *   *   Don't know   *   *   To some extent   *   *   Clear and broadly shared

Are employees encouraged to respond proactively to situations involving risk?

No   *   *   Depends on the situation   *   *   Yes, that is expected

Do employees have the authority to take timely action in response to risk without going through managers?

No   *   *   Depends on the situation   *   *   Yes

Do people in your organization believe it is insulated from risk because of its leadership, superior market position or resources?

Yes   *   *   No opinion   *   *   No

Are the risk attitudes of employees aligned with your organization's overall risk strategy?

No   *   *   Don't know   *   *   Yes

If your marks fall to the left, your organization may lack a coherent risk strategy or it may be devoting more resources to internal controls than to establishing a strong risk culture. When organizations neglect to develop a robust risk culture, they are vulnerable to potentially crippling consequences hindering the achievement of both operational and strategic goals.

Sources and Causes of Failure

Risk culture failures can range from the relatively mundane, such as a lapse in a routine safety procedure, to the catastrophic such as a gas pipeline explosion or 100-year flood. Whether triggered by an internal problem or an external event, risk culture failures often result from a long-standing cultural weakness or weaknesses that have been incubating over time. Common causes of risk culture failure identified by *GRCxperts Enterprise Solutions*, a company specializing in governance and risk management, include:[5]

Weak governance Inadequate oversight and poor decision-making leading to strategic errors, reduced employee morale and loss of trust. When governance is weak, organizations lack the foundation to effectively manage risk.	**Overemphasis on efficiency** An overemphasis on efficiency causing organizations to cut corners and overlook potential risks. Operational efficiency is not a substitute for robust risk assessment and management.
Undeliverable strategies When organizations pursue strategies that are unrealistic or unachievable, employee confidence can take a hit and culture failure is a possible outcome.	**Limited executive experience** Lack of experienced leadership resulting in poor decision-making. Executives who don't fully understand the nature and scope of risks their organization is facing are prone to flawed choices
Toxic risk culture A toxic culture stifles innovation, reduces engagement and promotes irresponsible behavior. Toxic environments are psychologically unsafe and limit employee engagement with risk.	**Lack of transparency** When there is a lack of clear communication and openness about risk and management strategy, employees are hindered from understanding and acting on risk.
Underdeveloped ERM programs Organizations with an immature ERM program lack the tools, processes and culture needed for effective risk management. This can lead to haphazard decision-making and inability to respond to risks proactively.	**Irresponsible risk-taking** Risk-taking without adequate risk assessment can have devastating consequences. From financial losses to reputational harm, heedless risk-taking undermines risk management and weakens cultural bonds.

Weak governance. In poorly governed organizations, responsibility and accountability are often misaligned—everyone is responsible, but no one is accountable. When there is a disconnect between responsibility and accountability, roles and expectations are not clearly defined—a circumstance which can lead to dereliction of responsibility for risk. Lack of accountability is a clear sign of a *toxic culture* which can inhibit employee participation in risk strategy.[6] Employees feeling unheard and undervalued in a culture that doesn't value open communication may fulfill their job tasks but pass on responsibility for risk. *Lack of transparency* is among the most insidious of risk management failures.[7] When communication channels are unclear or information is kept under wraps, the cost is a loss of faith in leaders and the organization. Lacking information about risk and its relationship to their work, employees may disengage from an organization's strategic thrust and fail to take responsibility for risk.

Operational efficiency is crucial for the success of any organization. An overemphasis on efficiency, however, can lead to cutting corners—a recipe for risk management failure. When processes are subjected to excessive streamlining, important checks may be skipped allowing risks to go undetected or unmanaged. Leaders in pursuit of efficiency may fail to invest in risk management technologies and employee training programs, considering them to be costs rather than long-term investments.[8] Among the casualties of operational efficiency are *ERM programs* which are easy targets of cost-cutting initiatives.[9] If ERM is seen as a compliance exercise, its focus may be reduced to operational risk in contrast to the bigger picture of strategic risk. A consequence could be *irresponsible risk-taking*—taking risks without adequate assessment of conditions in the environment. Imprudent risk behavior, if allowed to spread without checks and balances, can render an organization vulnerable to costly mistakes and severly damage its brand and image.

Risk management failures often occur on the watch of *leaders with limited risk experience.* Uninformed leaders may fail to recognize early warning signs or make decisions without fully considering potential hazards. Worse yet, they may downplay or even deny the existence of hazards which may heighten vulnerability to risk. Short-term gains without adequate assessment may be favored over long-term strategy—a circumstance that could result in suboptimal strategic choices.

Snapshots of Risk Culture Failure

Snapshots of risk culture in four organizations within my realm of experience are presented below. Each is an example of what can happen when risk is mismanaged because of culture failure. As you read the snapshots, put yourself in the position of an employee and consider your inclination to engage with risk.

College A: Operational Efficiency by Fiat

The CFO in this urban college was the de facto president. The operating budget reposed in his head—unpublished and invisible to all employees including executive officers. All major expenditures were subject to CFO approval toward a goal of building financial reserves through operating efficiency. Travel funds were

tightly controlled as were expenditures for professional development, capital equipment and part-time instruction. Risk management was viewed as an unnecessary cost in an institution deemed
impervious to risk. A false xsense of security pervaded the institution. The CFO was in charge of the purse strings and had the
resources necessary to handle any and all risks.

College B: The C-Suite Bubble

This southeastern college was led by a long-serving president who
viewed executive office as the bastion of a privileged few. Authority
and power were concentrated in the hands of a few battle-hard-
ened lieutenants who controlled management functions throughout
the institution. The president held an imperial view of executive
office. Strategic matters and critical information were the province
of executives and not shared beyond the C-Suite. Decision-making
was insular with less-than-optimal choices made because of a lack
of diverse perspectives. The disconnect between C-Suite executives
and employees fanned resentment and created a culture of disengagement. In the words of an employee: "The president and executive team make all of the decisions. They do not listen and do not
know what is going on in the trenches. Why get involved when
you will not be heard and your effort will not be valued?"

College C: The Inconvenience of Transparency

This small midwestern college was led by a long-serving baronial
president who viewed resources and information as his personal
preserve. Decision-making was top-down and a chunk of the
College budget remained under his direct control unbeknownst
to staff. The president was a power broker. His management style
was old school and paternalistic. He operated on a need-to-know
basis with little regard for transparency. "If I think you need to
know something, I will tell you—otherwise go about your work."
Staff became accustomed to the lack of transparency—it was how
the president did business. If problems arose, the president would
shield the institution from harm. There was no need to engage
with risk. Everything was taken care of. On the president's watch,
the college was impervious to harm.

College D: Leadership Gone Astray

This midwestern college rapidly evolved from a single campus institution to a multi-campus system. Its culture was rooted in tradition nurtured and maintained by long-serving, change- resistant faculty. In the mid-1970s, a new CEO came on board and immediately initiated a process of organizational change based on an administrative model he had used in the institution of his previous employ. Long-standing cultural norms were ignored, traditional ways of doing business were altered, and key staff were replaced as part of a management restructuring. The CEO quickly became the enemy of tradition. A culture of hostility and resistance took hold and the institution turned in on itself. Forward progress stopped and its risk focus shifted from external challenges to internal dynamics. The CEO became the face of risk. Two years after taking office he was on his way out.

When culture fails, risk management can go downstream quickly. Risk management in savvy organizations is a holistic process encompassing everything from tone at the top to processes at the operational level that enhance their ability to absorb shocks.[10] Organizations that adopt a holistic approach to risk management tend to be more resilient, adaptable and strategically aligned leading to better overall outcomes than their more passive counterparts.

Strong and Weak Risk Cultures

Organizations with a strong risk culture have a strategic understanding of risk and have developed three interdependent components critical to their ability to manage risk: risk mindsets, risk practices and contributing behaviors.[11] Risk mindsets are the assumptions about risk that individuals hold within an organization, risk practices are the day-to-day actions that determine the effectiveness of risk management, and contributing behaviors are the collective actions that give rise to risk attitude.[12] Management consulting firms *McKinsey & Company* and *Deloitte* have identified ten dimensions of risk culture which can be used to gauge the strength of an organization's approach to risk:[13]

■ ***Insight:*** understanding of risks present in the industry

- ***Awareness:*** understanding of an organization's exposure and vulnerability to risk
- ***Responsiveness:*** speed of reaction to threats
- ***Communication:*** the degree to which warning signs of external and internal risks are shared
- ***Openness:*** the extent to which management and employees exchange bad news or learning from mistakes
- ***Cognizance:*** cognizance of the appropriateness and accuracy of others' attitudes and actions toward risk
- ***Tolerance:*** understanding of risk appetite and its linkage to strategy and decision-making
- ***Alignment:*** alignment of individuals' risk attitudes to the overall risk strategy of the organization
- ***Accountability:*** acknowledgment and acceptance of responsibility for identification, assessment and reporting of risk
- ***Modeling:*** understanding the importance of modeling appropriate behavior in situations involving risk

Cultural Differences

Differences between organizations that acknowledge and act on risk and those that do not are stark. Consider, for example, two manufacturing companies facing similar industry risks and sharing a similar appetite for risk. The first overhauled internal controls and systems coming out of the pandemic, but considered this step to be piecemeal in response to risk.[14] It understood the importance of people and culture and worked diligently to build a culture that valued anticipation and adaptation to changing conditions. This involved instilling a common set of values among employees that shaped how they handled threats. Employees were expected to identify and report risks upon observation, to share information with coworkers and managers and to respond proactively—for example, to halt production upon noticing a violation that could compromise safety. The risk posture of this company boiled down to a declaration of war against risk: "If we see it, identify it, report it, and figure out its intensity and scope, we'll manage and overcome it."

The second company had a defensive and reactive culture—one focused more on staying out of trouble and making sure all compliance boxes were checked.[15] It put its faith in internal controls and managers who were content to keep production moving without rocking the boat. Leaders and managers were not interested in knowing what they didn't know and adopted a philosophy that no news is good news. They ignored potential threats because managing them would demand time and attention that might affect production. This company's stance was: "Let's keep moving until something gets in our way, because we have the talent and resources to overcome challenges."

The 2007 subprime mortgage crisis is an excellent example of the peril of reckless neglect. Some financial institutions were led by executives who rejected models which accurately predicted the severity of conditions to come.[16] They knew that if the models were correct, they would experience challenges they were not equipped to handle. They looked past the models in the hope that the risk would crest and fall before the model's estimates came true. Even as the crisis unfolded, they continued to believe they were safer than they really were. In the end, their refusal to acknowledge and address risk left their institutions vulnerable to catastrophe.

In mid-career I worked with a college that exhibited a similar mindset, but for reason of lack of awareness. The college occupied an expensive parcel of land in the center of a city experiencing explosive growth. Its personnel were entrenched in the ambiance of an attractive campus and insulated from change by an elitist culture and established way of doing business. A deep sense of collective satisfaction prevailed that obscured awareness of the growth happening around them. Growth was a double-edged sword of opportunity and risk—opportunity in the form resources that would be forthcoming through economic development and risk in the form of competitors poised to grab enrollment and resources if the college failed to change with the times. Analytically speaking, it didn't take much to see what was happening and what it would mean for the college.

> *The college was surrounded by a ring of like-type institutions poised to compete for its enrollment if it failed to extend its operations to areas of projected growth. The inevitability of growth was hardly a secret. Development was everywhere to be seen—business expansion, commercial and residential construction, new malls and highways, airport expansion and an outer-belt under construction. If the growth projections held true, the logistics of work would change to accommodate more of everything. More learners, more facilities, more equipment and more work. Satellite campuses would be built to absorb new learners in areas of rapid growth—an occurrence that would dramatically alter workload and delivery of instruction. Instructors accustomed to teaching in one location*

would be rotated among multiple campuses which for some would mean longer travel distances to work. Beyond the discomfort of rotation among campuses, would be expansion of teaching loads to accommodate additional learners—a red flag for instructors in an established culture.

Faculty and staff could not get their arms around the specter of change that would be part of growth so they looked past the growth. Even with growing evidence of physical changes in the service region and graphic evidence of the potential for enrollment loss to competitors instructors resisted proposals to extend campus operations. It took executive action from college leaders and the board of trustees to move the college on a path of expansion.

The Power of Transparency

Organizations that are confident in their ability to manage transparency are more likely to share information that signals a risk event and empower personnel to act before it becomes a crisis. They focus on sources of risk and encourage staff to be vigilant as a precursor to action. In the subprime mortgage crisis and college planning examples above, leaders in a strong risk culture would have broadly shared information about emerging conditions and the peril of standing still. They would have detailed the impact of unanswered risk on the organization, actions necessary to head off a potential crisis, and mobilized personnel to action. Instead, they operated in reverse gear. Warning signs of risk were not shared, leaders did not develop or communicate a clear risk strategy, and personnel neglected responsibility for risk. The risk culture in these organizations was marked by:[17]

- disengagement because of lack of understanding and exposure to risk
- reluctance to pass on bad news to superiors
- apathy due to bad faith or a feeling of powerlessness
- lack of confidence in management
- misalignment between individual risk attitudes and organizational risk strategy

Separating organizations with strong and weak risk cultures is the understanding leaders and employees have of risk. In a strong risk culture, employees across the organization grasp the risk landscape. They understand the nature of risk and take responsibility for managing it in their daily activities. This mindset enables them to make informed risk decisions and encourages others to do the same. In weak cultures, employees lack understanding of risk due to a lack of clear guidelines and poor communication—a deficit not of their making but of leader neglect.

Gauging Risk Culture

Risk culture assessments provide critical information about an organization's approach to risk and the attitudes and behavior of employees toward risk. They are not a compliance exercise—their value lies in the insights they provide into an organization's risk management strategy:

- Is the organization risk tolerant or risk-averse?
- Do leaders and employees embrace common purpose and values related to risk?
- Is information about risk widely shared?
- When, how and to whom are risks communicated?
- Do employees take personal responsibility for managing risk?
- Are employees empowered to act on risk?

Management consulting firms and risk professionals have designed approaches to assessment of risk culture based on the attitudes of people and organizational behavior in five dimensions of risk: ***Synergy***, ***Awareness***, ***Transparency***, ***Responsiveness*** and ***Accountability***.[18] These dimensions are bidirectional as they are both the behavioral product of culture and structural properties on which culture is built. Synergy, for example, is an attribute of risk culture predisposing individuals to collaboration in order to achieve an outcome which cannot be achieved alone. When consistently practiced by individuals, it is simultaneously a product of, and contributor to, an organization's risk culture.

Risk Culture Framework

Using models developed by *McKinsey & Company* and *Deloitte*, a multi-dimensional Risk Culture Framework (RCF) can be crafted for risk culture assessment.[19] The RCF consists of 14 risk culture indicators aligned with five risk culture dimensions as presented in Figure 9.1.

Figure 9.1   Risk Culture Framework

Synergy is a function of common purpose—people coming together to achieve a result greater than the sum of their individual efforts. Employees are the first line of defense against risk. The extent to which they collectively understand an organization's approach to risk, adopt its risk management policies and take responsibility for managing risk contribute in important ways to its risk culture. Indicators of Synergy are *common purpose and values, universal adoption of risk strategy* and *collective responsibility for risk management.* The importance of Synergy is self-evident as described by Levy, Lamarre and Twining in *Taking Control of Organizational Risk Culture* and illustrated in the actions of a global investment bank in the aftermath of the 2008 financial crisis:[20]

Recognizing the importance of risk culture in preventing future failures, the bank developed a comprehensive risk strategy that was communicated transparently across the organization. This strategy outlined the bank's risk appetite, risk tolerance, and risk management principles. The senior leadership team visibly aligned and engaged around this strategy and urged employees to adopt the strategy and to share information and insights related to risk. Employees were encouraged to take responsibility for risk, to raise red flags promptly when they identified potential risks, and to model appropriate behavior in response to risk. The bank's commitment to synergy paid off. It prevented catastrophic failures going forward and enhanced the overall resilience of the institution.

Awareness is a measure of risk perception among people in an organization. A risk-aware organization interprets risk in ways that are clear to all employees and promotes a shared understanding of risk. Informed employees are conversant with risk and have insight into actual and potential risks facing the organization. Indicators of Awareness are *understanding of risk* and *insight into potential risks*. The transformation of a global bank after a major financial scandal highlights the importance of awareness:[21]

Suffering reputational damage from a scandal involving fraudulent accounts, the bank completely revamped its risk culture. It actively sought feedback from employees at all levels and encouraged open communication channels, allowing staff to voice concerns and share insights related to risk management. To build awareness of actual and potential risks, it conducted regular risk training programs for employees covering risk concepts, causes and consequences, best practices, and practical scenarios. The bank integrated aspects of governance and compliance to improve risk awareness across different functions and established explicit lines of authority to ensure that employees understood their roles and responsibilities in managing risk.

Transparency in the context of risk culture refers to the openness and precision with which risks are identified, communicated and reported.[22] Indicators of Transparency are *Openness*, *Communication* and *Clarity*. The best cultures actively seek information and insight into risk through procedures, detailed risk reporting and shared authority to communicate potential issues. Transparent communication ensures that everyone understands risks the organization faces, their potential impact and strategies to mitigate them. In a strong risk culture, employees openly discuss and share information about risk and learn from mistakes.

> *When Mary Barra became CEO of General Motors in 2014, she had no idea that her first order of business would be to preside over a faulty ignition switch problem that had festered in the organization since as early as 2004. In 2005, the company's engineers met to discuss the problem and decided against a fix because it would take too long and cost too much. The issue was not elevated to the highest levels of the company......Shortly after her appointment, Barra was called before the Senate to testify. The Senate found that the faulty ignition switch in GM cars had significant repercussions and constituted a breach of trust with the American public. The company issued 84 recalls involving 30.4 million vehicles in Barra's first year, and enacted policies to encourage a "speak up" culture in which workers reported problems directly upon encountering them.[23]*

Responsiveness is a measure of an organization's ability to swiftly and effectively address risks as they arise. It encompasses timely action, adaptability and open dialogue. Organizations with a strong risk culture adjust strategy and processes based on changing risk landscapes and swiftly adapt to new information or unexpected threats. Open dialogue about risk is encouraged among employees, and they are expected to report risks directly upon encountering them. Indicators of Responsiveness are *Adaptability, Dialogue* and *Speed of Response*.

> *Imagine an organization where employees promptly report suspicious activities or potential risks they encounter. When they notice an anomaly, it is immediately elevated to higher levels in the organization. The Swiss electricity network has integrated risk management into the daily lives of all employees by fostering a culture where risk awareness is pervasive, efforts toward identification and assessment are unremitting, and reporting is instantaneous.[24] Rather than limiting risk to a specific department, Swissgrid focuses on managing a wide range of risks, and employees are encouraged to approach risk from a holistic perspective. Employees are educated about risks and their potential consequences, how to assess and*

report them and how to respond to them. Safety-related incidents and findings are analyzed and lessons learned are integrated into ongoing training and development.

Accountability in risk culture refers to the responsibility that individuals have for managing and mitigating risks. Employees understand that risk management is everyone's duty and there are consequences for action (and inaction) related to risk. Training ensures that employees understand risk policies and procedures and active oversight ensures compliance with risk guidelines. Individuals are encouraged to question the assumptions, decisions and actions of others, including authority figures. They model appropriate behavior and proactively involve others. Indicators of Accountability are *Individual Responsibility, Willingness to Challenge Others* and *Modeling Behavior.* An exemplar of accountability is Swissgrid, Switzerland's network energy operator. As described by Kaplan and Mikes in "Enterprise Risk Management in a Digital Age" (2018):[25]

> *Swissgrid uses two parallel management processes to identify and mitigate strategic and external risks. For each business unit, it convenes recurring and interactive risk workshops. Employees review previously and newly identified risks, evaluate each risk using structured scales, and set priorities for resources and actions that reduce their likelihood and impact. It supplements these meetings with a low-threshold issue-reporting app that all employees carry. This app makes it easy for employees to report, anonymously if they wish, any issue that could adversely affect corporate strategy and operations. Employees, in less than a minute, can submit a message that is geo-tagged, date-stamped, and with an option to attach a photograph of a potentially dangerous situation. Employees can use natural language, not risk management jargon, and are not required to classify or set a priority for the problems they report.*

Strengthening Risk Culture

Diagnostic surveys and interviews with employees are useful tools for measuring an organization's risk culture. Survey results and interview findings can be analyzed on a dimension-by-dimension basis to illustrate the risk culture challenges an organization faces and interventions necessary to address the causes of culture weakness. A hypothetical example follows of the Risk Culture Framework and how it can be used to strengthen risk culture.[26]

COVID-19 and the Food Service Industry

The food service industry was among the hardest hit industries during the pandemic. According to Statista, the food services industry lost $130 billion in revenue between March and October 2020 as shelter-in-place orders and limits on capacity curbed their ability to serve people.[27] This translated into a loss of 2.1 million jobs and the closure of an estimated 110,000 restaurants either permanently or long term.[28] Those that survived did so largely on takeout, outdoor dining options and indoor dining with limited capacity—strategies that decimated their operating base and revenue.

> Two restaurants in a popular suburban mall were blindsided and deeply impacted by the pandemic. Each had an established customer base and steady revenue stream leading up to the pandemic. Their pandemic experience, however, was markedly different. One restaurant closed permanently and the other continued to operate although with limited capacity. Both restaurants used the Risk Culture Framework prior to the pandemic to assess their risk culture. Three phases of operation were assessed:
>
> - *customer-facing operations:* customer service, waitstaff training, scheduling and communication
> - *the customer experience:* customer satisfaction and staff alignment with business goals
> - *employee morale:* transparency, manager-employee relations, openness of communication and involvement in decision-making
>
> Each restaurant displayed relative strengths on the RCF on dimensions of Awareness (understanding of risk) and Responsiveness (speed of response). Differences were noted, however, on dimensions of Synergy (common purpose and commitment), Transparency (openness and communication) and Accountability (individual responsibility). One factor, in particular, separated them as revealed in interviews with staff: *employee morale and engagement with risk.* The failed restaurant was part of a national chain with corporate offices in a distant state. It was described

by employees as having a toxic work culture. Management was centralized and decision-making was top-down leaving employees with little or no voice. Risk was seen as the province of risk professionals in the corporate office and as getting in the way of work in a high-pressure environment. The successful restaurant was locally owned and operated and staffed by employees committed to a business model of common purpose and open communication. Information about risk was widely shared and employees were expected to elevate risk issues to a higher level directly upon encountering them. Their role and responsibility in risk management was clear, and they were empowered to act in situations where immediate action was necessary. Everyone had a stake in the business, and risk was everyone's responsibility.

Given obvious risk culture differences between the restaurants, it is no surprise that their pandemic experience was markedly different. One laid off all of its employees and ceased operations while the other continued to operate. The interventions necessary to save the failed restaurant are self-evident:

1. **Build a sense of common purpose** so that leaders and employees are on the same page with risk.
2. **Develop and present a coherent approach to risk and a clear risk strategy** to ensure that everyone understands the organization's risk objectives and tolerance.
3. **Share information about risk widely throughout the organization** to remove the burden of risk from one department and enhance employee understanding and engagement.
4. **Open channels of communication** to foster employee participation in risk management and engage them in early detection.
5. **Cultivate employee understanding of their role and responsibility in risk management** to help them understand how their actions impact the organization's risk profile and to integrate risk management into their work and decision-making.
6. **Empower employees to report and act on risk** to tap into their insights and expertise and encourage them to take ownership of the risks they encounter.

The good news for organizations is that assessment of risk culture using an instrument and structured interviews is not rocket science. Weaknesses are readily apparent and actions that can be taken to strengthen culture are obvious. The difficulty is in the interventions—overcoming resistance and making corrective actions work. Some organizations will pursue and successfully implement change to reduce their vulnerability to risk. Others will continue to be vulnerable as an unavoidable part of their DNA.[29] It is inconceivable, for example, that a hospital can avoid risk associated with complex surgeries or that a technology company can avoid new product risk. Organizations choosing to forego efforts to fortify their risk culture will pay a price of continuing vulnerability to self-inflicted wounds whether they be insider threats, over-reliance on internal controls, reputational harm or issues related to cybersecurity.

Risk Management to Risk Intelligence

Risk intelligence—a prominent feature of forward-thinking organizations—is the new frontier of risk management. In the words of Columbia University professor Leo Tillman, risk intelligent organizations think holistically about risk and uncertainty, speak a common risk language and effectively use forward-looking concepts and tools in making decisions about risk.[30] These organizations engage people throughout the enterprise in managing risk. Everyone understands the organization's approach to risk, takes personal responsibility to manage it in everything they do and encourages others to follow their example. The difference between a *risk culture* and *risk intelligent culture* is one of awareness. Employees in a risk culture are generally aware of the risks their organization faces. In a risk intelligent culture, their awareness, understanding and attitude toward risk enable them to anticipate risk and make incisive and informed decisions.[31]

Risk intelligence is a strategic imperative. It equips organizations with new ways of seeing the future amidst the anxiety and uncertainty of a post-pandemic world. In Tillman's conception:[32]

> *Within organizations, a desire for new value propositions and broader social relevance is set against a backdrop of a changing risk universe. Climate change is exacting a fearsome toll on quality of life as global warming threatens health and well-being. A tele-everything world has emerged where digital connections play a*

crucial role in work, education, healthcare and social interactions.
Economic disparities are widening as tech savvy individuals benefit
from technological advances and workers are displaced from jobs
by automation. Social stability, rational deliberation, and evidence-
based policy making are at risk as authoritarians and polarized
groups engage in information warfare and spread misinformation.

These trends make risk a kaleidoscope of events, conditions, perceptions
and emotions that bring into question the effectiveness of internal controls.
Beyond policies and procedures, it is entirely possible that organizations
may be better off investing in their human capabilities—strong leadership
and a culture where open communication is encouraged, bearers of unwelcome news are rewarded, and everyone is responsible for management
of risk.[33] Employees in risk intelligent organizations have capabilities that
extend beyond internal controls. They bring a human touch to risk identification and assessment, and they understand risk protocols and management processes. They also have the analytical and technological capability
to "connect the dots" within a holistic framework that lends itself to effective
action.[34]

Risk management is an opportunity to unify vision, strategy, communication and organizational development. When organizations holistically unite
critical activities in a risk intelligent enterprise, they position themselves to
navigate the complexity and uncertainty surrounding them. They envision
the environment differently out of which emerges new ways of thinking
about leadership—the subject of the closing chapter in this book.

Notes

1. Risk Culture. "Institute of Risk Management." https://www.theirm.org/what-we
   -say/thought- leadership. Retrieved: February 2, 2024.
2. Cultivating a Risk Intelligent Culture: Understand, Measure, Strengthen and
   Report. "Deloitte." https://www2.deloitte.com/content/dam/Deloitte/us/Doc.
   Retrieved: February 6, 2024.
3. Levy, C., Lamarre, E. and Twining, J. *Taking Control of Organizational Risk
   Culture.* New York: McKinsey & Company, Report Number 16. February, 2010.
       Confidential Working Paper Number 16, *Taking Control of Organizational
   Risk Culture*, authored by McKinsey & Company risk experts Cindy Levy, Eric
   Lamarre and James Twining served as an important source of information

about risk culture and management throughout the chapter. It is cited on a continuing basis when specific elements of information presented in chapter narrative relate directly to content in Working Paper 16.

4. Levy, C., Lamarre, E. and Twining, J. *Taking Control of Organizational Risk Culture.* New York: McKinsey & Company, Report Number 16. February, 2010.

5. GRCxperts Enterprise Solutions. *8 Common Risk Management Failure and How to Avoid Them.* GRCxperts Enterprise Solutions, Dubai, October 27, 2023. Retrieved: February 11, 2023.

6. Clark, T. "The Hazards of a 'Nice' Company Culture." *Harvard Business Review.* June 25 2021.

7. Levy, C., Lamarre, E, and Twining, J. *Taking Control of Organizational Risk Culture.* New York: McKinsey & Company, Report Number 16. February, 2010.

8. GRCxperts Enterprise Solutions. *8 Common Risk Management Failure and How to Avoid Them.* GRCxperts Enterprise Solutions, October 27, 2023.

9. GRCxperts Enterprise Solutions. *8 Common Risk Management Failure and How to Avoid Them.* GRCxperts Enterprise Solutions, October 27, 2023.

10. Gius, D., Mieszala, J-C., Panayiotou, E., and Poppensieker, T. "Value and Resilience Through Better Risk Management." *McKinsey & Company,* October 1, 2018.

11. Higgins, R., Liou, G., Maurenbrecher, S., Poppensieker, T., and White, O. "Strengthening Institutional Risk and Integrity Culture." *McKinsey & Company,* November 2, 2020.

12. Higgins, R., Liou, G., Maurenbrecher, S., Poppensieker, T., and White, O. "Strengthening Institutional Risk and Integrity Culture." *McKinsey & Company,* November 2, 2020.

13. Higgins, R., Liou, G., Maurenbrecher, S., Poppensieker, T., and White, O. "Strengthening Institutional Risk and Integrity Culture." *McKinsey & Company,* November 2, 2020.

14. The case illustrations of organizations employing strong and weak risk management practices are drawn from "Managing the People Side of Risk" authored by Alexis Krivkovic and Cindy Levy and published by McKinsey & Company in May, 2015.

15. The case illustrations of organizations employing strong and weak risk management practices are drawn from "Managing the People Side of Risk" authored by Alexis Krivkovic and Cindy Levy and published by McKinsey & Company in May, 2015.

16. Krivkovic, A. and Levy, C. *Managing the People Side of Risk.* New York: McKinsey & Company May 1, 2015.

17. Levy, C., Lamarre, E., and Twining, J. Taking Control of Organizational Risk Culture. New York: McKinsey & Company, Report Number 16. February, 2010.

18. Levy, C., Lamarre, E., and Twining, J. Taking Control of Organizational Risk Culture. New York: McKinsey & Company, Report Number 16. February, 2010.

19. Levy, C., Lamarre, E., and Twining, J. Taking Control of Organizational Risk Culture. New York: McKinsey & Company, Report Number 16. February, 2010.

Two industry risk models were combined to create the Risk Culture Framework: 1) a diagnostic risk model developed by McKinsey & Company risk experts Cindy Levy, Eric Lamarre and James Twining and presented in *Taking Control of Organizational Risk Culture* (Confidential Working Paper Number 16, February 2010) and 2) a Risk Culture Framework developed by Deloitte and presented in *Cultivating a Risk Intelligent Culture.*

20. Levy, C., Lamarre, E., and Twining, J. Taking Control of Organizational Risk Culture. New York: McKinsey & Company, Report Number 16. February, 2010.
21. Levy, C., Lamarre, E., and Twining, J. Taking Control of Organizational Risk Culture. New York: McKinsey & Company, Report Number 16. February, 2010.
22. Levy, C., Lamarre, E., and Twining, J. Taking Control of Organizational Risk Culture. New York: McKinsey & Company, Report Number 16. February, 2010.
23. Lareau, J. "GM's Ignition Switch Crisis Created Culture Shift to Spot Defects." *Detroit Free Press,* October 6, 2019.
24. Kaplan, R. and Mikes, A. "Swissgrid: Enterprise Risk Management in a Digital Age." *Harvard Business School Case 119-045*, November 2018.
25. Kaplan, R. and Mikes, A. "Swissgrid: Enterprise Risk Management in a Digital Age." *Harvard Business School Case 119-045*, November 2018.
26. Streicher, B., Bielefeld, M., and Eller, E. "The Risk Culture Framework: Introducing an Integrative Framework for Holistic Risk Analysis." *SAGE Journals* (August 10, 2023) DOI: 10.1177/21582440231191789.
27. Rosenfeld, J. "The 10 Industries That Have Been Impacted the Most by COVID-19." *Statista,* March 10, 2021.
28. Rosenfeld, J. "The 10 Industries That Have Been Impacted the Most by COVID-19." *Statista,* March 10, 2021.
29. Levy, C. Lamarre, E., and Twining, J. *Taking Control of Organizational Risk Culture.* New York: McKinsey & Company, Report Number 16. February, 2010
30. Tilman, L. and Jacoby, C. *Agility: How to Navigate the Unknown and Seize Opportunity in a World of Disruption.* Tom Rath Publishing, New York, NY, October 15, 2019.
31. Tilman, L. and Jacoby, C. *Agility: How to Navigate the Unknown and Seize Opportunity in a World of Disruption.* Tom Rath Publishing, October 15, 2019.
32. Tilman, L. and Jacoby, C. *Agility: How to Navigate the Unknown and Seize Opportunity in a World of Disruption.* Tom Rath Publishing, October 15, 2019.
33. Tilman, L. *Risk Intelligence: A Bedrock of Dynamism and Lasting Value Creation.* Tilman & Company, New York, NY, December 28, 2013.
34. Tilman, L. *Risk Intelligence: A Bedrock of Dynamism and Lasting Value Creation.* Tilman & Company, December 28, 2013.

Chapter 10

The Asymmetry of Leading

Leaders who make a difference have an ability to find opportunity in risk—to create symmetry from asymmetry.

Anonymous

Leaders are being challenged to step up and manage the moving pieces that make risk a growing challenge for organizations. Modern risk is complex with consequences that can be catastrophic and long-lasting. Its complexity requires a fusion of macro and micro thinking—an ability to see risk as a multifaceted phenomenon and to manage it as a singular event. The skill that sets leaders apart is an ability to balance *holism*—the big picture of risk as a multifaceted phenomenon—and *reduction*—the small parts that contribute to the big picture. Insightful leaders navigate risk by segmenting its elements into manageable pieces. Simultaneously, they have a capacity to see risk as a whole thereby enhancing their ability to understand cause and effect and craft strategies for mitigation.

In the pages that follow, leading in the new landscape of risk is approached from the perspective of biases standing in the way of leader understanding and skill in managing it. The basis of analysis is simple: one cannot effectively manage what one does not fully understand. As humans, we have a natural desire for balance and consistency. When things are out of balance, the resulting asymmetry can affect our behavior and decision-making. Leaders are not exempt from a need for balance. In the new environment of risk, much of their success will depend on their ability to create symmetry from asymmetry.

DOI: 10.4324/9781003335658-13

Challenges and Obstacles

The capacity to balance holism and reduction seemingly would amount to perfect logic. Who would argue that a capacity to see risk holistically and to reduce it to manageable parts *is not* an important skill? It is important, but obstacles stand in the way that must be overcome:

- The complexity and unpredictability of ***humanly created risk*** and the multifaceted challenge it poses to organizations and leaders.
- The challenge that ***asymmetry*** poses to leaders in managing stakeholders with diverse attitudes toward risk.
- ***Framing***—the tendency to make decisions based on the thought and behavior of others and the way a situation is presented, rather than on actual characteristics of the situation.
- ***Cognitive biases*** that leave leaders ill-equipped to manage modern risk.

Humanly Created Risk

Shortly after 1 a.m. EDT on March 26, 2024, a Singapore-flagged container ship, the Dali, was traveling down the Patapsco River in Baltimore on its way to Sri Lanka.[1] At 1:24 a.m. it experienced a total power failure and lost control over its propulsion, steering and electrical systems. Three minutes later, at 1:27 a.m., the Dali struck a pier of the Francis Scott Key Bridge, collapsing almost the entire structure into the water and killing six workers. Shortly before impact, a first responder on emergency radio picked up a mayday call from the ship's crew and dispatched officers to halt traffic onto the bridge. Without their fast work, the scale of the disaster would have been far greater, even during early morning hours when vehicular travel is relatively light. The Key Bridge disaster was the worst U.S. bridge collapse since 2007, when a design error caused the I-35W bridge in Minneapolis to plunge into the Mississippi River killing 13 people.[2]

The Key Bridge disaster is emblematic of the widening risk landscape facing organizations and leaders. The Dali and the Key Bridge were man-made, the power unit on the ship was man-made, the ship was guided by humanly created technology, and it was piloted by a trained crew. It is a powerful illustration of how human ingenuity and actions have changed the risk landscape compared to earlier times. Differences between yesterday and today include:

■ Interconnections among risks in multiple domains that cannot be addressed in silos and necessitate a holistic approach.
■ Leader capability that is challenged by risk antecedents and events that cannot be seen or predicted.
■ A widening ecosystem of stakeholders playing an ever-larger role in risk management.
■ A panoply of risk attitudes among stakeholders that make risk management more complex.
■ The emergence of asymmetry as a critical challenge to leaders facing a wide spectrum of risk attitudes.

Organizations face intersecting risks from multiple sources which are difficult to predict and manage. A single event disrupting one part of an interconnected system can ripple to other parts. Intersecting risks are dangerous because leaders tend to underprepare for their combined impact. Corporate risk management practices are designed to track and mitigate individual threats. Rarely do they assess the impact and consequences of primary, secondary and tertiary shocks occurring simultaneously.

The Discord of Asymmetry

COVID-19 killed more than 15 million people globally by early 2022, but its impact extended far beyond that figure.[3] The effects of the pandemic touched nearly every facet of society in the United States including health, the economy and human behavior. It lowered global life expectancy by 1.6 years.[4] Further, its rapidly unfolding effect yielded long-term changes in the way people interacted and how they handled stress. Most telling was its impact on the personal lives of people evidenced in rising rates of affective polarization and asymmetry resulting from emotional attachment to partisan groups.[5]

The pandemic elicited diverse attitudes in Americans, shaped by situational factors, personality traits and social context. The resulting asymmetry was most evident in the coping strategies people used to adapt to the pandemic. Some focused on practical solutions to pandemic challenges, others avoided pandemic issues altogether. Some dealt with emotions and stress through self-reflection and emotional expression, while others sought support from family, friends and community. People responded in different ways to social distancing guidelines. Some complied with mask-wearing and hygiene protocols while others actively resisted such protocols.. Some worried about infecting others or being infected themselves, while others ignored the possibility of infection. Some placed full trust in information provided by scientific experts and government officials while others rejected such information. Some exhibited empathy toward people infected with COVID-19 while others discriminated against them.

Asymmetry is a fundamental part of human nature. Commonly understood as a lack of equivalence between parts of a whole, it is a critical factor in the risk landscape of organizations.[6] Some individuals hold more power than others, have more information than others, possess greater expertise than others or interact in ways that lead to advantage over others. In the world of risk, asymmetry refers to differentiation in attitude toward risk as a result of distribution of power, group membership and access to information. Differences among individuals in what they know, the power they possess and the groups to which they belong combine to shape attitude in two important ways: how risk is perceived and the way in which individuals respond to it.

When the risk disposition of individuals varies widely across an organization, asymmetry is in full bloom. In most organizations, two polar perspectives exist which challenge leader ability to manage it—individuals who are risk-averse and those who are risk-embracing.[7] Risk-embracers engage risk head-on and address it as part of their work. Avoiders steer clear and see risk as the responsibility of others. Variation in attitude comes with a host of problems. Among them are confusion and conflict arising among employees responding differently to risk communication and tension within teams when members with different mindsets run head-long into each other in decision-making.

Framing

> *The Deepwater Horizon oil platform blowout in 2010 sent toxic fluids and gas shooting up the well, leading to an explosion on board the rig that killed 11 people and injured 115 crew members, some seriously.[8] Two days later the rig sank, breaking off the pipe connection to the well and jettisoning 134 million gallons of oil into*

the Gulf of Mexico for a period of nearly three months until it could be contained. The disaster became the worst oil spill in the history of the United States, far exceeding the Exxon Valdez tanker spill of 10.8 million gallons in 1989.[9]

On February 3, 2023, 38 cars of a Norfolk Southern train carrying hazardous materials and combustible liquids derailed.[10] *Several railcars burned for more than two days, with emergency crews eventually conducting a controlled burn of additional railcars which released hydrogen chloride and phosgene into the air. Residents within a one-mile radius were evacuated and emergency response teams were mobilized from Ohio, Pennsylvania, West Virginia and Virginia. Preliminary findings suggested a mechanical problem on one of the railcar's trucks prior to the derailment.*

Post-disaster investigation of the Deep Horizon oil rig explosion revealed regulatory oversight to be woefully inadequate and coordination lacking among BP, Transocean and Haliburton employees.[11] There was an absence of contingency planning by the companies and the U.S. Coast Guard on what to do in the event of an emergency. Gross negligence on the part of BP and its partners was revealed through evidence presented in regulatory hearings following the disaster. Safety was compromised by an emphasis among collaborating organizations on short-term profits over sound drilling practices.

The train derailment in East Palestine upended lives and led to partisan finger-pointing in a town of 5000 residents near the Ohio-Pennsylvania border. Norfolk Southern executives and government agencies were blamed for a derailment that could have been avoided through better company supervision and more stringent government regulations.[12] Norfolk Southern executives were accused of advocating deregulation in their own interests and the U.S. Department of Transportation and Environmental Protection Agency of employing bureaucratic measures that stifled corporate innovation. Blame was also assigned to public officials for a lack of information and answers about health issues resulting from the controlled release of toxic vinyl chloride. Tests conducted by the Environmental Protection Agency showing air quality to be acceptable and water safe to drink were met with skepticism by residents experiencing headaches, nausea, dizziness, and nose, throat and lung irritation.

The cause of the Deep Horizon oil rig disaster and East Palestine derailment was not equipment failure per se. Root cause can be traced back to the accommodating relationship and pattern of reciprocating influence between company executives, government agency heads and public officials—a relationship and pattern of influence which shaped company strategy and operations. Cozy relationships come with adverse effects including insufficient oversight, inadequate safety measures and conflicts of interest. In the Deepwater Horizon and East Palestine disasters, critical issues underlying company operations were not addressed leaving a trail of unanswered questions: What is more important—short-term profits or safety? Why were the vested interests of company executives in deregulation permitted to forestall government initiatives to make oil drilling and railroads safer? Why did government agencies relax monitoring standards and procedures for oil drilling and rail transport of hazardous materials? Why did company owners, government agencies and subcontractors fail to establish contingency plans?[13]

Cognitive Bias

Comprehensive risk assessments across a variety of industries reveal a vulnerability rooted in the cognitive biases of leaders—from how they see risk to how they manage it. Cognitive biases which skew leader understanding of risk have become a subject of increasing interest among researchers and business consultants. Among the more interesting analyses of bias is a description of leader predispositions toward risk that heighten organizational vulnerability by Matthew Cramer:[14]

- *Overconfidence.* Statements like "it could never happen here" reveal a false sense of security among leaders in the future of an organization. When destructive events are referred to as "outliers" and discussion focuses on the low likelihood of such events, rather than their consequences, overconfidence is in full bloom. Overconfidence comes with a cost: neglect of important information in risk assessment.
- *Confirmation bias.* The tendency to seek out and favor evidence that aligns with personal belief is a natural tendency in human behavior.[15] It becomes problematic for leaders when beliefs about risk lead to neglect of alternative perspectives or relevant data—a circumstance that can lead to flawed decisions.
- *Leading with assumptions.* "Crossing the net" is a term used in analysis of interpersonal communication.[16] On one side of the net is a leader

with a distinctly personal view of risk and on the other side are others holding views that diverge from the leader. When a leader "crosses the net," assumptions are made about the motivations and values of others that depart from reality. Relationships weaken and the potential for a unified approach to risk diminishes.

■ *Anchoring.* Anchoring occurs when leaders rely on an initial piece of information as a basis for subsequent judgments.[17] This tendency can be detrimental when the potential for risk is predicted using past information. The absence of a risk event in the past has no bearing on assessments of future risk. Insightful leaders curb the effect of anchoring by recognizing its influence and gathering information from diverse sources.

■ *Attribution bias.* Attribution bias refers to a tendency to explain a circumstance by characteristics of the circumstance rather than root cause and consequences.[18] In the context of risk, bias can lead to inaccurate assessments of cause based on experience, emotion and cognitive processes—a circumstance that can result in neglect of contributing factors and misunderstanding of the totality of a risk event.

■ *Escalating commitment.* Escalating commitment is best understood as the tendency of leaders to elevate commitment to an existing course of action, even when objective evidence indicates otherwise.[19] The reasons are many—overestimating one's ability to influence outcomes, fear of losing what has already been invested, assuming others agree with a decision. Escalating commitment to inadequate solutions ignores root cause leaving organizations exposed to greater risk.

■ *Groupthink.* Groupthink occurs when the desire of leaders for harmony and conformity leads to irrational decision-making.[20] This can happen within groups when background experience among members is different or a leader is new to an organization. A newly arrived CEO, for example, may be reluctant to challenge the judgment of a team holding a different opinion, for fear of being impertinent. When aspects of risk are pushed under the table in the name of conformity, creative thought can be suppressed leading to flawed analysis and short-sighted decision-making.

■ *Dunning-Kruger effect.* Bias in which individuals with limited competence in a particular domain overestimate their abilities.[21] Leaders affected by this effect may think they excel, when, in reality, they lack competence. In the world of risk, leaders may overestimate their skill in assessing and managing risk thereby creating a credibility gap.

- *Planning fallacy.* A tendency to make unrealistic assumptions about risk with serious consequences for an organization.[22] Leaders may underestimate the consequences of risk and overestimate the benefits of their actions in managing it leading to suboptimal decisions.
- *Normalization of deviance.* Deviance is normalized when leaders become accustomed to behavior that deviates from what is expected in the absence of negative feedback.[23] In the world of risk, leaders may fall into a trap of normalizing behavior that deviates from internal controls but hasn't led to an accident. Over time, seemingly insignificant deviations can lead to small failures which eventually may cause a catastrophic failure.

A critical step for leaders in eliminating cognitive biases involves awareness of the extent to which risk exists in their operating environment and periodic examination of their own biases. Savvy leaders avoid mental traps by seeking diverse perspectives and fostering open communication. By doing so, they build analytical and reflective capacity and sharpen defense against their greatest nemesis—themselves.

The Challenge of Asymmetry

Leaders striving to reduce their organizations' exposure to risk invariably encounter asymmetries of attitude, control and style. In organizational theory, asymmetry refers to an inequity among individuals in power, authority and influence.[24] In the context of risk, it is not a function of inequity, but rather of incongruity in how people see risk and how leaders manage it. Leaders come face-to-face with asymmetry in the form of contradiction in attitudes toward risk, approaches to managing it and their leadership style. These asymmetries reduce a tension between aversion and acceptance in risk *attitude*; people and process in *managing* risk; and transaction and holism in *style*. Reduced to its core, asymmetry is a paradox of leading and managing—of enabling and controlling—in which leaders are expected to motivate others toward responsibility for risk while coordinating their actions through administrative controls.

The asymmetries leaders experience in relationship to risk unfold in three interrelated ways:

■ *Asymmetries of attitude:* Leaders encountering a diversity of risk attitudes among employees which influence their behavior and decision-making.
■ *Asymmetries of managing:* Leaders experiencing tension in decision-making about how to manage employees in high risk environments.
■ *Asymmetries of style:* Leaders exploring and employing alternative approaches to leading in environments of high risk.

Asymmetries of Attitude

Multiple risk attitudes are at play in organizations at any one time. Ingram and Thompson (2012) have classified feelings toward risk into four distinct attitudes: *Pragmatists* who see the world as uncertain and unpredictable; *Conservators* whose worldview is one of peril and high risk; *Maximizers* who see the world as low risk and fundamentally self-correcting; and *Managers* whose perspective on risk is guided by how effectively it is managed.[25] The typology of risk attitudes presented in Chapter 8 classified risk attitudes into three frames based on symmetry (**Flow**, **Asymmetry**, and **Paradox**) and seven categories of attitude (*Embracer, Avoider, Joiner, Conformist, Follower, Nonconformist* and *Compartmentalist*). In a state of flow, individuals see risk in an exclusively positive or negative way whereas in a state of asymmetry risk attitudes can vary depending on situation and circumstance. Individuals in a state of paradox have a unique ability to maintain simultaneously contradictory attitudes toward risk through compartmentalization. These classifications of attitude are speculative and may or may not hold up across organizations. Their utility, however, rests in the realization that leaders must navigate diverse employee attitudes toward risk and, while doing so, balance their own cognitive biases with those of employees.

In an ideal world, managing risk would be a matter of symmetry—controls and managerial styles employed by leaders would match the interests and preferences of employees. Reality, however, says something different. Unquestionably, internal controls play an important role in risk management, but their impact on employees can vary. If not carefully instituted, they can hinder empowerment and employee engagement in decision-making. Exercising responsibility for managing risk is very different from subjection to internal controls. For risk to be managed effectively, employees through-out the organization must be involved. Basically, every employee becomes a risk manager—a result best achieved when divergent attitudes toward risk are understood and allowed to stand but aligned in support of a common goal.

> *In 2016, Loomis a 160-year-old cash handling company, faced a challenge at the intersection of two forces; the rise of digital pay-ment methods and the persistent use of cash worldwide.*[26] *Loomis employed 25,000 people carrying out cash in transit and cash management services through an international network of more than 400 branches in over 20 countries. Loomis's customers were primarily banks and retailers—two industries that were being heav-ily disrupted by changing customer preferences and a new breed of competitors.*
>
> *To address this challenge, Loomis's CEO, Patrik Andersonn, initi-ated a strategy review process and established dedicated teams comprised of people from cross functional areas to explore the future trajectory of Loomis's businesses.*[27] *As cross functional teams went to work, Andersonn had one concern. How could he ensure that the options being explored would not become incremental and inter-nally focused? How could the teams be encouraged to weigh compet-ing interests and perspectives on risk and change and see diverse possibilities before converging on the best way forward? Rather than rushing to quick answers, Andersonn adopted a "leader" mindset. He challenged teams to break out of their comfort zones, expand their understanding of prevailing attitudes toward risk and areas of choice, and shape strategic options for the company's future.*[28] *By slowing down and understanding and embracing divergent atti-tudes and thinking, Loomis developed breakthrough ideas to change its trajectory, balancing traditional cash services with emerging digital trends.*

To manage with a "leader" mindset, leaders must adopt a learning attitude and challenge themselves and employees to step out of the comfort zone of long-held attitudes and beliefs about risk and change. By encouraging employees to think from multiple perspectives, divergent thinking has the power to harness wide-ranging attitudes into a cultural understanding that makes asymmetry work for an organization.

Asymmetries of Managing

Leaders in high-risk environments grapple with ongoing tensions related to managing employees, one of which is balancing command and control and empowerment. At first glance, control and empowerment appear to be opposite sides of the leadership coin, i.e., leaders and managers compensate for internal controls requiring employee compliance through lip service to engagement in decision-making. Symmetry is implied because the balance between control and empowerment provides each group with something it wants.

A closer look at managing, however, suggests a need to rethink the relationship between control and empowerment in asymmetrical terms. Asymmetry in the relationship would occur when employee discontent with internal controls outweighs the efforts of leaders to include employees in decision-making. A number of factors can derail the symmetry between control and empowerment—heavy-handed controls that constrain employees in their work, a mismatch between controls and organizational culture, and perception of unfairness to name a few. However, despite modern-day enthusiasm for empowerment and increased transparency in management, there is ambivalence about the relationship between control and empowerment. Both are important in an organization's risk management arsenal, but they must be in balance to be effective. Controls are important. They help organizations avoid costly and time-consuming oversights by providing systematic checks and balances that deliver results in real time. Empowerment, on the other hand, is a human dynamic of giving trust and decision-making authority to employees. It promotes engagement, but benefits take longer to realize and empowered employees need guidance and support which may work against organizational efficiency.

All of this would suggest that asymmetries of managing, in particular of control and empowerment and the importance of balance, may be driven by organizational mimicry—a tendency of organizations to emulate the practices of other organizations.[29] Mimicry can involve replicating specific practices not because they are better, but because they have met with success in other organizations. Essentially, it is a process in which organizations become similar to other organizations to gain legitimacy but continue to rely on tried-and-true management practices to do their heavy lifting. Command and control in managing persists because it delivers benefits of efficiency and enhanced ability to manage uncertainty and complexity. Empowerment is valued because it is the choice of progressive organizations—"the right thing to do." For leaders, therefore, managing is not about viewing control and empowerment as opposing forces but about engaging in both simultaneously.

- *Microsoft* has adapted its management practices to remain competitive in the fast-moving tech industry by partnering with and copying the behavior of pioneering organizations like OpenAI.[30] It employs different approaches to management with different business groups. The hierarchy is a continuing basis for organizing company-wide, but it is balanced by elements of empowerment in fast-moving business units such as Cloud and AI, Experiences and Devices, and Gaming.
- *Toyota*'s success is attributed in large part to its Toyota Production System (TPS), a "hard" innovation that improves manufacturing processes.[31] However, equally important is Toyota's "soft" innovation related to corporate culture. Toyota deliberately fosters contradictory viewpoints in the organization, challenging employees to find solutions by transcending differences rather than compromising. Its culture blends control and empowerment to generate innovative ideas to remain ahead of competitors.

Change journeys are unique, but these company examples of mimicry and managerial asymmetry illustrate how learning from successful companies can drive change without throwing the baby out with the bath water.

Asymmetries of Leadership Style

The influence of asymmetry extends beyond managing to the manner in which leaders lead—their *leadership style*. The challenge for leaders is how to lead in a high-risk environment—what style to adopt, when to change style and how to go about changing style when circumstances dictate. Understanding context is critical. Leaders in high-risk environments need to make timely decisions. More often than not, they will employ an analytical approach and factor information about external conditions, organizational dynamics and business cycles into decision-making. In uncertain times, however, information is not always available. When this happens, leaders must turn to intuition.

Analysis and intuition involve capabilities that work in different ways in leading. For intuition to work, one must trust one's instincts—a dynamic requiring self-confidence. For analysis to be effective, one must have access to reliable information and trust that information—a dynamic requiring confidence in the integrity of information. These capabilities play out differently for leaders depending on context and situation as illustrated in research by Daniel Goleman on leadership style.[32] Known for his work on emotional intelligence, Goleman identified six leadership styles used by leaders based on context:[33]

- *Authoritative leadership*, which involves decisiveness, clear direction and compliance.
- *Visionary leadership*, which is about mobilizing people toward a vision.
- *Pacesetting leadership*, which involves setting standards and leading by example.
- *Affiliative leadership*, which centers around building emotional bonds.
- *Democratic leadership*, which involves collaboration and decision-making by consensus.
- *Coaching leadership*, which focuses on individual growth and development.

On the surface, these leadership styles would appear to be asymmetrical. *Authoritative* leadership based on compliance is an entirely different animal than *democratic* leadership based on collaboration. *Pacesetting* leadership involving standards is a different animal than *coaching* leadership focused on individual development and growth. These differences lead to questions about leader capacity to fit style to context in a high-risk environment:

> *Having adopted a style of leadership appropriate to an environment in which the likelihood of risk is low, how can leaders change course and adopt a different leadership style to meet the demands of a high-risk environment?*

> *Is it possible that leaders resolve the asymmetry of incompatible styles by dividing their outlook on leadership into compartments?*

According to Goleman, effective leaders don't rely on just one approach to leadership; they adapt style to different contexts.[34] Effective leaders move flexibly among leadership styles as needed. They are keenly aware of the impact they have on others and seamlessly adjust their style to get the best results.

Changing leadership style in an environment of high risk would have the look and feel of driving on a switchback road up a steep slope. When launching internal controls and cultural initiatives to enhance an organization's risk management capability, a leader would use an authoritative style where clear direction and decisiveness are required to bring people together toward a common goal. A coaching style would be adopted with employees experiencing difficulty in adapting to new controls and initiatives. And a pacesetting style would be used to drive change to completion. This amounts to perfect logic, but changing leadership style to fit different circumstances is easier said than done. It begs the question of whether leaders accustomed to a particular style of leadership can take on a new and different style, let alone multiple leadership styles? Said another way: Are leaders capable of tolerating asymmetry by compartmentalizing style? In this perspective, asymmetry would not be resolved by choosing one style over another, but by moving back and forth between styles depending on context.

Leadership is not a static skill that leaders master once and for all. It is dynamic and evolving and requires constant adaptation and innovation. Movement between styles discloses the functional importance of asymmetry while matching style to context discloses the situational importance of symmetry. In this way, leading is a dynamic learning process involving both asymmetry and symmetry to meet changing conditions in an unpredictable landscape.

Asymmetric Leadership

Put yourself in the position of CEO of Finnish telecommunications giant Nokia when Apple launched its iPhone. From its establishment as the Nokia Corporation in 1967, your company has been running on cruise control as the world's largest mobile phone handset maker.[35] But along came the iPhone in 2007 and everything changed. You failed to read the threat to your keypad-based product from touchscreen smartphones. After years of declining sales, you sold what was left of Nokia to Microsoft in 2013.[36] Questions abound:

- Why did this happen?
- How could Nokia have missed the threat to its keypad-based products from touchscreen smartphones?

- Did the company fail because it overestimated its market position and failed to anticipate market shifts?
- Was failure a result of complacency after years of market leadership?
- Was failure due to organizational and management problems that rendered the company unable to adapt?
- Were the company's problems caused by leaders with fixed ideas about how to lead which prevented them from recognizing the shift from product-based competition to platforms?

In periods of fast change and growing risk, organizations and leaders must "look beyond what they see" and get in front of change. Nokia crashed because of inferior technology, a failure to innovate and keep pace with changing technology and arrogance of its leaders.[37] Its demise was rooted in a closed culture which restricted inflow and outflow of information.[38] Interactions occurred principally among employees in a culture of status leading to an atmosphere of shared fear. Employees were in fear of reprimands from demanding leaders and middle managers. Managers feared not meeting quarterly targets. Senior leaders feared losing investors and customers if they acknowledged technological inferiority. The sum total of fears added up to a toxic culture.

Lessons for leaders from Nokia are many. Chief among them is the *human factor* in leading: maintain a close relationship with employees, be aware of their emotional makeup and state of mind and foster trust and positivity. Transformational leadership is critical in a high-risk environment. Closed doors are costly and leaders must work at listening to their employees. In order to understand employees, however, leaders must first understand their own cognitive biases.

Modeling Asymmetric Leadership

Asymmetry poses a significant challenge to leaders in high-risk environments. They grapple with an array of attitudes toward risk among stakeholders, tension between control and empowerment in managing, and fitting style to context. Effective leaders understand asymmetry. They are aware of their bias toward risk and contextual dynamics that shape an organization's ability to manage risk. As shown in Figure 10.1, they possess capabilities that uniquely suit them to address the challenge of asymmetry. The first two involve comprehension of external forces and organizational dynamics contributing to

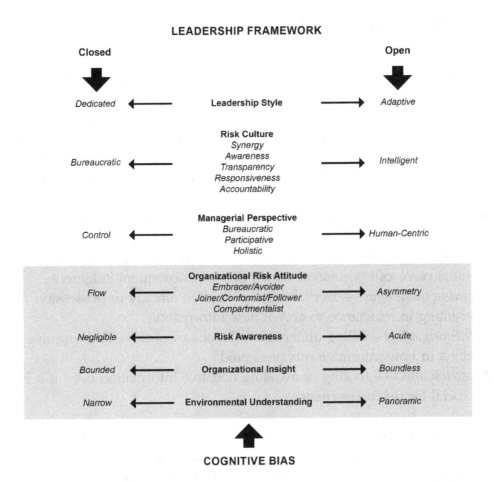

Figure 10.1 Asymmetric Leadership Model

risk. The next pair reflect awareness of risk and risk attitudes throughout the organization. The final group involves elements of culture, management and leadership style that enhance leader capability in managing risk.

In high-risk environments, leaders need to be able to move back and forth between asymmetries of culture, managerial perspective and leadership style. In shaded frames of the model—*environmental understanding, organizational insight, awareness of risk* and *risk attitudes*—asymmetry is dysfunctional. Leaders who lack insight into their own cognitive bias, environmental and organizational dynamics, and risk attitudes are ill-equipped to navigate risk. There is no room for sub-optimal performance.

Awareness of Cognitive Bias

Cognition is a driving force in the risk behavior of leaders. Cognitive biases are subtle and can narrow understanding of risk if not recognized. Common biases include:[39]

- *confirmation bias*—seeking information that aligns with existing beliefs
- *availability bias*—relying on immediate, easily accessible information
- *overconfidence*—underestimation of risk and overestimation of ability to manage it
- *recency bias*—distortion of risk assessment by giving undue weight to recent events
- *anchoring bias*—distortion of risk assessment through fixation on an initial piece of information which distorts subsequent judgments
- *endowment effect*—overvaluing information already in possession resulting in reluctance to accept new information
- *framing effect*—falling under the influence of positive and negative effect in how information is presented
- *ostrich effect*—ignoring or avoiding negative information even if it is crucial for risk assessment

Nokia's leaders played a significant role in the decline of the company. Despite possessing a wealth of resources and technical expertise, they failed to envision the transformative power of smartphones and the imminent shift in consumer preferences. Believing that its dominance in the mobile phone market would be enough to stave off competitors, Nokia's leaders fell victim to overconfidence and confirmation bias. Its culture of status created an atmosphere of shared fear grounded in the arrogance and temperament of top executives.[40] When fear permeated the organization, rank and file employees turned inward to protect resources thereby hindering Nokia's ability to innovate and adapt to emerging trends.

Nokia's failure illustrates a common shortcoming of leaders in fast-change industries: success breeds hubris which, over time, results in neglect of the human factor in management. Leaders operating with a mindset of past success can fall into a trap of looking past their own bias and losing sight of the emotions and motivation of their employees. Confirmation bias—seeking and using information aligned with one's beliefs—can lead to neglect of employee input and foreclose consideration of alternative solutions in decision-making. Anchoring and recency bias can foreclose decision alternatives because they withdraw critical information in decision-making through over-reliance on prior information and events. The outcome, more often than not, is sub-optimal decision-making.

Deep Understanding of the External Environment

Knowledge of the external environment enables leaders to navigate uncertainty, seize opportunities and guide their organizations toward success. At a minimum, leaders should have information about economic, social, political, technological and regulatory trends as well as information about risk, consumer preferences, competitor behavior and environmental challenges. Less obvious, but equally important, is forward-looking intelligence in an increasingly complex landscape.

> *Competitive intelligence and bold intention shaped the rise of Netflix.[41] Early on, its business centered on shipping DVDs to customers' homes. Years before, its cofounder and then-CEO Reed Hastings had articulated a dramatically different future: "The dream 20 years from now will be to have a global entertainment distribution company that provides a unique channel for film producers and studios."[42] Netflix's leaders planted that vision deep into the company's culture. As the company began streaming content directly to users, it stopped distributing DVDs and launched its own production arm. In doing so, Netflix restructured the entertainment industry and created enormous value for its stakeholders. By 2019, almost one-half of its total business was production and the company had tripled its revenue and increased earnings 32-fold.[43]*

Netflix's leaders used a combination of external trend analysis and industry foresight to create an organization that would bring the entertainment market to its vision of the industry. It gathered extensive data about consumer preferences, scoured the practices of competitors and dove into the world of advancing technology to identify a niche that would shape the future of entertainment. Contrast this with Nokia's failure to adopt to changing consumer preferences that put it behind Android competitors Apple and Samsung. Nokia's leaders were slow to recognize the potential of smartphones and consumer preference for touchscreen devices with advanced capabilities such as app ecosystems. Rather than capitalizing on the evolving landscape of smartphones, Nokia's leaders turned back the clock and tried to strengthen company position by enhancing existing software. This lack of strategic foresight eroded market share and cost the company market advantage.

Sensitivity to Organizational Dynamics

Organizational dynamics involve intricate interactions among people, processes and structures that drive outcomes. Leaders who are sensitive to dynamics know their organizations inside-out. They value awareness and learning—diving into and fully understanding talent, strengths, resources and ideas critical to the organization while also understanding weaknesses and vulnerabilities. Leaders tuned into organizational dynamics know their cognitive biases—a capability that enables them to move beyond controllers with a mindset of certainty to coaches with a mindset of exploration and learning.

> *Financial software company Intuit shifted to a learning organization when it found itself plateauing after its initial success with desktop financial software for consumers.[44] Senior leaders doubled down on innovation and design, fostering a cultural shift to experimentation with fast learning and fast failure at its heart. Senior executives, beginning with the CEO, published their own performance reviews, admitting mistakes and seeking feedback.[45] Employees were given 10 percent of unstructured time to experiment, and good ideas were given funding. Decision-making was streamlined and accelerated, with clear responsibilities and processes based on both data and dialogue. This shift helped the company evolve into an innovative learning organization with numerous experiments running at any one time. From 2009 to 2019, Intuit doubled its customer base to 50 million, tripled its earnings, and increased its value from $10 billion to $60 billion.[46]*

Contrast Intuit's culture of learning based on awareness of internal strengths and weaknesses with Nokia's culture of status leading to an atmosphere of shared fear. Headstrong leaders lacking sensitivity to organizational dynamics weakened company culture rendering it vulnerable to fast-moving competitors. Employees turning inward to protect resources squandered its ability to innovate thereby hastening its decline.

Cognizance of Risk

Leaders who understand risk make informed decisions that align resources with organizational goals. By recognizing potential threats and acting quickly they reduce exposure to peril and protect the organization from harm. At first glance, recognition and timely response would seem simple enough—keep your antenna up and act decisively when a threat is identified. Successful leaders have the ability to detect risks from their beginning as bumps in the road to their evolution into full-scale problems. They know when to act in response to a threat and when to take a safe approach. They are masters at balancing opportunity and caution when it comes to risk.

- *Indra Nooyi*, the former CEO of PepsiCo, significantly reshaped Pepsi's strategic direction by emphasizing healthier products and sustainability.[47] Fully aware of changing consumer preferences and the risks involved in product rebranding, she classified Pepsi's products into three categories: "fun for you" (regular soda and potato chips), "better for you" (diet or low-fat versions), and "good for you" (Quaker Oats oatmeal). Nooyi introduced design thinking into Pepsi's innovation process and coined the term "Performance with a Purpose" as its mantra acknowledging corporate accountability.
- *Satya Nadella*, Microsoft's CEO, led the company's transformation from a software giant to a cloud-first organization.[48] Aware of the risk of clinging to legacy models, he shifted Microsoft's focus from legacy on premises businesses to a cloud-first platform. He enhanced Microsoft's internal culture and customer focus by doubling down on AI and social networking and making Windows free for devices with a screen nine inches or smaller—a significant departure from traditional software licensing models.
- *Jeff Bezos*, the founder and former CEO of Amazon, revolutionized the way people shop and set new standards for competition.[49] His understanding of risk and insight into consumer shopping preferences pushed Amazon to continually challenge the boundaries of shopping convenience. Features like two-day free shipping through Amazon Prime, one-click ordering and voice-based shopping via devices like Echo became industry standards. Bezos's awareness of risk involved in industry disruption worked to Amazon's advantage by setting new standards in e-commerce and logistics and reshaping consumer expectations.

Juxtapose these examples against the risk perspective of Nokia's leaders and their actions in navigating risk. Hubris, a lack of vision and aversion to change were the trinity of leader errors that led to Nokia's downfall. Rather than embracing the transformative power of smartphones, Nokia's leaders overestimated its market position and continued to invest in traditional technology—a strategy that hindered the company's ability to respond to market shifts. Complacency built on hubris was the enemy of change. In the mindset of its leaders, Nokia was a successful company—it did not need to change. It could not fail—a belief that made it hard for leaders to objectively assess the competitive threats emerging around them.

Awareness of Risk Attitudes

People are the X factor in risk management. They are subject to multiple influences, both explicit and covert, which shape attitude toward risk on a continuum ranging from aversion (uncomfortable with uncertainty), to acceptance (neutrality), to risk-seeking (welcoming), to many shades in-between. For organizations and leaders, the implications of multifaceted risk attitudes are clear: attitudes shape behavior and dysfunctionalities in risk attitude among employees can hinder achievement of organizational goals. In the competitive hotel and restaurant industry, for example, risk-averse employees could hamper the early detection capability of a hotel and damage its reputation. Risk-taking managers in the financial services industry could ignore market signals and place their organizations in jeopardy. Employees with an aversion to risk in a hospital or clinic could jeopardize patient safety and result in legal claims. Attitudes toward risk are varied and they have a valence. If not understood and managed, they can wreak havoc on an organization.

> *Founded in 1999, Plum Healthcare aimed to create a healthcare company without the persistent problems often seen in the industry.[50] Its strategy involved acquiring and transforming dysfunctional long-term care and rehabilitation facilities. However, it faced deep challenges due to divergent risk attitudes among continuing and new employees which affected decision-making and collaboration. To grow, it needed to overhaul its culture to a people-centric approach—a move beyond its internal capability to achieve. Assistance was sought from Arbinger, an organization specializing in mindset shifts and cultural transformation.[51] Arbinger provided*

strategic consulting, virtual coaching, customized training pro-grams, facilitator certification and transformation tools for each newly acquired facility. It developed a strategic roadmap for cultural transformation during and after each facility acquisition includ-ing assessment of employee attitudes toward change and blending them into an outward mindset culture. The attitude transformation strategy worked. Plum achieved remarkable growth—increasing the number of facilities and employees by almost 500 percent and expanding to operate 63 skilled nursing facilities and 5 home health and hospice facilities strategically located throughout California, Arizona and Utah up to the time of its sale in 2021.[52]

A culture in which leaders lack awareness of risk attitudes can work against an organization's effectiveness in managing risk. When organizational poli-cies and goals set by leaders based on their personal attitude toward risk clash with the risk attitudes of employees, a double bind can be created for employees. Tension between leader expectations for conformity to con-trols and employee preference for self-expression can place employees in a double bind of adherence to controls and personal desire to openly share their feelings about risk. Solutions to the double bind of conflicting expecta-tions around risk begin with leader interest in learning the risk attitudes of employees, and their motivation to create a supportive environment where employees understand the organization's approach to risk and take personal responsibility for managing it.

Managerial Perspective

The widening environment of risk has extended the range of decisions that leaders must make from big picture thinking to careful execution, from control to empowerment, and from planning for the long term to operating in the short term. What is acceptable in managing has also changed from "either/or" to "both/and." To succeed in an environment of rapid change, leaders need to employ different approaches to managing—authoritative and transactional, bureaucratic and transformative, and transactional and human-centric. They need to embrace asymmetry in how they manage and move back and forth between different approaches based on situation and context.

Kaplan and Mikes (2012) illustrated the importance of asymmetry in managing risk by developing a categorization of risk that enabled lead-ers to determine which risks could be managed through a rules-based control model and which required open discourse typical of human-centric models.[53] They divided the risk landscape organizations face into three categories:

- *Preventable risks:* internal risks rising from within an organization that are controllable and can be managed through operational controls.
- *Strategy risks:* internal events that disrupt an organization's ability to achieve its goals that cannot be managed through rules-based control.
- *External risks:* risks rising from events outside the organization that are beyond its influence and control.

All organizations are subject to risk in these categories, and each requires a different approach to management.[54] Preventable risks, rising from within, are monitored and controlled through rules and controls which require compliance. In contrast, strategy risks and external risks require processes that encourage leaders and employees to openly discuss risk and find ways to reduce the likelihood of risk events and mitigate their consequences. Facing risks in different categories, leaders have no choice but to tailor management to the nature of risk in each category. While a compliance-based approach may be effective for managing preventable risks, it is wholly inadequate for strategy and external risks, which require open and explicit discussion. Which approach is appropriate depends largely on context.

Matching managerial approach to context is easier said than done. When organizations face simultaneously occurring risks in different categories, leaders must manage them in real time. Cognitive biases intervene by narrowing choice to preferred ways of managing. Leaders may rely on past experience (anchoring) when making decisions about how to manage employees. Confirmation bias may further compound decision-making by impelling leaders to favor ideas that support their preferred way(s) of managing and reject ideas that contradict their preferences. And there is the possibility that groupthink may also be at work—suppression of specific ideas about managing out of a desire for group consensus. Collectively, these biases help to explain why so many leaders migrate to a preferred approach to managing even when events and circumstances dictate otherwise.

> The mission of the LEGO Group is to "Inspire and develop the builders of tomorrow."[55] Company leaders use an innovation strategy and a multi-method risk management strategy to achieve its mission. Risk management involves elements of control, risk ownership

*and employee engagement: (1) Enterprise Risk Management (ERM)
processes and controls requiring compliance and accountability
for results, (2) Monte Carlo Simulations involving employees in risk
modeling and helping them understand uncertainties and potential
outcomes, (3) Active Risk and Opportunity Planning (AROP) which
engages employees in risk planning and strategic decision-making
and (4) Preparation for Uncertainty—identifying and testing risk
scenarios and management strategies using industry and world
trend data.[56] By using multiple methods to manage risk and aligning management with business strategy, the LEGO Group ensures a
holistic approach to risk that merges principles of control, engagement and empowerment to achieve optimal results.*

Focus of Risk Culture

Risk culture—a blend of attitudes and beliefs that define how an organization and its leaders perceive, respond to and manage risks—is a corner-
stone of effective management in a high-risk environment.[57] Its key elements
include: (1) disposition toward risk guiding an organization's approach to
threats, (2) processes guiding how risks are assessed and mitigated and (3)
communication with stakeholders about their role and responsibility in managing risk. A strong risk culture starts through tone at the top and modeling
of risk-aware behavior by leaders.

In the wake of COVID-19, many organizations put oversight processes in
place to detect risks long before they become full-blown disasters. Yet processes are only part of an organization's risk management arsenal. Crises can
continue to emerge when leaders neglect to manage the behaviors that are
part of an organization's risk culture—its first line of defense against risk.
Leaders with a record of success in managing risk foster robust risk cultures
in which employees understand the organization's approach to risk, take
personal responsibility for managing it and encourage others to follow their
example.

The differences between organizations that invest in a robust culture
and those that do not are stark. Consider the case of global aerospace giant
Boeing whose culture contributed to the 737 MAX disaster. A detailed case
study of the disaster was authored by Tahir Abbas and published in June,
2023.[58] Abbas' account follows:

In 2018 and 2019, Boeing was confronted with a crisis of its own making that called into question its resilience and reputation—the crash of two 737 MAX aircraft killing 346 people. Designed for fuel efficiency and enhanced performance, the MAX was an attractive choice for airlines seeking to modernize their fleets. Boeing marketed the MAX as a seamless transition for pilots already trained on early generation 737s—a step that offered airlines an opportunity to minimize training costs and streamline operations when introducing new aircraft into their fleets. To expedite launch, Boeing employed a strategy of "minimum change, maximum benefit" involving nominal alterations to the existing 737 design while maximizing performance through new engines and aerodynamics.[59]

Growing Pressure. *As development progressed, Boeing faced pressure to bring the MAX to market swiftly. Intense competition with Airbus and the demand for more fuel-efficient aircraft led to a compressed timeline which put strain on engineering and certification processes. The Federal Aviation administration granted certification to the MAX in March 2017, paving the way for deliveries to airlines. The MAX took to the air in 2018 and within months made headlines following the crash of Lion Air Flight 610 in October 2018 killing 189 passengers and crew and the crash of Ethiopian Airlines Flight 302 in March 2019 killing 157 passengers and crew.*[60] *Investigations into both crashes revealed a common cause: erroneous data from a faulty angle of attack sensor that triggered the aircraft's Maneuvering Characteristics Augmentation Systems (MCAS) leading to a nosedive that pilots were unable to counteract.*[61]

Investigation and Results. *These devastating crashes prompted worldwide alarm and raised serious questions about the safety of the MAX. Multiple investigations were launched to determine root cause of the accidents with a primary focus on understanding the design and functionality of the MCAS, the training provided to the pilots, the certification process, and potential lapses in safety oversight rooted in Boeing's risk culture. The investigations revealed critical issues including shortcomings in the design and operation of the MCAS system, inadequate pilot training regarding the system's functionality and potential failure modes, and concerns about regulatory processes and Boeing's culture.*[62]

Boeing's Risk Culture. *Boeing's handling of the MAX crisis was met with widespread criticism and scrutiny. Its initial response was perceived as slow and lacking in transparency. It took several days for the company to release a statement expressing condolences and acknowledging the tragedies. The delay eroded public trust and called into question Boeing's commitment to transparency and accountability. The company was described in a congressional investigation as having a "culture of concealment" evidenced in its unwillingness to share technical details contributing to the fatal crashes.[63] It was further described as having a culture of "mismatched management expectations" that led to cutting corners and breakdowns in the engineering and development process—a fault revealed in evidence that the company had not disclosed the existence of the MCAS system to pilots or airlines prior to the accidents.[64]*

The 737 MAX crisis severely damaged Boeing's reputation and eroded trust among key stakeholders including airlines, passengers, regulators and the general public. Its culture and risk management practices were called into question and its reputation tarnished. In retrospect, Boeing lacked key elements of a robust risk culture:[65]

- *a clear and consistently communicated outlook on risk*
- *commonality of values and ethics*
- *universal adoption and application of internal controls*
- *timely, transparent and honest communication*
- *information sharing across the organization*
- *rapid identification and escalation of threats and concerns*
- *individual and collective responsibility for managing risk*
- *visible and consistent role modeling of desirable risk behavior*

These attributes nurture and sustain standards of rigor and discipline that define an organization's approach to risk. In robust cultures, processes, systems and leader behavior align to encourage people to make the right risk-related decisions and exhibit appropriate risk behavior. Consequently, disasters such as that experienced by Boeing, more often than not have their origin in organizational cultures that allow risks to take root and grow on the watch of leaders who lack vigilance.[66]

Leadership Style

By setting tone and reinforcing desirable behavior, leaders have a powerful influence on how risk is managed. The important place they occupy in risk management, however, does not mean that they are better prepared. When attention is occupied by immediate concerns and pressing issues, leaders may overlook warning signs that can morph into threats. Worse yet, they may mismatch leadership style with organizational need and exacerbate the effects of risk.

Arguably, the ability to manage risk is a crucible of leader effectiveness. Failure to develop a risk-savvy culture and provide guidance to employees can sink a company if not addressed. This was apparent before, during and after the 2008 financial crisis as profiled in research by Western University Ivey Business School professors Jeffrey Gandz and Gerard Seijts.[67] Some organizations and leaders were ill-prepared to manage the risks they built up over the previous decade of dramatically expanded leverage. Others recognized the risks and either avoided them or developed robust cultures that enabled them to survive or even prosper when the immediate crisis was over. Gandz and Seijts' research disclosed that differentiating factors between organizations that collapsed and survived could be found in organizational risk management competencies and leadership.[68]

Case studies involving two Canadian institutions developed and published by Gandz and Seijts in 2013 further illustrate the effect of leadership on risk management:[69]

> **TD Bank.** *In 2002, new leadership at TD Bank decided to redefine its risk management appetite.[70] This shift in risk strategy followed many years of uneven performance during which the bank experienced significant credit losses because of over exposure to specific industry sectors. Over the next decade, the bank exited risky and complex synthetic investment products, reduced its reliance on concentrated industry lending and built out its retail banking and wealth management businesses. These moves shifted its risks from those over which it had little or no control to those it could better understand and manage. From 2002–2012, TD Bank Group moved from being the 55th largest North American bank in terms of market capitalization to become the 6th largest.[71] It did so under the leadership of a CEO and executive team that created and sustained a risk culture that had a powerful influence on risk*

behavior at all levels in the company. TD's CEO talked constantly about the bank's risk appetite—what it was doing to ensure that practice complied with goals and successes it was having. He instituted formal executive- and management-development programs in which risk strategy and management and the role of senior managers and executives as risk leaders were discussed with senior leaders and cascaded down to lower-level managers and non-managerial employees. The CEO stayed on point by avoiding strategic drift and instituting formalized governance and risk management systems which focused employees on their responsibility in managing risk.

Maple Leaf Foods. *A $1.6 billion food processing company with 5 billion in annual sales in 2012, Maple Leaf Foods experienced a serious setback in 2008, when processed meats sold by the company under its major brand names were implicated in the deaths of 23 people from Listeria monocytogenes, a food-borne bacterium that had colonized in meat slicers in one of the company's plants.[72] The direct and indirect costs of this event and its reputational aftermath shook consumer confidence in Maple Leaf's brands, depressed the company's brand shares by 50 percent, and left an indelible mark on many of the company's employees.[73] Following a low point in 2008–09, the company recovered its brand shares, restored its margins, and refreshed and reenergized its approach to food safety management through a world-leading food safety culture. Recovery came under the leadership of a CEO who redefined the company's risk appetite—zero tolerance for pathogens in products—and established control systems with strong management oversight. The CEO spoke about, wrote about, and blogged about food safety leadership as a strategy going forward years after the risk event. The CEO and senior leaders became highly visible in video messages, conferences, leadership development programs and press briefings. Inside the company, disciplinary action was taken in rare instances when employees, at any level, breached food-safety protocols. Centralized oversight of food safety was beefed up, while maintaining responsibility at the local plant level. Plant managers understood they "owned" the risks, but in the context of a business model where risk is centrally controlled, tracked and reported.*

In both of these organizations, senior leadership, led by the CEO and supported by management teams, created and sustained risk cultures that had a powerful influence on risk behavior at all levels in the organization. Led from the top, these cultures reinforced desirable behavior through structures, processes and behavioral modeling that cascaded throughout the organization. Central to the transformation in risk culture was the approach and style of leaders who rallied organizations in trouble to new heights of performance.

Ten Questions for the Future

Humanly created risk is an ongoing reality for any and all organizations. It is omnipresent and its arrival comes in forms known to us. Its sources are many, its occurrence is becoming more frequent, and its effects more severe. Yet, we're only at the beginning of a risk landscape that is continuing to evolve—a landscape that poses critical questions to organizations and leaders regarding preparedness:

- *Comprehension:* Do you have a full understanding of conditions inside and outside of your organization that lead to risk?
- *Awareness:* Are you aware of your organization's top risks, how severe their impact could be, and how likely they are to occur?
- *Blind Spots:* Are there risk-related "blind spots" in your organization warranting attention?
- *Crisis Response:* Does your organization have a crisis plan for response to unanticipated risks?
- *Social Dynamics:* Do you understand social dynamics underlying attitudes and behavior in relationship to risk and how they manifest in employees?
- *Cognitive Bias:* Are you aware of your cognitive bias toward risk and its impact on employees?
- *Risk Attitudes:* Do you have a full understanding of the risk attitudes of people in your organization?
- *Employee Response:* Is your understanding of risk attitudes sufficient to mobilize employees to take responsibility for risk?
- *Risk Intelligence:* Does your organization have a robust risk management culture?
  - a clearly communicated outlook on risk
  - shared values and ethics surrounding risk

– universal adoption and application of internal controls
– transparent and honest communication
– information sharing across the organization
– rapid identification and escalation of response to threats
– individual and collective responsibility for managing risk
– visible and consistent role modeling of desirable risk behavior
■ *Leadership Style:* Is your approach to leadership conducive to effective management of risk?
■ *Opportunities:* Are you aware of opportunities in risk and what can be gained from these opportunities?

These questions present a critical perspective on your ability to manage risk in an expanding risk universe. Their thesis is clear: risk is a multifaceted phenomenon and its management requires multiple perspectives. You will need a keen understanding of context and your cognitive biases to effectively manage it. You will also need to invest in building a robust risk culture. Implicit in all of this is a responsibility to bring vitality to your organization and to enhance the well-being of employees in a risk landscape that is changing how we live. The journey will be difficult and laden with obstacles, but it will be a journey in which you and your organization will flourish if you can find the opportunity in risk.

Notes

1. Kassam, A. and Michael, C. "Baltimore Bridge Collapse: At Least Six Missing as Biden Laments 'Terrible Accident.'" *The Guardian,* March 26, 2024.
2. WCCO News. "The I-35 W Bridge Collapse: What Happened, What's Changed." *CBS Minnesota,* July 30, 2017.
3. Rigby, J. "COVID Led to 15 Million Deaths Globally, Not the 5 Million Reported—WHO." *Reuters,* May 5, 2022.
4. Pare, S. "COVID Pandemic Knocked 1.6 Years Off Global Life Expectancy, Study Finds." *Live Science,* March 12, 2024.
5. Marysville University Home Blog. "Social Analysis of the Pandemic: How COVID-19 Impacted Society." February 25, 2022.
6. "Symmetry vs. Asymmetry: What's the Difference?" *Difference,* April 2, 2024.
7. Hillson, D. and Murray-Webster, R. *Understanding and Managing Risk Attitude,* 2nd ed. Farnham, Surrey: Gower Publishing, 2007.
8. Environmental Protection Agency. *Deepwater Horizon: BP Gulf of Mexico Oil Spill.* Environmental Protection Agency, Washington, D.C., August 14, 2023.
9. History.Com Editors. "Exxon Valdez Oil Spill." *History,* March 23, 2021.

10. Perkins, T. "Ohio Catastrophe Is 'Wake-Up Call' to Dangers of Deadly Train Derailments." *The Guardian*, February 11, 2023.
11. Ebinger, C. "6 Years from the BP Deepwater Horizon Oil Spill: What We've Learned and What We Shouldn't Understand." *Broking*, April 20, 2016.
12. Yamanouchi, K. "NTSB Criticizes Decisions in the Ohio Norfolk Southern Derailment, Pushes Reforms." *The Spokesman-Review*, June 26, 2024.
13. Ocasio, V. "Contingency Planning: Why It's Important and Who Should Have It." *Blog*, February 25, 2023.
14. Cramer, M. "How 6 Psychological Biases Are Leaving Companies Exposed to Catastrophic Risk." *Hatch*, October 31, 2019.
15. Cramer, M. "How 6 Psychological Biases Are Leaving Companies Exposed to Catastrophic Risk." *Hatch,* October 31, 2019.
16. Ethier, M. "Inside "Touchy Feely,' Stanford's Iconic MBA Course." *Poets and Quants*, July 22, 2018.
17. Cramer, M. "How 6 Psychological Biases Are Leaving Companies Exposed to Catastrophic Risk." *Hatch*, October 31, 2019.
18. Mcleod, S. "Fundamental Attribution Error in Psychology." *Simply Psychology*, June 15, 2023.
19. Cramer, M. "How 6 Psychological Biases Are Leaving Companies Exposed to Catastrophic Risk." *Hatch,* October 31, 2019.
20. Cramer, M. "How 6 Psychological Biases Are Leaving Companies Exposed to Catastrophic Risk." *Hatch,* October 31, 2019.
21. Vandergriendt, C. "The Dunning-Kruger Effect Explained." *Healthline*, March 11, 2022.
22. Nikolopoulou, K. "What Is the Planning Fallacy: Definition and Examples." *Scribbr*, August 28, 2023.
23. Cramer, M. "How 6 Psychological Biases Are Leaving Companies Exposed to Catastrophic Risk." *Hatch,* October 31, 2019
24. Fousiani, K. "Power Asymmetry, Negotiations and Conflict Management in Organizations." In *Organizational Conflict-New Insights*, ed. J. Fahed-Sreih, London, England, UK, December 28, 2020.
25. Ingram, D. and Thompson, M. "What Is Your Risk Attitude? (And How Does It Affect Your Company?)." *Harvard Business Review*, June 11, 2012.
26. Wikipedia. *Loomis (company)*. Retrieved: June 12, 2024.
27. Loomis, A.B. "Loomis Launches 'Loomis Pay', A Complete Payment Solution for Cash, Cards and Other Digital Payments." *PR Newswire*, September 9, 2020.
28. Loomis, A.B. "Loomis Launches 'Loomis Pay', A Complete Payment Solution for Cash, Cards and Other Digital Payments." *PR Newswire,* September 9, 2020.
29. Sakib, N. "Institutional Isomorphism." *Springer Link*, April 30, 2020.
30. Tabrizi, B. "How Microsoft Became Innovative Again." *Harvard Business Review*, February 20, 2023.
31. Takeuchi, H., Osono, E., and Shimizu, N. "The Contradictions That Drive Toyota's Success." *Harvard Business Review*, June, 2008.
32. Goleman, D. "Leadership That Gets Results." *Harvard Business Review*, March–April 2000.

33. Knight, R. "6 Common Leadership Styles-And How to Decide Which to Use When." *Harvard Business Review*, April 9, 2024.

34. Knight, R. "6 Common Leadership Styles-And How to Decide Which to Use When." *Harvard Business Review*, April 9, 2024.

35. Special Report. "The Giant in the Palm of Your Hand." *The Economist*, February 10, 2005.

36. Nuttal, C. "Nokia Completes Phone Sale to Microsoft." *Financial Times*, April 25, 2014.

37. Uta, C. "Nokia's Failure: What Was Their Biggest Mistake?" *Brand Minds Blog*, July 10, 2018.

38. Uta, C. "Nokia's Failure: What Was Their Biggest Mistake?" *Brand Minds Blog*, July 10, 2018.

39. Cramer, M. "How 6 Psychological Biases Are Leaving Companies Exposed to Catastrophic Risk." *Hatch*, October 31, 2019.

40. Uta, C. "Nokia's Failure: What Was Their Biggest Mistake?" *Brand Minds Blog*, July 10, 2018.

41. Adams Funds. "How the Rise of Netflix Has Reshaped the Media Industry." *Adams Funds*, March 15, 2019.

42. .Westberg, P. and Karlsson, K. "Reed Hastings: The Architect of Netflix's Rise." *Quartr,* April 11, 2024.

43. Sherman, N. "Netflix: Four Things Which Have Driven Its Success." *BBC*, January 19, 2021.

44. Ivec, S. "Creating Transformative Learning Experiences: An Intuit Success Story." *ELB Learning*, August 22, 2023.

45. Colvin, G. "How Intuit Reinvents Itself." *Fortune*, October 20, 2017.

46. Intuit News Details. "Intuit Full Year Revenue Up 13 Percent." *Intuit*, August 25, 2020.

47. Jess. "Revolutionizing Pepsico: A Case Study on Indra Nooyi's Visionary Leadership." *Inspire Magazine*, February 25, 2024.

48. O'Brien, M. "Microsoft CEO Satya Nadella Caps a Decade of Change and Tremendous Growth." *Yahoo! Finance*, February 3, 2024.

49. Hall, A. "The Disruptive Visionary: Jeff Bezos' Leadership Style and Amazon's Success." *Aaron Hall*, August 18, 2023.

50. Arbinger. "Plum Healthcare: How One Company Engaged Arbinger, the Remarkable Culture They Created, and the Industry Leading Results They Achieve." *Case Study*, June 30, 2024.

51. Arbinger. "Plum Healthcare: How One Company Engaged Arbinger, the Remarkable Culture They Created, and the Industry Leading Results They Achieve." *Case Study*, June 30, 2024.

52. Arbinger. "Plum Healthcare: How One Company Engaged Arbinger, the Remarkable Culture They Created, and the Industry Leading Results They Achieve." *Case Study*, June 30, 2024.

53. Kaplan, R. and Mikes, A. "Managing Risks: A New Framework." *Harvard Business Review*, June 2012.

54. .Kaplan, R. and Mikes, A. "Managing Risks: A New Framework." *Harvard Business Review,* June 2012.
55. Frigo, M. and Laessoe, H. "Strategic Risk Management at the LEGO Group." *Strategic Finance,* February 2012.
56. Frigo, M. and Laessoe, H. "Strategic Risk Management at the LEGO Group." *Strategic Finance,* February 2012.
57. Institute of Risk Management. "Risk Culture." *Enterprise Risk Magazine,* June 30, 2024.
58. Detailed analysis of the Boeing 737 MAX disaster presented in this chapter was drawn directly from a case study created by Tahir Abbas under the title: *Boeing Crisis Management Case Study: A Detailed Analysis.* Abbas's case study was published in the June 9, 2023, issue of *Change Management Insight* and offers detailed insight into technical, cultural and management aspects of Boeing's business model underlying the 737 MAX disaster.
59. Detailed analysis of the Boeing 737 MAX disaster presented in this chapter was drawn directly from a case study created by Tahir Abbas under the title: *Boeing Crisis Management Case Study: A Detailed Analysis.* Abbas's case study was published in the June 9, 2023, issue of *Change Management Insight* and offers detailed insight into technical, cultural and management aspects of Boeing's business model underlying the 737 MAX disaster.
60. Kesslen, B. "737 MA Crashes That Killed 346 Were 'Result of Horrific Culmination' of Failures by Boeing and FAA, House Report Says." *NBC News,* September 16, 2020.
61. Abbas, T. *Boeing Crisis Management Case Study: A Detailed Analysis.* Change Management Insight, June 9, 2023
62. Kesslem, B. *737 MAX Crashes That Killed 346 Were "Result of a Horrific Culmination" of Errors by Boeing and FAA, House Report Says,* NBC News, September 16, 2020.
63. Burridge, T. "Boeing's 'Culture of Concealment' to Blame for 737 Crashes." *BBC,* September 16, 2020.
64. Shepardson, D. and Insinna, V. "Panel Finds Safety 'Disconnect' Between Boeing Management, Employees." *Reuters,* February 27, 2024.
65. Eight elements of intelligent risk culture were presented and described in Chapter 8 *Building Risk Intelligent Organizations.*
66. Levy, C., Lamarre, E., and Twining, J. "Taking Control of Organizational Risk Culture." *McKinsey & Company,* February 2010.
67. Gandz, J. and Seijts, G. "Leadership and Risk Culture." *Ivey Business Journal* (March/April 2013). https://iveybusinessjournal.com/publication/leadership-and -risk-culture/
68. Gandz, J. and Seijts, G. "Leadership and Risk Culture." *Ivey Business Journal* (March/April 2013). https://iveybusinessjournal.com/publication/leadership-and -risk-culture/

69. Analyses of the risk management disasters at TD Bank and Maple Leaf Foods presented in this chapter were drawn directly from case studies (Ivey Case 9B12C001 and Ivey Case 9B11C001) prepared by Jeffrey Gandz and Gerard Seitjts and published in the *Ivey Business Journal* in March/April 2013.

70. Analyses of the risk management disasters at TD Bank and Maple Leaf Foods presented in this chapter were drawn directly from case studies (Ivey Case 9B12C001 and Ivey Case 9B11C001) prepared by Jeffrey Gandz and Gerard Seitjts and published in the *Ivey Business Journal* in March/April 2013.

71. Analyses of the risk management disasters at TD Bank and Maple Leaf Foods presented in this chapter were drawn directly from case studies (Ivey Case 9B12C001 and Ivey Case 9B11C001) prepared by Jeffrey Gandz and Gerard Seitjts and published in the *Ivey Business Journal* in March/ April 2013.

72. Analyses of the risk management disasters at TD Bank and Maple Leaf Foods presented in this chapter were drawn directly from case studies (Ivey Case 9B12C001 and Ivey Case 9B11C001) prepared by Jeffrey Gandz and Gerard Seitjts and published in the *Ivey Business Journal* in March/April 2013.

73. Analyses of the risk management disasters at TD Bank and Maple Leaf Foods presented in this chapter were drawn directly from case studies (Ivey Case 9B12C001 and Ivey Case 9B11C001) prepared by Jeffrey Gandz and Gerard Seitjts and published in the *Ivey Business Journal* in March/April 2013.

Index

A

ACC, *see* Anterior cingulate cortex
Acute stress response, 72
Adrenaline, 37, 72
Advanced Studies in Culture Foundation
    (ASCF), 101
Aeronautical engineers, 128
Affiliative leadership, 210
Aggression, 37, 132
Agricultural herbicides, 30
Altruism, 91, 98, 103, 108
Ambiguity, 31–33
Ambiguous threats, 34
Anchoring bias, 214
Anomie
    cultural, 97
    definition, 91, 95
    mechanical, 96
    in modernity, 97–98
    organic, 96–97
    in theory, 96–97
Antecedents, 47, 200
Anterior cingulate cortex (ACC), 79
Antivax movement, 5
Artificial intelligence (AI)
    advance, 11–12
    change, 93
    dangers, 12–13
    safety and security, 30
    social dynamics, 22
ASCF, *see* Advanced Studies in Culture
    Foundation

Asymmetry, 165, 167–178
    of attitude, 205–207
    awareness of cognitive bias, 214–215
    awareness of risk attitudes, 218–219
    Canadian institutions, 224–226
    challenges, 205
    cognitive bias, 203–205
    cognizance of risk
        Bezos, Jeff, 217
        Nadella, Satya, 217
        Nooyi, Indra, 217
    discord of, 200–201
    external environment, 215–216
    framing, 201–203
    humanly created risk, 199–200
    leadership, 211–212
    leadership style, 224–226
    of managing, 208–209
    managing risk, 219–221
    modeling, 212–213
    obstacles, 199
    organizational dynamics, 216–216
    risk culture, 221–223
    risk landscape, 226–227
    of style, 209–211
Attentiveness, 37
Attraction-selection-attrition, 142
Attribution bias, 204
Authoritative leadership, 210
Automotive and aviation
    technologies, 30
Autonomic nervous system, 37, 77
Availability bias, 214

Printed in the United States
by Baker & Taylor Publisher Services